Sacramental Theology

Sacramental Theology

Theory and Practice from Multiple Perspectives

Special Issue Editor

Bruce T. Morrill

MDPI • Basel • Beijing • Wuhan • Barcelona • Belgrade

Special Issue Editor
Bruce T. Morrill
Vanderbilt University
USA

Editorial Office
MDPI
St. Alban-Anlage 66
4052 Basel, Switzerland

This is a reprint of articles from the Special Issue published online in the open access journal *Religions* (ISSN 2077-1444) in 2019 (available at: https://www.mdpi.com/journal/religions/special_issues/sacramental)

For citation purposes, cite each article independently as indicated on the article page online and as indicated below:

LastName, A.A.; LastName, B.B.; LastName, C.C. Article Title. *Journal Name* **Year**, *Article Number*, Page Range.

ISBN 978-3-03921-718-2 (Pbk)
ISBN 978-3-03921-719-9 (PDF)

Cover image courtesy of Bruce T. Morrill.

Contents

About the Special Issue Editor

Bruce T. Morrill, the Edward A. Malloy Professor of Roman Catholic Studies at Vanderbilt University (Nashville, Tennessee), specializes in sacramental–liturgical theology, drawing upon a range of interdisciplinary resources in the fields of systematic and historical theology, ritual studies, cultural anthropology, and biblical studies. His other strongly related interest is in political theologies investigating the problems of suffering in social contexts. This work has come together most comprehensively in his books *Divine Worship and Human Healing: Liturgical Theology at the Margins of Life and Death* (Liturgical Press, 2009) and *Anamnesis as Dangerous Memory: Political and Liturgical Theology in Dialogue* (Liturgical Press, 2000). More recent titles include *Encountering Christ in the Eucharist: The Paschal Mystery in People, Word, and Sacrament* (Paulist Press, 2012) and *The Essential Writings of Bernard Cooke: A Narrative Theology of Church, Sacrament, and Ministry* (Paulist Press, 2016). His current research and writing projects include a typology of liturgical remembering and a mystical–political theology of Easter. A Jesuit priest, his academic degrees include an M.A. in anthropology (Columbia University) and Ph.D. in religion (Emory University). He has lectured widely in North America, Europe, and Australia, and is currently president of the North American Academy of Liturgy.

Preface to "Sacramental Theology"

In the second half of the twentieth century, sacrament emerged as a vital topic within the *ressourcement* movements of Western European Catholic theology.   This overlapped with the ecumenical liturgical movement already in progress for a half-century.   Scholarship attentive to multiple sources in early Christianity—philosophical, historical, homiletic, liturgical, pastoral—rescued sacramental symbol and ritual from merely being an object of clerical ministration, passive lay reception, and canonical regulation to becoming a key for understanding divine human encounter in the mission of the church and the lives of its members. Recovering the ancient, as well as best of medieval, theology of sacramental rites as sacred mysteries, European and North American theologians enlisted contemporary phenomenological and hermeneutical philosophies to explain and promote sacraments not as clerically delivered objects but, rather, as profound human symbolic events of divine revelation.

By the turn of the twenty-first century, the need for attention to the actual performance of specific rites and, thus, the need for historical, social–scientific, and other human disciplines—in addition to philosophy—had become well established. This now makes the work of sacramental theology an ongoing point of attention in multiple cross-disciplinary theories attentive to actual contexts, both historical and contemporary, of sacramental–liturgical practices. Insofar as Christian sacraments only exist in symbolic–ritual performances, the field of liturgical studies (itself multidisciplinary, including ritual and performance theories) has proven increasingly integral to sacramental–theological work. Attention to historical and current practices of Christian symbol and ritual (liturgy and sacraments) nonetheless returns continuously to philosophical–theological theories that meet the intellectual need to reflect upon divine presence and absence, personal and communal experiences of God, of Christ, of the Spirit, scripture and tradition, the ecclesial or communal dimension of sacramental celebrations, types of power at work in the rites, liturgical participation, and more. Thus, sacramental theology proves expansive in the range of the Christian existence it addresses, even as the bodily nature of the subject matter requires constant theoretical reconsiderations attentive to historical, social, and cultural contexts.

The essays in this volume begin with profound philosophical perspectives on personal and communal sacramental experience, expanding from traditional cosmology to evolutionary and chaos theories of our planetary existence, continuing with shifts—especially among youth—to interreligious and non-institutional perspectives, then on to change in popular notions of guilt and social–ethical issues in relation to liturgical theology, so as finally to return to fundamental theological reflection on human sacramentality and divine revelation.

Bruce T. Morrill
Special Issue Editor

Article

Mystery Manifested: Toward a Phenomenology of the Eucharist in Its Liturgical Context

Christina M. Gschwandtner

Department of Philosophy, Fordham University, Bronx, NY 10458, USA; gschwandtner@fordham.edu

Received: 15 April 2019; Accepted: 6 May 2019; Published: 9 May 2019

Abstract: This article explores three contemporary phenomenological analyses of the Eucharist by the French phenomenologists Jean-Luc Marion, Jean-Yves Lacoste, and Emmanuel Falque, arguing that their descriptions are too excessive and individual, failing to take into account the broader liturgical context for eucharistic experience. The second part of the discussion seeks to develop an alternate phenomenological account of eucharistic experience that takes Eucharist seriously as a corporeal and communal phenomenon that is encountered within a liturgical horizon and which requires a liturgical intentionality to be prepared for and directed toward it.

Keywords: Eucharist; liturgy; phenomenology; Jean-Luc Marion; Jean-Yves Lacoste; Emmanuel Falque

---

Philosophical reflection on the sacraments—especially the Eucharist—has a long history. Aquinas employs and alters Aristotelian categories of substance and accidents for his account of a eucharistic ontology; Descartes discusses the impact of new insights in physics on the epistemology of the Eucharist in several letters to Marin de Mersenne; Leibniz tries to reconcile Lutherans and Calvinists with a "monadic" interpretation of eucharistic substance; Hegel employs a natural philosophy of the living organism as an argument for a Lutheran interpretation of the Eucharist as sacramental reality (Alexandrescu 2007; Backus 2011; Fouke 1992; Finn 2015–2016). Such philosophical explications of the sacraments have been metaphysical, ontological, epistemological, physical or biological, even hermeneutic. Maybe the most recent and surely one of the most fruitful approaches is phenomenological. Several contemporary French philosophers have employed phenomenological tools derived from Edmund Husserl and Martin Heidegger in order to articulate a philosophical account of religious experience, in which analyses of the sacrament of the Eucharist play a prominent role.

What can phenomenology bring to our understanding of and encounter with the sacraments? Phenomenology is the study of our experience of phenomena, of their modes of manifestation and revelation, the ways in which we apprehend and experience them. Unlike approaches in the social sciences, phenomenology is not primarily concerned with empirical experience—how this or that person might experience a specific event at a particular moment—but rather with the broader structures of experience in order to ascertain what sort or kind of experience it is, its various modes of manifestation, and how it reveals something about the human condition. Early philosophical phenomenology often excluded any considerations of religious experience, which it deemed too esoteric or transcendent, in order to focus on issues of perception, imagination, or memory and the ways in which phenomena are experienced via temporality, spatiality, corporeality, affectivity, i.e., the very structures within and through which experience occurs.[1] Increasingly, contemporary philosophers like Paul Ricoeur,

---

[1] This is true of "classical" philosophical phenomenologists like Husserl, Heidegger, Sartre, and Merleau-Ponty. Other thinkers, both philosophers like Scheler, Stein, and Walther or those in other fields like Otto, Eliade, Kristensen, and van der Leeuw, did draw on phenomenology for analyses of religious phenomena. See my brief survey of and introduction to these thinkers (Gschwandtner 2019), especially Part I. (Part II focuses on the French thinkers, some of whom are discussed in the present essay.) One should note also Robert Sokolowski's book on eucharistic manifestation (Sokolowski 1994), which draws on Husserl's phenomenology.

Michel Henry, Jean-Luc Marion, Jean-Yves Lacoste, Jean-Louis Chrétien, Emmanuel Falque, and others, have suggested that a phenomenological approach might also be profitable for analyzing religious experience, faith, and the sacraments. References to the Eucharist in particular can be found in almost all of these thinkers.

This contribution will focus on three of the fullest phenomenological analyses of the Eucharist, that of Marion, Lacoste, and Falque, suggesting that each highlights some aspect of its phenomenality, how the phenomenon is given, how the phenomenon is received, and how it involves and illuminates a particular notion of corporeality. The essay will set forth and critically evaluate these proposals, showing that they are still too prone to consider the Eucharist in isolation from its liturgical and ritual context. For this reason, these analyses of the phenomenality of the Eucharist tend to describe it as a solitary and excessive phenomenon, disregarding the corporate, corporeal, and communal dimensions of eucharistic experience within its liturgical setting. It will be proposed, instead, that paying more attention to how Eucharist is experienced in its spatial, temporal, corporeal, and affective dimensions within the communal, ecclesial setting will provide a fuller and more adequate phenomenological account of it as genuinely *human* religious experience. Such an account might also tone down some of the emphasis on the excessive and extraordinary nature of this phenomenon, which often implies that if sacraments are not experienced in such intense fashion the person does not have genuine belief or is somehow at fault. A broader account of the liturgical setting for eucharistic experience will reveal not only how its "mystery" is manifested through and within the "ordinary" or even mundane experience, but also how such liturgical experience directs toward and prepares for eucharistic participation. That is to say, a phenomenological analysis of eucharistic experience requires an account of liturgical intentionality.

1. Jean-Luc Marion: Eucharist as Abundant and Abandoned Gift

The Eucharist is a frequent theme in Marion's writings. Already in his early *God without Being*—primarily a polemic tract against a certain kind of Heideggerianism in France—he argues for a *theo*-logy grounded in the event of the Eucharist (Marion 1991, pp. 139–58).[2] The essay thus does not necessarily focus on Eucharist as religious experience but instead employs it to say something about the activity of theologizing. Marion proposes a "eucharistic hermeneutics" that would allow God to pronounce "correct" interpretation from the Word revealed in the "eucharistic moment" (Marion 1991, pp. 151, 153).[3] He urges the theologian to move over to "God's point of view" and to speak theology only from this (essentially episcopal) perspective (Marion 1991, pp. 149–52).[4] In a subsequent chapter in the same book, he provides an analysis of eucharistic presence that seeks to defend a particular account of transubstantiation in the face of interpretations that focus on the reception by the community in the attempt to combine a "subjective" and an "objective" perspective (Marion 1991, pp. 161–82).[5] These two accounts have been extensively criticized, especially for their heavily hierarchical tenor (e.g.,

---

2   See also his essay "The Gift of a Presence" (Marion 2002a, pp. 124–52). This text analyzes the ascension narratives.

3   Or, in more detail: "The Word intervenes in person in the Eucharist (in person, because only then does he manifest and perform his filiation) to accomplish in this way the hermeneutic. The Eucharist alone completes the hermeneutic; the hermeneutic culminates in the Eucharist: the one assures the other its condition of possibility" (1991, p. 150). He explores this in more detail in his analysis of the story of the Emmaus disciples, which culminates in the recognition of Christ when he breaks the bread (and disappears). Here, also, Christ provides the correct interpretation and "intentionality" for what the overwhelmed intuition of the disciples cannot grasp. (Marion 2017, pp. 136–43).

4   Or, more succinctly: "If, first, theology as *theo*logy attempts the hermeneutic of the words in view, hence also, from the point of view of the Word, if the Eucharist offers the only correct hermeneutic site where the Word can be said in person in the blessing, if finally only the celebrant receives authority to go beyond the words as far as the Word, because he alone finds himself invested by the *persona Christi*, then one must conclude that *only the bishop merits, in the full sense, the title of theologian*" (1991, p. 153; emphasis his).

5   The language of unifying the subjective and the objective is employed on page 181. Interestingly, this second piece is "outside" the regular text (in an afterword called "Hors-Texte"), while the other essay on the Eucharist is the final chapter "inside" the text. Neither of the essays yet employs explicitly phenomenological language. In fact, in the second essay he says clearly that his "task here remains theological" (1991, p. 171).

Mackinlay 2004; Wallenfang 2010).[6] After developing his phenomenological approach much more fully in such works as *Being Given: Toward a Phenomenology of Givenness* or *In Excess: Studies of Saturated Phenomena* (Marion 2002c), Marion's later work returns to the topic of the Eucharist in several much more explicitly phenomenological essays (Marion 2017, especially chapters 8, 10, and 11).[7]

Probably the fullest account is his "The Phenomenality of the Sacrament," which can be said to represent his mature position (Marion 2017, pp. 102–15).[8] He begins by contending that phenomenology is an appropriate method for Christian theology and the phenomena of Christian experience, because both phenomenology and Christianity start with the central notion of revelation or manifestation and seek to unfold its meaning. The Eucharist brings together visible and invisible—the invisible manifesting in some way through the visible elements—in a quintessentially phenomenological way.[9] It is thus not inappropriate to speak of the Eucharist as a phenomenon. Marion explicates traditional models of the sacrament—as invisible substance in visible accidents, as invisible cause of a visible effect, or as visible sign of an invisible reality—and finds their phenomenological kernel to be that of a fully abandoned gift: In each case, the sacrament *"gives itself without withdrawal* to the point of abandon" (Marion 2017, pp. 106–8; the same phrase is reiterated after the analysis of each model). He concludes from this that "to define the phenomenality of the sacrament, one must see that within it the invisible is translated, delivers itself up, and abandons itself to the visible to the point of appearing in it as the invisible that it remains" (2017, p. 108). The gift of revelation can appear in the Eucharist precisely because it is given so fully that it protects its invisibility by being kenotically exhausted in the visible. We can never point to body and blood of Christ—they remain invisible—precisely because they are wholly manifested within the visible species of bread and wine. Incarnation is accomplished entirely and in full immanence; no remainder of pure transcendence is withheld, but all of it is given and delivered over.

This is of a piece with Marion's broader phenomenological project, which seeks to articulate a phenomenology in which the phenomenon takes the initiative and its manifestation and meaning are unfolded entirely from how it gives itself, rather than imposed on it by the consciousness of the one experiencing it. That is to say, some phenomena—such as rich cultural events, beautiful works of art, the intimate touch of loving flesh, the face of the human neighbor, or the manifestation of the divine—come to us in such overwhelming ways that we cannot impose categories or parameters upon them, but experience them as they give themselves in abundant, surprising, unpredictable ways, without being able to exercise control over them.[10] Marion calls such experiences "saturated"

---

[6] Marion defends himself against some of these critiques in his interview with Richard Kearney (Kearney 2004, pp. 15–32, especially pp. 21–22). See also my analysis of Marin's "spirituality of adoration" (Gschwandtner 2017, pp. 188–217) and the final chapter of my *Degrees of Givenness* (Gschwandtner 2014, pp. 170–92).

[7] Many of the pieces included in this text (2017), as well as those in an earlier collection (Marion 2008), were originally articles in the Roman Catholic journal *Communio*. Marion was the first co-editor of the Francophone edition of *Communio*. The essays were thus originally conceived as theological pieces written for a Roman Catholic audience.

[8] What follows in the rest of this paragraph is a brief summary of this essay. The essay was first published in 2001; it is confirmed by similar arguments in 2008 and his Gifford Lectures (albeit focused on the Trinity not on sacraments), published as *Givenness and Revelation* in 2016.

[9] See also his analysis of *mysterion* and *apokalysis* in the Gifford lectures (Marion 2016, pp. 76–77). (An anonymous reviewer suggested that there might be a hidden Palamite influence in Marion's work, such that God's essence remains entirely transcendent and mysterious while manifestation occurs through the divine energies. It is certainly true that Marion stresses that we have no access to God as such and that the divine must always remain incomprehensible, while he also affirms that God is revealed and "effective" within phenomenality. Yet, although Marion often appeals to Dionysius the Areopagite and occasionally Gregory of Nyssa, he does not engage the later eastern patristic tradition and is occasionally quite dismissive of contemporary eastern Orthodoxy. He also rigorously rejects any language of *ousia*, essence, substance, or being for the divine and is critical of the Aristotelian language of *energeia*, especially as it relates to act and potency. Jones explores the patristic sources of Marion's thought in detail (Jones 2011).

[10] He summarizes this also in the present essay: "By givenness, one must here understand the ultimate accomplishment of phenomenality, indubitable because it is perfectly reduced to immanence, such that it makes it possible to calibrate and accommodate all the degrees of presence, evidence, reality, and actuality, yet without itself being returned to them. The phenomenon thus recovers the sovereignty of its appearance only while being phenomenalized of and by *itself*, in showing *itself* from *itself*. Yet it attests this *self* only when the appearance enters into its appearing. And it enters into the appearing and commits to appear only if it gives *itself*. Nothing shows *itself* that does not first give *itself*. This rule of

phenomena, because they "saturate" (that is, entirely fill and overwhelm) our intuition, rather than having to be constituted through the intentionality of consciousness.[11] His overall project seeks to articulate a phenomenology of givenness in which such intense, rich, saturated phenomena could appear and their modes of manifestation be articulated via the impact they have on the recipient. The phenomenon gives itself fully to us, entirely on its own terms, thus effecting what he calls a "counter-experience," in which the recipient no longer imposes categories upon the phenomenon or directs his or her intentionality toward it in order to constitute it, but instead receives it as a surprising, unpredictable, unforeseeable, uncategorizable event.[12] The Eucharist manifests even more fully and purely as such a phenomenon given completely and utterly as gift (*don/donné*), abandoned (*abandonné*) wholly to its recipients without remainder.

Indeed, Marion speaks of the Eucharist most often and most fundamentally as gift.[13] Already in *God without Being* he stresses this dimension: "Eucharistic presence must be understood starting most certainly from the present, but the present must be understood first as a gift that is given. One must measure the dimensions of eucharistic presence against the fullness of this gift" (Marion 1991, p. 171).[14] In other places, too, he discusses the Eucharist as a loving gift, given entirely and abundantly by God, to be received by us in similar kenotic abandon.[15] In the breaking of the bread, Christ "gives himself to the point of abandoning himself like bread is distributed, abandoning himself like bread, like *this* bread, can concentrate all his presence in a gift, whether in a fleshly body or by taking body of the bread, always without any reserve whatsoever" (2002a, p. 133). The recognition of "unbearable glory" that occurs in the Eucharist, heightened by Christ's apparent absence or withdrawal, requires that we must now become models of Christ, playing a "trinitarian role" of "the place, the role, and the charge of Christ" (2002a, pp. 144–45). Christ is given so entirely in the gift that he is fully abandoned to it and does not remain isolable from it, to the point of withdrawing from straight-forward visibility (as in his disappearance at Emmaus). Like the saturated phenomenon, we are blinded by the appearance, must recognize it obliquely (e.g., in the breaking of the bread), and respond to it in kenotic abandon.

In "The Recognition of the Gift" he suggests that the Eucharist constitutes the supreme instance of gift or givenness, because in it Christ is wholly given to the point of death, in such a way that the gift can be continually regiven in the eucharistic elements (Marion 2017, p. 132). The Eucharist is the most perfect gift because "the real presence actually *de-realizes* the matter of the gift, which, paradoxically, in turn phenomenalizes the giver and allows the entire process of givenness to appear" (2017, p. 134; emphasis his).[16] Eucharist thus displays the fullest kind of phenomenality, one that can serve as a paradigm for all phenomena (Marion 2017, pp. 133–35). Phenomena, as Marion has attempted to show throughout his work, give themselves to us; the more overwhelming and saturated they are,

---

phenomenality in general measures the legitimacy and possibility for any phenomenon to show itself according to the measure of givenness." (2017, pp. 110–11.)

[11] As occurs in everyday or what Marion calls "poor" phenomena, where intuition only supplies some elements (e.g., the front of a book or side of an object, where we constitute the phenomenon by supplying the "back side" or reverse that is not intuited directly or the constitution of a circle where we have no intuition of a perfectly circular phenomenon at all, at least via perception). Marion contends that in these cases intention supplies the signification that is missing via concepts, while this is impossible in the case of saturated phenomena both because they are so overwhelming that they cannot be grasped via concepts and because it is fully given to intuition and thus nothing has to be supplied for its apprehension.

[12] This is worked out most fully in *Being Given*, but also pursued in several subsequent texts.

[13] For his broader analyses of the gift, see the "Sketch of a Phenomenological Concept of Gift" (Marion 2008, chapter 5, pp. 80–100), Book II of *Being Given* (Marion 2002b, pp. 71–118), and chapters III and IV of *Negative Certainties* (Marion 2015, pp. 83–154).

[14] See also the section on "The Gift of Presence" (2017, pp. 176–78). The same title is employed for his essay on the ascension narratives in *Prolegomena to Charity*.

[15] "The presence of Christ, and therefore also that of the Father, discloses itself by a gift: it can therefore be recognized only by a blessing. A presence, which gives itself by grace and identifies itself with this gift, can therefore be seen only in being received, and be received only in being blessed" (2002a, p. 129). This becomes the supreme task of the disciples, the church, and ultimately all of humanity (2002a, p. 130).

[16] He also reiterates here the idea that we must see the gift from the point of view of the giver, God, thus applying "the proper hermeneutical decision," that is, "the hermeneutics of givenness" (2017, p. 135).

the less they are open to prediction or manipulation (or constitution) from the experiencer and the more abundantly they come and displace, unsettle, overwhelm, bedazzle the one exposed to their arrival. Eucharist is the most intense, most saturated, most overwhelming, most bedazzling of such phenomena to the point that it may appear no longer as a saturated (*saturé*) phenomenon, but as an erased (*raturé*) phenomenon.[17] It gives itself so fully that nothing remains of it.

Eucharist, for Marion, thus phenomenalizes as gift, as supremely saturated phenomenon, that is to say, as a phenomenon that overwhelms us with its givenness, startles and bedazzles us, presents as infinitely more than we can grasp, and yet at the same time gives itself so wholly that it withholds nothing, that the entire divine abundance is offered within it. The sacrament therefore reorients us, makes us devoted or given over to it (*adonné*), as we receive its abandon as far as we are able without exercising control over it, imposing concepts upon it, or determining it in some fashion—all of which would be impossible due to its overwhelming character. Its dazzling and abundant character is not always visible, however, both because this invisible abundance is hidden within or behind the visible and because we are not always able to bear it. We can only receive—and thus allow to manifest as a phenomenon—what we can bear or are able to see. In that respect, although the phenomenon of revelation offers itself entirely and we are unable to impose parameters upon it or control its manifestation, it still requires a recipient to serve as the screen of manifestation, someone to respond to Eucharist in awe and adoration, hence to "phenomenalize" it. Marion offers us a phenomenology of the Eucharist that is focused almost exclusively on how the phenomenon is given to us, namely as saturated, overwhelming, bedazzling, abundant gift, to which we are called to become wholly devoted.

2. Jean-Yves Lacoste: Eucharist as Eschatological Anticipation

Lacoste has also returned to the topic of the Eucharist several times. Drawing heavily on Heidegger for his phenomenological parameters and presuppositions, Lacoste focuses on several dimensions of the eucharistic experience, such as the phenomenological status of the elements, the affectivity (*Befindlichkeit*) involved in the experience, how intuition is at work in sacramental apprehension, and the "logic" of the sacrament as one transcending death and challenging the "logic" of the world. Lacoste's overall project posits itself as a phenomenology of "liturgy," but this does not refer to ritual or worship (i.e., what is meant by liturgy in theology); instead it designates a broader phenomenological "being" before the Absolute.[18] This is essentially an analysis of ascetic experience as wholly kenotic, defined by radical abnegation, liminality, and dispossession. Throughout Lacoste relies heavily on Heidegger, taking his analysis of Dasein or being-in-the-world as the "secular" or neutral starting point for the human condition and envisioning a confrontation with the divine from that basis, while also suggesting that such an encounter with the Absolute may lead to the displacement or reorientation of human being-in-the-world and our being-toward-death. Eucharist is a boundary experience that resituates us vis-à-vis the world and everyday life.

In one of his early essays, Lacoste actually explores liturgy not simply as existence *coram Deo*, but refers more explicitly to ecclesial liturgical elements (Lacoste 2005, pp. 93–103). He argues that there are neither subjects nor objects in liturgy; the things of liturgy "appear by refusing their objectification"; they "appear in a play that excludes all grasping, whether this be in the mode of representation or taking possession" (2005, p. 97). They are not objects or tools, because they break with our regular experience of the world.[19] There is no "representational consciousness" in liturgy. He thus agrees with Marion that

---

17 He also claims this of orgasm and for the erotic phenomenon more broadly (Marion 2007, pp. 138, 144, 153).
18 "The reader who has seen the term [liturgy] arise in the table of contents of this work must therefore be advised: what 'liturgy' designates in these pages is, in fact, as convention would have it, the logic that presides over the encounter between man and God writ large. I am not denying that this encounter is also attested to in worship, or that worship has an order and that this order is rule governed. But the limits of what I understand here by 'liturgy' exceeds the limits of worship." (Lacoste 2004, p. 2).
19 "Things in general, and those of the liturgy in particular, are such by virtue of a rupture or a separation" (2005, p. 97). Instead, like art, "they are signs and symbols" (2005, p. 97).

traditional phenomenological modes of experiencing phenomena do not apply to our being before God: The phenomena of liturgy cannot be constituted via our intentionality or as representations within consciousness. We must disqualify objectifying manipulation and representational consciousness, and instead approach liturgical phenomena with "vigilance and a respect" (2005, p. 98). Drawing again on Heidegger, Lacoste also argues for a coaffective experience of the "we" (*Mitbefindlichkeit*) in liturgy.[20] Heidegger stressed that we always find ourselves in the world already among and with others. Liturgy, in Lacoste's view, disqualifies these "'everyday' modes of the 'with'," but can instead propose a different kind of shared experience of affect, at least by anticipation, in terms of a "desire for communion" (2005, pp. 99–100). Although Lacoste does no analysis specific to Eucharist in this essay, it is already clear that he does not regard the eucharistic elements as objects or even tools. We experience them otherwise and must come to them with a different sort of affectivity, namely approaching them with awe and veneration, maybe even with joy.

He addresses sacramental experience more explicitly in other contexts, all of which stress that eucharistic experience cuts across our field of experience and points to an existence that would be neither mortal nor existential, thus undoing our condition as being-in-the-world and being-toward-death in the Heideggerian sense (Lacoste 2011, p. 301). Lacoste reiterates repeatedly that sacramental experience, although "parousial" in character, is limited to this world; no sacraments are needed in the afterlife because we will be immediately in God's presence. Although the sacrament must be talked about in terms of presence, this presence ruptures the closure of the world and undoes the logic of the object (Lacoste 2011, p. 302).[21] This sacramental presence is not sensed, however; it is not a matter of theophany, but rather a "cryptic" revelation. Presence is sensed within the limits of the present, such as the species of bread and wine, yet cannot really be apprehended there securely. Joy over this abundant gift would always be partial and in anticipation only.[22] Our affective responses to the infinite remain limited and the phenomenon must unsettle (rather than comfort) us in some way.[23]

For Lacoste, this is always a matter disrupting the order of the world and of undoing its logic, pointing to a beyond the world, and beyond time.[24] Thus, "the sacrament sanctions our finitude, for there are sacraments only for mortal beings. All the same, in the world of life, for the one who recognizes it, the sacrament opens a space in in which this finitude, whether it is unsettled or tastes the joys of quietude, is initiated into a duration which is not defined as being-toward-death. This bracketing of being-toward-death in the experience of the sacrament is as fragile as can be" (2011, pp. 306–7). Because phenomenology only deals with the appearing of the visible within the world and history, it can never reveal the invisible or what is beyond the world and history. The sacrament opens a way to "transcend our being-in-the-world and our historiality," but only in the most tentative of senses.[25] For Lacoste, life is always "caught between quietude and disquietude," thus "the limits of 'spiritual' experience always escape us" (2011, p. 311). Ultimately, sacramental experience is a non-experience, because it cannot be sensed or articulated within earthly parameters of emotion, affect, objectivity, place, time, or other conditions of experience.[26]

---

[20] "And about men who want to associate liturgically with angelic praises, it must be conceded that they are a little bit more than just together" (2005, p. 99).

[21] E.g., "where there is sacrament there is henceforth no longer any object" (2011, p. 302).

[22] "No more than absolute knowing there is no absolute affectivity" (2011, p. 303).

[23] "The infirmity of affections toward the infinite that it can only grasp partially certainly does not give rise to (or cannot give rise to) a disaster of the believing consciousness. All the same, it does give rise to a kind of disquietude (and we should be worried if that were not the case): we encounter here a phenomenon in its most exemplary reality" (2011, p. 304).

[24] "Nevertheless, within the world of life, it points to the irruption of a beyond the world and, if we limit life to its world, a beyond life" (2011, p. 304).

[25] "We can all the same do better and respect what gives itself in the sacrament to the double experience of affectivity and thought. And doing better would thus mean to admit that the sacrament and everything that participates in its logic makes it possible for us to transcend our being-in-the world and our historiality" (2011, p. 308).

[26] The idea of nonexperience (including the non-place and non-time of liturgy) is worked out most fully in chapter 3 of *Experience and the Absolute* (Lacoste 2004).

Lacoste's fullest account of the Eucharist is in an essay on "sacramental intuition" (Lacoste 2015, pp. 59–95). This essay explores what he explicitly calls "the phenomenality of the sacrament" (2015, p. 71). Like Marion he employs the traditional idea of the visible referring to an invisible reality, that is to say, appearance or manifestation is here actually a matter of disappearance or of what does not appear visibly. Although bread and wine clearly are phenomena that can be seen, touched, and tasted, as Eucharist they must always appear as more or other than themselves. They are not simply objects; a phenomenology of the sacrament has to go beyond both ontological (or epistemological) language, as well as the logic of sacrifice or offering. While bread and wine appear "within the world," the sacrament points beyond the world and its logic (2015, p. 76). The sacramental and the corporeal order are linked, yet the sacrament "belongs to an economy of the provisional" (2015, p. 79). We do not have a straightforward affectivity or sensation or "sentiment" in the phenomenological experience of sacramentality, but rather a "presentiment" or anticipation. There is nothing necessarily "felt" directly in our experience of the sacrament, but something is anticipated via faith (2015, pp. 80–81). The sacrament instantiates a constant play between presence and absence, appearance and disappearance, history and eschaton, world and parousia.

Here Lacoste differs from Marion: Although he agrees that sacramental experience is difficult to phenomenalize, this is not the case because it is so overwhelming, but because it goes beyond any experience of being in the world. It is not that too much intuition is given that our intentionality could not grasp or constitute, but rather that there is no intuition involved at all, that intentionality is utterly incapable of apprehending the Absolute (2015, p. 86). It is not that God is given so fully that we become too overwhelmed to bear this revelation, but that the Absolute is so kenotically absent that no experience can appear in our present world at all. We would have to step across the liminal line to the eschaton and that can only be anticipated in the most elusive fashion. It would require a radical reorientation and disintegration of all our present parameters of perception or apprehension. Lacoste therefore insists on a context of faith for an experience of the Eucharist; "sacramental experience presupposes a world where man exists already before God," which is not the present world. Thus, he finds it a truism that "sacramental intuition cannot be our first experience of God" (2015, p. 87). We must believe in the "world of faith" in order for sacramental experience to "happen"; faith must prepare us; there is no "primordial sacramental position" (2015, p. 89).[27] He insists over and over again that sacramental intuition always cuts across the world and puts it into question: Sacramental intuition is that "of a limit and of our impossibility of getting across it here and now" (2015, p. 92). Thus, for Lacoste, this is a phenomenality of believing rather than of experiencing (2015, p. 93).

For Lacoste, the experience of Eucharist or sacrament is of a piece with his broader phenomenological analysis of being-before-God or the Absolute. It cannot be experienced or described within the traditional (in this case primarily Heideggerian) parameters, because the Absolute never appears or is experienced within "normal" time and place, objects or sensory perception. Rather, such encounter always presents a challenge to our regular way of being and unsettles it radically. It undoes death in the anticipation of eschatological life, undoes time via the parousia, undoes place and the logic of the world by pointing to an elsewhere. Ascetic, kenotic, or eucharistic "non-experience" provides a tantalizing hint of this anticipation, yet it can never really be experienced or encountered in this present life within this world, but remains wholly mysterious.

Although for Lacoste the experience of "liturgy" or sacrament is thus always a non-experience or an experience of abnegation or dispossession, rather than one of fullness, excess, or saturation as in Marion, ultimately their accounts of response to the phenomenon are quite close: For both, the eucharistic (or ascetic) recipient must give him- or herself over to the Absolute in total kenotic abandon and neither allows for intentionality or processes of constitution in regard to the eucharistic

---

27   Although I cannot explore this further in the present context, I would say instead that liturgy can prepare for and cultivate faith and thus may well function in primordial ways.

phenomenon. Lacoste does actually sometimes use language of gift, excess, and an ambivalent presence in ways that parallel Marion's descriptions. Yet, he exacerbates the tension between visible and invisible even more strongly than Marion; almost everything is deferred to eschaton and parousia, even though there will be no Eucharist or sacraments there. Lacoste's analysis thus can be said to focus almost exclusively on eucharistic reception: The ways in which it is a wholly liminal experience that challenges our ordinary ways of being and calls us to an utterly kenotic existence of total abnegation, albeit one that cannot be lived here and now, is always only hinted at in the most elusive fashion. Ultimately, there cannot really be a phenomenality *of* the Eucharist for Lacoste, but only an undoing of phenomenality *by* Eucharist, an anticipatory displacement or dissolution of our experience and its phenomenological parameters.

3. Emmanuel Falque: Eucharist as Erotic Participation and Incorporation

In many ways, Falque can be said to be responding to these rather extreme and liminal accounts of religious experience, attempting to temper their excess and recover a stronger sense of the immanence of Christian experience as fundamentally incarnational, especially in regard to the sacrament of the Eucharist.[28] He also considers the (Roman Catholic) liturgical context more fully, even explicitly quoting from the liturgical texts for the eucharistic liturgy of the mass. In general, philosophy (as phenomenology) and theology are much more fully linked in Falque's writings; he even suggests that "the more we theologize, the better we philosophize" (and the reverse) (Falque 2016, p. 148).[29] Two texts are especially important here. His essay "This is my Body" is explicitly focused on developing a "philosophy of the Eucharist," that links an analysis of eucharistic "incorporation" with those of the erotic and the suffering body "spread out" (as on a bed) (Falque 2015a, pp. 279–94). In his book on the *Wedding Feast of the Lamb* he develops a phenomenology of the body that culminates in a theology of Christian marriage and a theologico-phenomenological analysis of the Eucharist (Falque 2015b).

His eucharistic discussion considers four aspects of the experience, what he calls its heritage (the lamb), its content (the body), its modality (eros), and its aim (abiding).[30] He suggests that this experience can only be expressed by questioning and pushing beyond the limits of philosophy, holding philosophy and theology together or even transgressing the boundaries between them. He criticizes the preceding French phenomenological tradition for having separated "body" and "flesh" in such a way as to reinstitute the distinction between body and soul they originally sought to overcome by simply attributing to the flesh what was traditionally predicated of the soul. To get beyond this dichotomy, he develops the notion of the *corps épandu*, that is, the body as "spread" or "splayed" out. He employs this as a notion of the body that takes account of both its organic and its experienced dimensions, neither an "extended" body (*corps étendu*) in Descartes' sense nor the "lived body" (*corps vécu*, *Leib*, often translated into French as *chair*/flesh) in Husserl's sense. We should not privilege the lived experience of the body over the organicity of the body, as recent philosophy has done.

Falque suggests that the body stretched out on the cross is phenomenologically parallel to the body splayed out on the sickbed or the body spread out on the nuptial bed.[31] They are connected through what he calls our "animality," our fully embodied experience of the chemical and organic substructures of the body, the psychological "chaos" of passions, impulses, and emotions, and our biological physicality, especially in its breakdown of illness, aging, and death. The Eucharist affirms

---

[28] His most explicit response to a variety of phenomenological thinkers is found in his *Loving Struggle* (Falque 2018).

[29] In a sense this is the central thesis of the entire book.

[30] "It is therefore advisable to question the entirety of human experience, everything involved in the Eucharist, in order to be transformed by God: animality (Eucharistic heritage [the figure of the lamb]), the body (Eucharistic content [this is my body]), eros (Eucharistic modality [a body given]), and finally abiding (Eucharistic aim [remain in me and I in you])" (Falque 2015a, p. 280).

[31] One should note that eros as it occurs within marriage and only via a traditional heterosexual union is central to his analysis of such nuptials. This entails for him a particular account of sexual difference as complementarity that allows women to be more fully "feminine" and men more fully "masculine."

not that God becomes an animal (cf. the prohibition of portraying Christ as an animal at the Council of Trullo), but does claim that God enters our animality, as the mode of access to human corporeality (2015a, pp. 282–83). Christ assumes the full "chaos" of our passions and impulses (2015a, p. 283). Falque distinguishes this animality (as organicity) from bestiality (a descent into sin) and from a transformation into a full humanity or even divinity via the resurrection. We must return to a full affirmation of Christ's body and its real materiality; he assures us that this leads neither to cannibalism nor to a purely symbolic interpretation (2015a, pp. 286–87). Thus, this affirmation of Christ's corporeality in the Eucharist can be likened to the experience of the body in illness or within erotic experience. In these cases, there is a sharing of forces, in which two bodies become a single flesh via spousal union or sexual difference, which prefigure the Eucharist (2015a, pp. 290–93).

Falque pushes this further in the third book of his trilogy on the Paschal Triduum, *The Wedding Feast of the Lamb*, in which he equates the "modality of eros" with the "modality of eucharisticized body"; indeed, eros emerges as a form of eucharistic sacrifice (Falque 2015b, pp. 47–49). He again reiterates that Eucharist transforms our embodiedness from mere animality to full humanity (2015b, p. 199). Holding on to the notion of transubstantiation as giving an account of real presence, he suggests that there must be a real conversion of the bread/body: "*This is my body* points above all to a body made of flesh and blood that is the body of the Word incarnate, one that is in another mode (not localized but transubstantiated) and has another presence (of the Resurrected Christ and not simply of the historic Jesus). To take communion is to participate in the life of the Resurrected One, not to share fragments of a flesh that it would be forbidden to chew" (2015b, p. 201). It is significant for him that Christ's body is given as bread, thus as nourishment.[32] Thus, Falque suggests a reversal is at work here: "the *becoming-flesh of the body* (Resurrection)" corresponds to "the *becoming body of the flesh* (Eucharist)" (2015b, p. 203). We eat Christ and are eaten by God in what he calls a phenomenology of "anti-digestion" and "ingurgitation," inasmuch as it functions to assimilate and incorporate us into the divine life without losing its physical and visceral connotations of chewing and digesting.[33]

He explicitly labels this account phenomenological and contends that phenomenology can help clarify what we might mean by incorporation.[34] This again brings together philosophical and theological dimensions: "In presenting myself for communion, and this time in the mode of incorporation and not simply of assimilation, I do not simply bring forward my own concerns and the sufferings of my flesh; he brings forward his divine mode of being in his body, through which he embraces and takes responsibility for all the sufferings of our flesh" (2015b, p. 208). We must be "integrated and transformed in God" via a double movement, "that by which the Word is incorporated or assimilated into the bread in its kenosis (subjective genitive), and that by which we are ourselves caught in this act of integration and transformation (objective genitive). ... the eucharistic sacrifice ensures that we are ourselves offered, rather than that we consume it" (2015b, p. 209). He concludes by stressing again that Eucharist is able to transform our animality into a fuller humanity: "transubstantiation, incorporation, and consecration constitute three stages of a *this is my body* that is capable of taking on and transforming our humanity, and indeed also our animality, in the expectation of an adoration that can bring us back to our nature as created humans and that integrates us in a definitive and radical filiation" (2015b, p. 209). We have thus moved significantly from the initial affirmation of organicity and animality as full (albeit secular) humanity to an important distinction in which only Christian and explicitly eucharistic experience (including of suffering and resurrection) constitutes true humanity; the "atheist" experience remains a lesser "animality" only. This sort of slippage occurs frequently in Falque's work,

---

[32] "In making his body a *this*, the Christ given for us, in his humility or as his *humus* (earth), borrows the path of the thing, just as the bread given to us serves as nourishment to fortify us" (2015b, p. 202; trans. lightly modified).

[33] "Nobody simply eats God, but we are always in some respect eaten by him" (2015b, p. 205). "That which is assimilated by us, in the unique case of the body of Christ, is what assimilates us; or rather, paradoxically, it incorporates us even into Christ-there whom we eat" (2015b, p. 206).

[34] "We can say that what goes for phenomenological intentionality applies also to eucharistic incorporation" (2015b, p. 207).

which always wants to start with the "human as such" (*l'homme tout court*) as shared philosophical basis and yet frequently thinks of the Christian experience as more fully phenomenological and more fully human.

In either case, he maintains that the Eucharist reactualizes the mystery as phenomenon each time we participate in it: "Because we participate in the Mass consciously, or rather, through our consciousness, we are inclined to forget the silent experience of the body-to-body [referring to hand-to-hand combat, as in Jacob's struggle with the angel] of human and God that should guide us here" (2015b, p. 210). Our whole body must participate in this.[35] Falque stresses that this involves not only eating the body, but also seeing and loving God through it in order to achieve "incorruptibility."[36] Here we have moved back to a theological analysis, as presumably phenomenology has no access to an experience of incorruptibility. At the same time, Falque continues to stress the sensory dimensions of the experience: "In the eucharistic Adoration, none of our senses, up to and including that of sight, will be forgotten as we try to come to an understanding of the One who, by the act of manducation, will be tasted" (2015b, p. 213). They are, however, always quickly assimilated to theological affirmations: "After all, when I see him, in his body and under the stable form of the species of bread, I think—no, I believe—that he sees me: me, in my body that lives and shares with him that mute experience of a body-to-body, where my sense and my interior Chaos will emerge so that I take responsibility for them and they are changed" (2015b, p. 215). Here also he ends by superimposing his account of the Eucharist on an account of marriage or sexual difference and references to illness (2015b, p. 223).[37]

Thus, although Falque's discussion is far more attentive to the concrete ecclesial instantiation of Eucharist (citing from the texts of the Roman mass) and its theological heritage (with frequent references to theological controversies, patristic and medieval texts, and various historical eucharistic positions) and also stresses its sensory and affective phenomenality far more fully than either Marion or Lacoste do (via the analysis of organicity and animality), the constant conflation of these two dimensions is problematic, because it makes the argument by assimilation or even wholesale merging of phenomenological and theological assertions rather than by showing how these dimensions are actually parallel or linked. We slip from phenomenological corporeality or animality to theological transformation into incorruptibility rather too smoothly, in a way that certainly cannot be sustained on purely phenomenological terms. The phenomenological parameters are here employed in order to justify essentially theological positions without further phenomenological description of Eucharist as encountered or lived in human experience. Theological affirmations about the meaning of Eucharist are simply assumed and superimposed on the phenomenological interpretation of corporeality. Sometimes the reverse occurs, phenomenological assumptions about human corporeality are imposed on the theological event and simply taken to be present and applicable there without showing in any substantive fashion how that might be the case. Although the "Rubicon" between philosophy and theology is surely crossed here, such crossing may have been too hasty.

The superimposition of erotic and palliative experiences on Eucharist seems especially problematic. Does the body "spread out on the hospital bed" really function like the body in erotic experience and can both be likened to what body means phenomenologically or how body is experienced when one participates in the Eucharist? That seems highly questionable. The hospitalized body is not experienced as an eroticized body; indeed, it would be quite problematic if that were the case. Although they

---

[35] "The eucharistic memory cannot then remain indifferent to the body, to its weight and its wounds that are endlessly reactualized; otherwise, it risks being held and kept simply by the consciousness, as the memory of a past that has been superseded. Everything is inscribed in our bodies, and nothing has been forgotten of the body of the Resurrected One in the total of the eucharisticized bodies. By eating his body and drinking his blood, we don't simply celebrate the memory of an event, even if that event was foundational for all humanity. We drink the blood of *his* life that flows as far as our veins, and we eat the flesh of *his* body that feeds us even in our inmost organs" (2015b, p. 212).

[36] "It is not enough to *eat* him to participate in this mode of incorruptibility. We can still, and we should still, lead ourselves to *see* him and to love him as the power of transformation" (2015b, p. 213).

[37] These superimpositions or conflations also return in an essay on palliative care: (Falque 2019, pp. 91–116).

may share a kind of vulnerability that cannot be expressed either in terms of extension or purely affective flesh, it has not been shown that this vulnerability is experienced in the same way, or is phenomenologically of the same sort. Neither is Christ's "body" (or the bread) experienced as either hospitalized (like the sick or dying body) or eroticized (like the body of the beloved). Do we "intend" these bodies in the same way, are directed toward them as phenomena in parallel fashion? Or are their intuitive experiences significantly alike? Surely our experience of chewing the bread—even in all its visceral physicality—is quite unlike our experience of touching or dressing someone's wounds or our experience of caressing or copulating with beloved flesh. These phenomena are neither of the same kind (*Wesen*), nor are they experienced in a similar fashion as regards their phenomenality, whether in terms of intuition or intentionality. There is little meaningful similarity here that could be phenomenologically discerned within the horizons of the experience. Thus, although Falque's eucharistic phenomenology certainly stresses its corporeal dimensions far more than Marion or Lacoste do, this corporeality comes with problematic assumptions that conflate different types of corporeal experience in a way that does not necessarily illuminate how corporeality is at stake in eucharistic experience specifically. How else, then, might a phenomenological analysis proceed?

4. The Phenomenality of Eucharistic Experience in Its Liturgical Context

How might it be possible to describe the experience of Eucharist in purely philosophical terms, that is, in terms of how it appears to human consciousness? Can a religious phenomenality, such as that of sacramental experience, be discerned and depicted philosophically? An analysis might proceed in three steps: First of all, Eucharist is a fully corporeal, sensory, and affective *phenomenon* that occurs within specific temporal and spatial dimensions of human experience, usually in the context of a "religious" (normally ecclesial) setting. Secondly, in a way ignored by almost all the philosophical accounts (and sometimes even by theological ones), Eucharist almost always happens within the specific rites of various Christian liturgical traditions, thus within a broader context of liturgical experience, what we might call phenomenologically its *horizon* of experience. Third, this liturgical context or horizon gives rise to or at least seeks to shape a particular kind of *intentionality* that is directed toward the phenomenon of the Eucharist in specific ways. How might such an analysis and depiction be useful? A phenomenological analysis of the human dimensions of participating in this religious ritual may enable us on the one hand to understand more fully why humans engage in such rituals, that is, enrich our *philosophical* understanding of the meaning of human experience. On the other hand, it may also provide methodological tools for a *theological* interpretation of Eucharist (although that implication is not pursued in the present essay, but left to the theologian to explore further). Let us take each of the three (interrelated) dimensions in turn and then draw out some preliminary philosophical implications.

4.1. Eucharist as Phenomenon

How does the phenomenon of eucharistic participation present itself to our consciousness? How do we sense, perceive, experience, or apprehend it? How do we experience the elements? How do we see, touch, or taste them, in what manner do they impact our perceiving or apprehending? What are the concrete parameters within which this sacramental experience appears as Eucharist? In its most mundane sense, Eucharist is experienced first of all as a concrete phenomenon within the world that has tactile, sensorial dimensions: The plate and chalice are seen; the institutional texts or anaphora are heard; the bread and wine are tasted, even smelled; depending on the tradition, various elements (the host, the chalice, a spoon) are touched with either hands or lips. These sensory elements can be observed and described; they can be likened to other experiences of sensing, touching, tasting and distinguished from them via imaginative variation, by examining how they appear to consciousness similarly or differently. In each case, this would not be a description primarily of a purely subjective experience of the sacrament at a specific moment, but an analysis of how it generally or usually appears, how it is experienced within the parameters that make it the sort of experience that manifests in recognizable ways.

The sensory experience also arouses emotions and affects. The participants "feel" the eucharistic bread and wine not only in a purely tactile sense, but also in terms of its affectivity. Often the experience is approached with awe and veneration, sometimes it generates joy or peace, almost always is it experienced with other people and thus as a communal event in which affect is shaped significantly by what transpires within the participating group and not just the individual. Eucharist is also always experienced at a specific time and place, even when it is taken to a hospital or sickroom rather than consumed in church. Especially the ecclesial time and place function to situate the experience of the Eucharist; contra Lacoste, it is never a disembodied, atemporal, aspatial experience, but always one that involves setting aside time, coming into a place, as well as corporeal movement and gesture. This corporeal dimension is immensely important: Participants bow or kneel, fold their hands or open them for reception, come forward, cross themselves or fold their hands over their chest, kneel at an altar rail, and ultimately return to their seats or place to stand, finally leaving the church altogether, yet maybe with the taste of wine and bread still on their lips. Eucharist thus involves our bodies, how we move and position ourselves, the gestures with which we celebrate and receive, and obviously the activities of physically receiving, chewing, drinking, swallowing. Furthermore, the eucharistic elements are not simply contemplated (except in the Roman Catholic practice of eucharistic adoration), they are eaten and consumed, ingested into our bodies, thus become part of us in some form.

These "elements" thus clearly do not appear simply as objects that can be moved around or manipulated at will (in this respect Lacoste is entirely correct). Nor do they manifest primarily as tools that are useable or useful in a kind of utilitarian fashion. But they do not simply come "over" us or fall upon us. Rather, our experience of them is evidenced by the way we treat them: We process with them, hold them up for veneration, approach them with awe or reverence, touch them with a mixture of reluctance and eagerness. We also do not leave them as they are, but speak signifying words over them, break and pour them, ultimately consume them. We share them; Eucharist is essentially plural and communal experience. The physicality of the elements is clearly significant (highlighted by some of the liturgical texts used for the rite in several traditions); otherwise we would not treat them in this fashion. Falque is right to stress the corporeal dimension; Eucharist is not a purely "spiritual" experience but involves physical bread and wine, eating and drinking. Eucharist manifests to consciousness in physical, visceral, material ways, but at the same time conveys a significance within the experience that suggests that this is not *mere* physicality, but that the physical conveys a meaning that is broader than its "objectivity" or materiality. These two dimensions cannot be separated in eucharistic experience: It is not that there is the "visible" and physical on the one hand (bread and wine) and the "invisible" or spiritual on the other (body and blood of Christ), but it is precisely the physical or material that signifies as more than itself. Materiality signifies as "sacred" (i.e., set apart) in some fashion and this is conveyed within and through the concrete (albeit not purely subjective) experience.

Such an analysis of the phenomenon can be deepened by examining how it appears to memory, anticipation, or imagination, not merely to concrete sensory perception. That is to say, Eucharist signifies not only via the moment in which it is consumed and the tactile dimension of that experience, but also through the ways in which that experience is prepared through the memory of previous eucharistic participation and the anticipation of future partaking. More narrowly, the moment of touching and tasting is informed through the retention in memory of the anaphora or institution narrative that has just been proclaimed, the resonance of the Lord's Prayer that has often just been prayed, the lingering memory of the exchange of peace, the touching of hands or embrace. The anticipation of participation, as one stands in line waiting for others to drink from the same cup, is similarly a significant part of the experience of Eucharist in many Christian traditions. The "moment" of eucharistic participation is thus distended through memory and anticipation. All these and surely many other dimensions can be depicted and unfolded in much more detail and described as part of the phenomenon of eucharistic experience.

4.2. The Liturgical Horizon

Yet, maybe even more significantly, Eucharist is always experienced within and against a larger liturgical horizon. The moment of eucharistic participation rarely happens in isolation; it occurs at the height of an entire ceremony, that is itself part of a larger liturgical experience encompassing the entire liturgical year with all its feasts and fasts and varied celebrations. Eucharist may well be experienced differently on a weekday than a Sunday, during advent rather than at the Paschal vigil. Some of its signification shifts through the meaning given by the specific liturgical context.[38] More fundamentally, Eucharist, as experienced within liturgy, requires entering a "sacred" building, i.e., a building set aside for this use and often decorated and prepared in lavish fashion; it involves positioning oneself in certain ways, cultivating a particular attitude that can be analyzed in terms of openness, of contrition, of celebration, and so forth. All the phenomenological dimensions just mentioned for the moment of eucharistic experience specifically are important elements of the larger liturgical context as well.

Spatiality and temporality are even far more significant here or at least emerge more fully. For example, the tension between anamnesis and eschatological expectation as they are expressed in various eucharistic anaphoras reflect a particular temporality within liturgical experience more broadly, as does the cycling between feasts and fasts throughout the liturgical calendar. The back-and-forth between celebration and contrition, the modes of liturgical repetition, the ways in which remembered past and anticipated future are brought into the present experience all shape the horizon against which Eucharist (and, indeed, other sacraments) is phenomenalized. They are not isolated instants frozen in time, but extended and repeated moments within a larger liturgical temporality that gives meaning to the particular experience. Similarly, the "sacred space" in which Eucharist is experienced provides a liturgical setting. We do not simply eat bread in a perfunctory or haphazard fashion, but we consume it after entering a space that has been set aside for liturgical gathering, a space that has been deliberately planned, organized, decorated over centuries of tradition, thus endowing it with an experience of spatiality that differs from other experiences of eating.

The same goes for corporeal, sensory, and affective dimensions. The liturgical context illuminates how we handle and treat and approach the elements, prepares us for their reception. The participants' bodies do not suddenly materialize out of nowhere when they go up to receive the bread and wine, but they have been standing, sitting, or kneeling throughout an entire rite that has prepared them for reception of the sacrament and provides a context for it. Particular movements, postures, and gestures have been exercised throughout the liturgy in meaningful fashion. Such postures and gestures orient us toward the sanctuary, express our veneration or our penitence, prepare our bodies by inscribing the liturgical movements upon them, often to the point where they become almost automatic and enter us deeply. We experience our bodies as oriented toward the eucharistic event and as prepared through listening to music, prayers, homily, as well as bells and other sounds, via seeing burning candles, beautiful chalices, colorful vestments, and other implements, via smelling incense, ultimately to touch and taste the eucharistic elements. The experience of affect is similarly not limited to the moment of the Eucharist itself, but the broader liturgical context prepares our affectivity in manifold and recognizable fashion; some emotions are explicitly generated by the rite (or at least the rite seems geared at generating such affect), some are involved in more subjective ways. We raise our hands with awe, we bow in veneration, we sing with exultation, we meditate with reflection; all these and many more are at work in liturgical and eucharistic experience. Isolating the eucharistic moment from the larger liturgical context fails to take seriously the ways in which consciousness is prepared to

---

[38] At the same time, it is worth noting that in most Christian traditions, the eucharistic liturgy itself undergoes the fewest changes and thus has the most stable signification. For example, vespers and matins (or vigil) in the Orthodox tradition have far more "moveable" elements that differ depending on the occasion than the eucharistic "divine liturgy." And although even the more scripted Western rites (e.g., Roman Catholic or Anglican) have now adopted a variety of eucharistic anaphoras and cycle between them, these are still fairly stable. Yet, the *experience* of Eucharist is clearly not wholly identical on every occasion but influenced by the temporality of the church year and even its spatiality (e.g., in a ceremony held outside).

experience or apprehend, how it is directed toward revelation or manifestation, how it becomes the very context for such manifestation.

It is also worth noting here that such sensory or affective dimensions are rarely of the utterly overwhelming character described by Marion; liturgy does not completely bedazzle us, totally sweep us away, but often has a far more mundane character. Regular participants in liturgy become habituated to it; its modes of repetition function to inscribe it on their bodies, generating consistent emotions or moods of expectation. In this way, the larger liturgical context forms a liturgical disposition that is marked in sensorial, affective, and corporeal ways. Our bodies and emotions become prepared for liturgy and Eucharist through the cycles of repetition and the habituation they engender. Indeed, the experience may be more "saturated," certainly richer and more meaningful, when it is carefully prepared and anticipated, when participants know what they are doing and how to orient themselves toward the experience. Nor is boredom—as Lacoste often insists must be involved because we are not yet in the eschaton—necessarily present only or primarily because we are too tied to the world and have not undone, annihilated, or suspended it. It may certainly be true that the logic of aspects of religious experience, including the Eucharist, challenges aspects of the "logic" of the "world" but it cannot annihilate it entirely or wholly, because otherwise no experience would be possible at all.[39]

Both in terms of the (extended, not punctual) moment of Eucharist itself and the broader liturgical context, the experience is almost always a communal one: One participates with others, in most Christian traditions all drink from the same cup and share the same bread; the community has gathered and sung and listened and venerated together. If theologically we affirm that both Eucharist and church in some way constitute "body of Christ" this is suggested on some level even by the experience itself inasmuch as it occurs within community, is received and passed on to others, gathers the congregation together and in visual, auditory, even tactile ways, links us to each other, shapes an experience that at least for a short time knits us together as one. Eucharist is rarely (and liturgy even more rarely) experienced as a purely individual event, but its very experience is shaped by the communal context within which it occurs. Like feasting, its experience requires the communal dimension of plural participation in order to function as experience of Eucharist. Its orientation and direction, even its temporality and spatiality, point to the plurality of fellowship.[40] The communal dimension is important even for how affect functions: Music impacts differently when it is sung by many voices; gathering together, embracing or passing the peace, all shape and provide a context for how liturgy and sacraments are experienced. These liturgical parameters and contexts obviously also need to be worked out far more fully, but this brief description provides at least some sense of the phenomenological horizon within which eucharistic experience can appear and become meaningful.[41]

4.3. Liturgical Intentionality

Third, the phenomenality of eucharistic experience, prepared and contextualized by the broader liturgical horizon, shapes a liturgical and eucharistic intentionality. Contra Marion, who wants to erase intentionality from religious phenomenality because it apparently imposes conditions, turns the recipient of revelation into a Cartesian subject constituting the phenomenon, or makes the phenomenon of revelation too predictable, intentionality is very much at stake and engaged in such experience. The liturgy forms a disposition and expectation, that is, an intentionality that prepares consciousness to intend and receive Eucharist in particular ways. We can prepare for liturgy and Eucharist, indeed, we *must* prepare for them, but that does not imply that we impose concepts on it arbitrarily or exercise total control over it. Such exercise of control is partly prevented through the fact that, experientially

---

[39] Indeed, theologically speaking, this would be Manichean and deny that the world is created good.
[40] Again, that is not to say that a particular person might feel out of sorts or even excluded during a rite, but to describe how the experience manifests structurally, i.e. through the parameters assumed, organized, and conveyed by the rite.
[41] I have attempted to give a fuller account of how liturgical experience manifests specifically in the Eastern Orthodox tradition (Gschwandtner 2020).

speaking, liturgy always precedes us, is often scripted for us, and is experienced as something into which we enter rather than something we manufacture. To form a dispositionality that allows for reception is not tantamount to forming a Cartesian subject in total control of the objects it encounters.[42]

The liturgical context shapes how consciousness becomes directed toward the phenomenon. Everything about the liturgical experience shows the importance and need for such preparation: Congregations meet at designated times, in elaborately prepared spaces, engage in complicated rituals developed and revised over long periods, often performed by carefully trained leaders, and do so over and over again, often with only slight variations. The rituals, whether sacramental or liturgical, signify precisely because of the weight of their history; a recently invented ritual means quite differently and while someone who unknowingly stumbles upon a ritual never before encountered might have an overwhelming experience, it is questionable whether it would signify in meaningful ways. Religious phenomena require preparation: physical, corporeal, mental, emotional, and spiritual. There is obviously no guarantee that the preparation will always "work"; even carefully and elaborately prepared ritual can fail. But preparation is inscribed upon the very phenomenality of liturgy, including via the aforementioned tension in which it holds anamnesis and anticipation.

To return more specifically to the Eucharist: The anaphora prayer in the liturgy of St. Basil in the Byzantine rite prays to "show" and manifest the bread as the body of Christ.[43] Here we have something much closer to a phenomenological than to a metaphysical or ontological claim. The liturgical rite orients its participants toward Eucharist as body and blood of Christ; our intentionality is shaped liturgically in such a way as to receive it as body and blood of Christ. Phenomenologically speaking we might say that the point is not to explain some magical metaphysical change in the elements, but to see how everything liturgically orients us to a certain kind of reception, to shaping consciousness to enable it to receive Eucharist as the gift of Christ. This also requires preparation; it cannot happen automatically or on its own. The whole liturgy is needed in order to prepare our minds, hearts, bodies, affects, and dispositions for eucharistic participation. It is not that this piece of bread or this sip of wine suddenly gives us the sensory perception of being in first-century Jerusalem, standing by the cross—indeed, even the most literal theological interpretations do not imply such time travel or a literal re-sacrificing of Christ—but the entire hermeneutic and phenomenological horizon of liturgy shapes an intentionality that hopes for God's presence, orients itself toward the divine in contrition and veneration, forms an attitude of expectation and receptivity for the gifts. They signify, that is to say, have meaning and can be intuitively received, within that prepared and intentional horizon of liturgy.

4.4. Phenomenological Implications

What, then, are we to make of these very (albeit not entirely) mundane aspects of experience: eating, moving, holding, gesturing, embracing? First, this implies that Eucharist, contra Lacoste, is also (or at least) an entirely human, material, physical, sensory activity.[44] Eucharist can never "mean" or "signify" without such mundane, earthy, physical dimensions. Yet, even within the ordinary, purely human, analysis of consciousness we can already detect that this experience is set apart in some form: We do not walk up to the altar in quite our usual stride, we do not simply grasp the bread but receive it from another, we usually dispense it in ornate cups or chalices set aside for special use, we bow or kneel for parts of the liturgical rite, sometimes even embrace, and we exercise all these gestures and motions in very deliberate, scripted ways. Even purely philosophically, something can, then, be "read off" from our experience here and, indeed, from how this experience is structured, what form it "usually" takes, what shape tradition has determined it "should" take (even as those traditions are plural and

---

[42] Indeed, that is probably a caricature even of what Descartes proposes, as Marion has shown in various places.

[43] Rather than praying for a transformation of the elements into body and blood of Christ, as does the liturgy of St. John Chrysostom and many Western eucharistic rites.

[44] Cyril of Jerusalem already stresses this sensory element in an oft-quoted injunction for the eucharistic participants to touch their lips still wet from the Eucharist and anoint their other senses (Cyril of Jerusalem 2017, V. 22, p. 135).

obviously undergo changes over time).[45] Experience is prepared and figured in certain deliberate ways in order to produce affect, corporeal sensation, disposition. If liturgy is meant to transform us, it has to mean a transformation—though not elimination or undoing—of our ordinary human experience, of our consciousness, of our awareness, of our disposition and orientation. This is obviously not purely mental (consciousness in phenomenology is not simply about the mental), but emotional, affective, corporeal, sensorial, heart-felt, and so forth. Consciousness in the phenomenological sense is the locus of any kind of experience, not just the seat of intelligence. We are speaking here also of an experience of the heart, and of the emotions (Steinbock 2014). Eucharist appeals to and is engaged in all of them and a full account must do justice to this.

More broadly, one must also conclude that, phenomenologically speaking, religious experience is not simply a matter of overwhelming intuition imposed on us by a bedazzling phenomenon of revelation, but involves an important dimension of the shaping of dispositions and intentionality. Religious experience, at least liturgical experience and specifically eucharistic experience, emerges as a very deliberate and intentional directedness toward the phenomena, as an elaborate preparation and formation of intentionality, as the inculcation of habits and dispositions that allow for receptivity. Religious experience, liturgical experience, or eucharistic experience, does not come out of nowhere, but is meaningful precisely because we anticipate it, prepare for it, are oriented toward it, engage in it repeatedly and habitually, and do so within a community that precedes, embraces, and follows upon us. Furthermore, eucharistic experience, maybe most religious experience, is plural experience, not singular or isolated experience, as most philosophical analyses of religion have tended to imply.

This might also suggest that a way to "protect" the "mystery" of the Eucharist (as *mysterion*) need not take a wholly apopathic path in which the phenomenon is either so overwhelming that it cannot be perceived, as in Marion, or so kenotic that it becomes a practically empty non-experience, as in Lacoste. Nor must it be (kataphatically?) conflated with other human experiences (of eros or illness) to bring out its corporeal character, as Falque seeks to do. It is precisely the phenomenality of the broader liturgical horizon and of the intentionality that is at work within liturgical experience that hints at the manifestation of mystery: The sense that no preparation—however elaborate, beautiful, and perfectly performed—is sufficient, that no level of contrition—however groveling or transparent—will ever make us wholly "worthy" of it, that no intensity of feasting—however enthusiastic and euphoric—will ever transport us into the eschaton. Even the most carefully scripted liturgical event still maintains elements of mystery; indeed, often it is precisely this elaborate and complicated scripting that conveys the tenor of mystery and unfathomability. To say that Eucharist or liturgy are experienced always within the temporal and spatial dimensions of this world, are experienced in fully corporeal, sensorial, and affective ways, does not erase any trace of mystery, does not deny the divine transcendence invoked within it, but instead opens up the human earthly, moral, finite dimensions to them. We bring to liturgy our finitude, our vulnerability, our precarity and make of them an offering to the one we hope will heal us, feed us, console us, meet us, yet never wholly, never in such a way that we are done and need no longer return. While a purely phenomenological analysis cannot identify the divine, not name a God who becomes revealed, it can surely depict how dimensions of the mysterious mark the structures of the manifest.

All this may also help the philosopher understand more fully why ritual experience has been such an important element of human culture for most of human history—and maybe why it seeks other venues, such as sports or politics, to express itself when the religious has been abandoned or is no longer experienced as meaningful. Humans seem to need ritual, on the one hand for its signifying

---

[45] To speak of "usually" or "general" here and above does not imply, phenomenologically, some sort of "least common denominator" or "average" of empirical experience, but instead tries to get at the character (or *Wesen*) of the phenomenon, the kind of phenomenon it manifests as, even when a particular empirical instance may go astray. That does not, however, turn it immediately into a normative claim about how Eucharist (or a religious phenomenon) "ought" to appear or how a rite should be structured or organized, but remains a descriptive claim.

dimensions—it gives meaning to human experiences, marks them as important, organizes them in ways that render them significant, opens us onto mysteries that transcend our ordinary experience and yet manifest at least partially within them—and on the other for its communal dimensions—many rituals are plural and public, they elevate us beyond ourselves, allow us to participate in something larger than ourselves, give meaning that transcends one's merely personal and subjective experience. And such a phenomenological analysis may ultimately also provide methodological resources for a more explicitly theological reflection, without itself becoming dependent on theological presuppositions or assumptions. In this way, phenomenology may be of use to the theologian while remaining true to its commitment to exploring important aspects of the human condition as they manifest within human experience.

Funding: This research received no external funding.

Conflicts of Interest: The author declares no conflict of interest.

References

Alexandrescu, Vlad. 2007. Descartes and Pascal on the Eucharist. *Perspective on Science* 15: 434–49. [CrossRef]

Backus, Irena. 2011. Leibniz's Concept of Substance and his Reception of John Calvin's Doctrine of the Eucharist. *British Journal of the History of Philosophy* 19: 917–33. [CrossRef]

Cyril of Jerusalem. 2017. *Lectures on the Christian Sacraments.* Translated by Maxwell E. Johnson. Yonkers: St. Vladimir's Seminary Press.

Falque, Emmanuel. 2015a. This is my Body: Contribution to a Philosophy of the Eucharist. In *Carnal Hermeneutics.* Edited by Richard Kearney and Brian Treanor. New York: Fordham University Press.

Falque, Emmanuel. 2015b. *The Wedding Feast of the Lamb: Eros, the Body, and the Eucharist.* Translated by Georges Hughes. New York: Fordham University Press.

Falque, Emmanuel. 2016. *Crossing the Rubicon: The Borderlands of Philosophy and Theology.* Translated by Reuben Shank. New York: Fordham University Press.

Falque, Emmanuel. 2018. *The Loving Struggle: Phenomenological and Theological Debates.* Translated by Bradley B. Onishi, and Lucas McCracken. London: Rowman & Littlefield.

Falque, Emmanuel. 2019. Toward an Ethics of the Spread Body. In *Somatic Desire: Recovering Corporeality in Contemporary Thought.* Edited by Sara Horton and et al. Lanham: Lexington.

Finn, Douglas. 2015–2016. Spiritual Consumption: Eating and the Christian Eucharist in Hegel. *The Owl of Minerva* 47: 109–67. [CrossRef]

Fouke, Daniel C. 1992. Metaphysics and the Eucharist in the Early Leibniz. *Studia Leibnitiana* 24: 145–59.

Gschwandtner, Christina M. 2014. *Degrees of Givenness: On Saturation in Jean-Luc Marion.* Bloomington: Indiana University Press.

Gschwandtner, Christina M. 2017. Jean-Luc Marion's Spirituality of Adoration and its Implications for a Phenomenology of Religion. In *Breached Horizons: The Philosophy of Jean-Luc Marion.* Edited by Steve Lofts and Antonio Calcagno. London: Rowman and Littlefield.

Gschwandtner, Christina M. 2019. What is Phenomenology of Religion? *Philosophy Compass* 14: e12566. [CrossRef]

Gschwandtner, Christina M. 2020. *Welcoming Finitude: Toward a Phenomenology of Orthodox Liturgy.* New York: Fordham University Press.

Jones, Tamsin. 2011. *A Genealogy of Marion's Philosophy of Religion: Apparent Darkness.* Bloomington: Indiana University Press.

Kearney, Richard, ed. 2004. *Debates in Continental Philosophy: Conversations with Contemporary Thinkers.* New York: Fordham University Press.

Lacoste, Jean-Yves. 2004. *Experience and the Absolute: Disputed Questions on the Humanity of Man.* Translated by Mark Raftery-Skeban. New York: Fordham University Press.

Lacoste, Jean-Yves. 2005. Liturgy and Coaffection. In *The Experience of God: A Postmodern Response.* Edited by Kevin Hart and Barbara Wall. New York: Fordham University Press.

Lacoste, Jean-Yves. 2011. *Être en danger.* Paris: Cerf.

Lacoste, Jean-Yves. 2015. *L'intuition sacramentelle et autres essais.* Paris: Ad Solem.

Mackinlay, Shane. 2004. Eyes Wide Shut: A Response to Marion's Account of the Journey to Emmaus. *Modern Theology* 20: 447–56. [CrossRef]

Marion, Jean-Luc. 1991. *God without Being*. Translated by Thomas A. Carlson. Chicago: University of Chicago Press.

Marion, Jean-Luc. 2002a. *Prolegomena to Charity*. Translated by Stephen E. Lewis. New York: Fordham University Press.

Marion, Jean-Luc. 2002b. *Being Given: Toward a Phenomenology of Givenness*. Translated by Jeffrey L. Kosky. Stanford: Stanford University Press.

Marion, Jean-Luc. 2002c. *In Excess: Studies of Saturated Phenomena*. Translated by Robyn Horner, and Vincent Berraud. New York: Fordham University Press.

Marion, Jean-Luc. 2007. *The Erotic Phenomenon*. Translated by Stephen E. Lewis. Chicago: University of Chicago Press.

Marion, Jean-Luc. 2008. *The Visible and the Revealed*. New York: Fordham University Press.

Marion, Jean-Luc. 2015. *Negative Certainties*. Translated by Stephen E. Lewis. Chicago: University of Chicago Press.

Marion, Jean-Luc. 2016. *Givenness and Revelation*. Translated by Stephen E. Lewis. Oxford: Oxford University Press, pp. 76–77.

Marion, Jean-Luc. 2017. *Believing in Order to See*. New York: Fordham University Press.

Sokolowski, Robert. 1994. *Eucharistic Presence: A Study in the Theology of Disclosure*. Washington, DC: Catholic University of America Press.

Steinbock, Anthony. 2014. *Moral Emotions: Reclaiming the Evidence of the Heart*. Evanston: Northwestern University Press.

Wallenfang, Donald W. 2010. Sacramental Givenness: The Notion of Givenness in Husserl, Heidegger, and Marion, and Its Import for Interpreting the Phenomenality of the Eucharist. *Philosophy and Theology* 22: 131–54. [CrossRef]

Article

Creaturely Communal Ontology in Practice: John Zizioulas in Dialogue with Ritual Theory

John W. Compton IV

Center for Biomedical Ethics and Society, Vanderbilt University Medical Center, Nashville, TN 37232, USA; john.w.compton.1@vumc.org

Received: 1 August 2019; Accepted: 25 August 2019; Published: 28 August 2019

Abstract: This article is born out of a deep concern for our current ecological crisis and serves as a beginning foundational work for how the Christian tradition can address global climate change. Our current way of being gives precedence to the autonomous individual, whose freedom is characterized by disregard for other creatures. John Zizioulas' communal ontology demonstrates that as the world was created out of God's loving will, it is comprised of relationship. Living into individuation and division is a refusal of this communion with other creatures and God, but the Eucharist serves as the ritual that brings Christians into communion through the remembrance of Christ. Ian McFarland's work on the theology of creation provides the helpful nuance that creaturely movement in communion must include the full diversity of creatures. I then turn to Bruce Morrill's work to demonstrate that the Eucharistic practice must have bearing beyond the walls of the church. It leads practitioners to live into eschatological hope and kenotic service to the world. John Seligman's ritual theory demonstrates that ritual practice can accomplish these goals because it creates a subjunctive 'as-if' world in the face of the world that is perceived as chaotic. Through the continuous practice of the ritual, participants are then formed to live into this subjunctive 'as-if' world without ritual precedence. In this way, the Eucharistic practice can prepare practitioners to live into the kenotic service to a world broken by individuation that has led to global climate change and creaturely destruction.

Keywords: John Zizioulas; communal ontology; ritual theory; creation; climate change

---

1. Introduction

One of the central characteristics of the late modern world is the primacy given to the autonomous individual, free to choose one's direction without societal strictures or consequences. This emphasis on the individual has been one of the contributing factors to the current ecological crisis manifest in global climate change: As humans see the individual as the only point of reference, any sense of relation to the rest of creation is ultimately forgotten. John D. Zizioulas' *Being as Communion: Studies in Personhood of the Church* demonstrates that from a Christian perspective true existence is only possible in relation with other persons and God. Though Zizioulas' communal ontology does have cosmological and practical dimensions, there is still the danger that such community does not involve the full richness of God's creation, such that these theories could never leave the walls of the church or the world of ideas. In this paper, I bring Zizioulas into conversation with Ian McFarland's notion of creaturely movement to sharpen this cosmological element in his communal, sacramental ontology. I then turn to Bruce Morrill's work to clearly understand the anamnestic character of the sacrament of the Eucharist. Finally, I bring this theological trajectory into practical focus through the ritual theoretical work of Adam Seligman and colleagues in *Ritual and Its Consequences: An Essay on the Limits of Sincerity*. This paper, then, serves as a foundation for exploring the ways in which Christian ritual practice can confront ecologically disastrous practices that are characteristic of late modern life.

2. Zizioulas: A Communal Ontology of Church and Sacraments

Zizioulas begins developing his notion of a communal ontology by turning to early arguments for Trinitarian Christian faith. In these attempts, the early Church Fathers faced the challenge of giving ontological content to each person of the Trinity while maintaining monotheistic biblical faith. The debates surrounding Trinitarian thought are well-known, but Zizioulas argues that what is most significant here is the philosophical revolution that took place when early Christians identified divine hypostasis with divine person (Zizioulas 2002). These arguments resulted in the philosophical notion that the person is constitutive of being and, therefore, that entities trace being back to the person, rather than being itself. These arguments could only be possible within Christian understanding of the world (Zizioulas 2002). Specifically, Zizioulas highlights that the world is not necessary in Christian cosmology. He writes that there is a "radical difference in ontology, to trace the world back to an ontology outside the world, that is, to God," which means that the world is a product of freedom, rather than necessity (Zizioulas 2002). In a Christian understanding of God, identifying the being of the world with the being of God means that, at its center, the world is fundamentally comprised by relationship. With the being of the world contingent on relationship to God, one must first understand God's relation to God's self. Therefore, Zizioulas emphasizes that for the Greek Fathers the unity of God consists in the person of the Father: "If God exists, He exists because the Father exists, that is, He who out of love freely begets the Son and brings forth the Spirit" (Zizioulas 2002). In this way, Christianity offers a unique understanding of ontology that situates the being of the world as a product of absolute freedom on behalf of the being of God that is the person of the Father.

A key element for understanding the weight of these arguments is Athanasius' response to Arianism. The first part of Athanasius' argument was his distinction between substance and will, which highlighted that the being of the Son is of the same substance as the Father and distinct from the being of the world (Zizioulas 2002). Zizioulas writes, "To say that the Son belongs to God's substance implies that substance *possesses almost by definition a relational character*" (Zizioulas 2002). In this way, then, relationality becomes an ontological category. Then, Zizioulas demonstrates that the Cappadocians identified the term hypostasis with *prosopon*. This last term is relational in nature, thereby making being in relation necessary for being at all (Zizioulas 2002). Consequently, the being of the world, even as it is a product of the will of God, is derived from the being of God. This distinction between substance and will, along with the Cappadocian development in relational ontology, leads Zizoulas to argue for a Christian understanding of the world as created by God out of freedom, rather than out of necessity.

Zizioulas maintains that this notion is not simply an academic idea abstracted from human experience. Because the being of the world is identified with the being of God, who creates in absolute freedom, there is a sense in which the world also shares in this freedom. Zizioulas, however, demonstrates that because creation is distinct from God, creatures experience the necessity of existence as a challenge to this freedom (Zizioulas 2002). He argues that for the human, there is a drive to transcend this necessity such that the human reality is a product of freedom, and yet, without a theological understanding of this freedom, this drive will inevitably end in nihilism (Zizioulas 2002).[1] Here, Zizioulas turns to theology to demonstrate that humans need an ontology rooted in that "which does not suffer from createdness" (Zizioulas 2002). Christ is the historical reality by which this sort ontology is possible for humanity. Because Christ was born of a virgin and is fully human and fully divine, he subsists in the same way that God the Father subsists: "Christology consequently is the proclamation to man that his nature can be 'assumed' and hypostasized in a manner free from ontological necessity of his biological hypostasis, which ... leads to individualism and death"

---

[1] See also Groppe (2005), who shows that, for Zizioulas, the most tragic aspect of human existence is that humans are unable to determine the beginning of their existence. Along these lines, Zizioulas, 42, points to Dostoyevsky, who proclaims through the character Kirilov in *The Possessed* that the only way for humans to obtain total freedom is through suicide.

(Zizioulas 2002). Zizioulas then turns to ritual to begin parsing out how humans are able to transcend biological necessity and enter into authentic personhood.

Through the sacramental ritual of baptism, humans come into a new relationship with the world as an ecclesial being. As such, their relation to the world is no longer limited to biological necessity. Zizioulas argues that since a human's baptism in Christ is the ritual death and resurrection of that individual, she or he dies to individuality and is resurrected into community: "The resurrectional aspect of baptism is therefore nothing other than *incorporation into the community*" (Zizioulas 2002). It is the relationships among these different people and with God that comprise humans as genuine persons, bringing them into an eschatological or sacramental hypostasis in the church. Zizioulas argues that in the ecclesial celebration of the Eucharist, humans are able to transcend the created necessity limiting whom one can love: "The Eucharist is the only historical context of human existence where the terms 'father,' 'brother,' etc., lose their biological exclusiveness and reveal ... relationships of free and universal love" (Zizioulas 2002). Encapsulated within the Eucharist is an eschatological dialectic in which humans feel a tension between the ecclesial and biological hypostasis. We feel a hope and desire to be fully that ecclesial being received from God while simultaneously living within the necessities of created biology. The body is not denied in the Eucharist and its eschatological hope. Instead, the body is ritually transformed, such that biological needs no longer determine the person's being: "The body, for its part as the hypostatic expression of the human person, is liberated from individualism and egocentricity and becomes a supreme expression of *community*—the Body of Christ, the body of the Church, the body of the eucharist" (Zizioulas 2002). The person, then, draws its being from the future, hoping for full realization of the resurrection-reality accomplished by Christ through participation in the ritual remembrance of the mystery of redemption in the Eucharist. This remembrance includes the living and the dead, such that the dead are not merely commemorated as passed away but, rather, there is an "assurance that the person has the final word over nature, in the same way that God the Creator as person and not nature had the very first word" (Zizioulas 2002).

The Eucharist is essential for Zizioulas' communal ontology because this ritualization is the place in which the truth of Christ is revealed to humanity through the very material of creation. In the Eucharist, the divisions among individuals are transcended, such that existence and communion are one—a truth coming from another world (Zizioulas 2002). The Eucharistic ritual accomplishes this reality through the embodied act of offering bread and wine to God for recapitulation. This patristic idea originates from Irenaeus and understands Christ as renewing all of creation through his incarnation. Through obedience to Christ, humanity undergoes the ongoing transformation until it is fully realized in the resurrection of the body.

Zizioulas then uses this idea to argue that within the Eucharist humans act as priests by connecting creation to God and, in so doing, make communion possible for nature, as well as for humanity (Zizioulas 2002). He argues that in being the priests of creation, humans recognize an ontological link between humanity and nature:

> The Eucharist consists in taking elements from the natural world, the bread and the wine which represent the created material world, and bringing them into the hands of the human being, the hands of Christ who is the man *par excellence* and the priest of creation, in order to refer them to God. (Zizioulas 2011, pp. 138–39)

Of essential importance in this statement is Zizioulas' identification of bread and wine with the material world, because these elements are the products of human labor. Before the world is ritually offered back to God, to whom the world belongs, it is transformed and developed through human hands.

Zizioulas' emphasis on communion is essential because it is the basis of truth and being.[2] He argues that creaturely truth is dependent truth requiring participation in God. What gives creation

---

[2] For a full historical theological survey of this idea, see (Zizioulas 2002, pp. 67–101).

its meaning is its movement from and toward its fulfillment in Christ, which is the *logos* of creation (Zizioulas 2002). As such, creation is inseparable from God's will, based in love rather than necessity, and the incarnation will be fully realized: "[Christ] represents the ultimate, unceasing will of the ecstatic love of God, who intends to lead created being into communion with His own life, to know Him and itself within this communion-event" (Zizioulas 2002). Practitioners experience communion as truth through the practiced freedom in the Eucharist, in which creatures are free from individualization and division and enter into communion. The Eucharist is a foretaste of this eschatological hope. Therefore, in the ritualization of the Eucharist, humans embody and live into the eschatological reality of authentic communal ontology by ritually bringing the world together and offering it to God in the Eucharistic communion.

Living into this authentic personhood and communion is distinct from the reality brought about by Original Sin. Zizioulas understands Original Sin as humans' refusal to live in communion with God, and instead understanding themselves as the ultimate point of reference for creation. He writes that from an ontological perspective "the fall consists in *the refusal to make being dependent on communion*, in a rupture between truth and communion" (Zizioulas 2002). Therefore, instead of being in communion with God, the true person who created the world, creation is referred to the finite, created human being limited by biological necessity. Through participating in the Eucharist, however, humans are ascetically trained to live beyond this necessity and refer creation back to God, with humans then serving as a link connecting God and creation (Zizioulas 2011). In other words, humans live into the truth of Christ that is practiced in the Eucharist and is conditioned by the epicletic (Spirit-invoked) and anamnetic (memory-invoking) character of that ritual (Zizioulas 2002). Zizioulas argues that the Spirit brings the *eschata* into history, transforming history from mere recollection of past events to a remembrance of the future. Bruce Morrill's work in *Anamnesis as Dangerous Memory: Political and Liturgical Theology in Dialogue* can provide some very helpful nuance to this eschatological understanding of the Eucharist by delving into the meaning of anamnesis and how it is practiced.

3. Eucharist: Eschatological Remembrance toward the Communion of All Creation

Morrill turns to the biblical scholarship of Nils Alstrup Dahl to demonstrate that in early Christian communities, anamnesis was "a recollection of the *gnosis* given to all those who have believed in the gospel, received baptism, and been incorporated into the church" (Morrill 2000). Specifically, Morrill shows that in the New Testament when Paul commands believers to remember their baptism, he is calling them to the remembrance of a knowledge known in an embodied way through the ritual of baptism. However, because the believers live in a fallen world, this knowledge remains a mystery, such that the life of the community must be continuously interrupted by the message of the Gospel (Morrill 2000). The Eucharist serves as this interruptive practice. Drawing upon the influential Orthodox theologian Alexander Schmemann, Morrill demonstrates that it is a break "from perceived reality of this fallen world [to] experience the vision of what God will yet bring about in the redeemed creation" (Morrill 2000). Morrill goes on to state that though this break is an interruption of time, it does not uphold a dichotomy between the profane and the sacred. Instead, the eschatological knowledge of a redeemed world is symbolically conveyed in the ritual. Nonetheless critical of the extent to which Schmemann believes eschatological vision to be so fully realized in the sacramental ritual, Morrill offers a helpful nuance by turning to Geoffrey Wainwright's demonstration (from early Christian literature) of how the Eucharist involves the expectation of both Christ's presence in the ritual and his final advent (Morrill 2000). Consequently, Morrill is able to highlight the eschatological dialectic within the Eucharist between the dangerous memory of Christ's suffering and the consolation of redemption it inaugurates (Morrill 2000). Morrill illustrates that the Eucharistic practice does more than simply console or train Christians to live as persons. In fact, the ritually engaged memory of the entirety of God's action in Christ draws Eucharistic participants into a dangerous memory, empowering them for lives of kenotic service to the world. Morrill's nuance demonstrates that this communal ontology cannot stay within the bounds of the ritual. Instead, it must push participants to engage more fully with the world.

This engagement with the world must, moreover, involve not just humans, but the entirety of creation. Zizioulas certainly has a cosmological sense in his understanding of the Eucharist, while Ian McFarland's notion of creaturely movement highlights the ways in which considering all of creation can substantiate a communal ontology. Like Zizioulas, McFarland argues that creation receives its being from God, with the Christian understanding of God as Triune imparting a relational understanding of God and, therefore, of creation. However, McFarland also highlights that one of the ways that creation is most distinct from God is its movement toward creaturely perfection (McFarland 2014). He shows that because God created that which is not God *ex nihilo*, creatures are not perfect, but that "it was possible … for creatures to attain a creaturely analogue to divine perfection over time as a gift from God" (McFarland 2014). Creatures' movement toward creaturely perfection is driven by a fundamental lack of the fullness of existence, which belongs only to the Triune God. In this movement, creatures are always dependent on God and other creatures: "These relationships shape the contours of creaturely movement, so that the process by which any creature becomes present to God is inseparable from its interactions with other creatures" (McFarland 2014). McFarland has a rich understanding of creation that includes humans, animals, microorganisms in soil, and even forces like electromagnetism and gravity (McFarland 2014). This understanding of a relational creation dependent on God and interdependent with other creatures deepens Zizioulas' communal ontology, expanding the ecclesial hypostasis from only interhuman relations to the rich diversity across creation. Such a view provides nuance to Zizioulas' understanding of the Eucharist as the place in which Christians practice the communal ontology.

Zizioulas is clear that in the Eucharist, humans act as the priests of creation by bringing the material world together and recapitulating it back to God. From this notion, Zizioulas avers that the protection of nature and the development of nature are not mutually exclusive: "The human being is the priest of creation in the sense that the material world he takes in his hands is *transformed* into something better than what it is *naturally*" (Zizioulas 2011). Zizioulas can thereby point to the Eucharist as the place in which humans symbolically gather all of creation through their labor of making bread from wheat and wine from grapes to offer it to God. McFarland's notion of creaturely movement is helpful here, showing the mutual involvement of all creatures in their movement toward communion, as theirs is a constitutive interdependence. Specifically, in preparing the bread and the wine, the human acting as the priest of creation is relating with a vast array of creatures, such as wheat, water, salt, yeast, and even bacteria on the practitioner's hands. By preparing the bread and the wine for the ritualization of the Eucharist, humans relate to one another and these creatures and, in doing so, participate in the movement toward creaturely perfection.

Zizioulas highlights the way that humans are integral for the development of creation (Zizioulas 2011),[3] while McFarland advances this understanding of the ways that the Eucharist ascetically trains Christians (Zizioulas's term), bringing believers into the eschatological dialectic Morrill described. By relating the production of wheat and grapes to bread and wine, humans acting as priests of creation are confronted by the uniqueness of these creatures, such that they cannot be developed into anything other than the possibilities of their endemic potential. To attempt to do otherwise refuses communion with those creatures and refers creation back to the human instead of God. Therefore, in the practice of preparing the elements, Christians are trained through their relation with these creatures and live beyond the biological necessity of createdness by bringing all of creation into communion with God. Relating to creatures in this way, moreover, refers back to Morrill's highlighting of the eschatological tension between the dangerous memory and consolation of Christ. By developing creation and offering

---

[3] Zizioulas argues here that humans occupy a unique place in creation, in that they are ontologically tied to it while simultaneously able to transcend it through freedom.

it to God, humans live in kenotic service to the world and live in hope for the full realization of the redeemed creation.

It must be noted here that the sacrament of the Eucharist rests on the sacramentality of the world. This idea means that while the ritual serves both as a practice of remembrance of God's redeeming work in the world and a way for Christians to live into that work, creation is full of God's grace. Alexander Schmemann succinctly states this idea thusly:

> ... the world, be it in its totality as cosmos, or in its life and becoming as time and history, is an *epiphany* of God, a means of His [sic] revelation, a rationally acceptable case of its existence, but only truly speaks of Him and is in itself an essential means both of knowledge of God and communion with Him, and to be so is its true nature and its ultimate destiny. (Schmemann 1973, p. 120)

Within this grace-filled context of the cosmos, Christians participate in the practice of the Eucharist. Practitioners use the very material of creation to produce the bread and the wine, gather as a community, and participate in the movement toward creaturely perfection. Kevin Irwin observes that creation's sacramentality reveals that "things matter and matter is not just a thing" and that sacramentality is the language of both. Irwin also notes that "In a sacramental world all is both graced and in need of complete redemption" (Irwin 2005). As members of the community of creation, Eucharistic practice confronts us with our constitutively relational condition that is both graced and in need of redemption.

Though such a communal ontology encapsulating (recapitulating) all of creation has significant merit, the danger of it becoming a set of beliefs that are only cognitively held without embodied practice remains. Here, the ritual theory of Adam Seligman and his colleagues, distinguishing between ritual and sincerity, can provide important nuances for this communal ontology.

4. Bringing Communal Ontology into Practical, Ritual Focus

Seligman argues that ritual creates a world out of participants' lived reality. He and his colleagues draw primarily from Jewish and Confucian sources to show that practicing ritual brings a sense of order to a world primarily experienced as chaotic. In this way, ritual creates a shared subjunctive 'as-if' world among participants (Seligman et al. 2008). Ritual is a distinctly different way of interacting with the world than what Seligman calls sincerity, by which he means the individual's having the right ideas in place before participating in the practice. Seligman succinctly makes distinction between ritual and sincerity as follows:

> In doing a ritual the whole issue of our internal states is often irrelevant. What you *are* is what you *are in the doing*, which is of course an external act. This is very different from modernist concerns with sincerity and authenticity ... Getting it *right* is not a matter of making outer acts conform to inner beliefs. Getting it right is doing it again and again and again—it is an act of world construction. (Seligman et al. 2008, p. 24)

In other words, ritual is the practice by which a community continuously constructs a shared 'as-if' world that gives them a sense of order in contrast to a lived experience that often feels chaotic. Sincerity, in contrast, involves an inward search for authenticity that is often removed from the work of ritual. In this way, then, ritual has a flexibility that sincerity does not. When the authentic beliefs that one holds in sincerity change, there is no subjunctive 'as-if' world to maintain order. Seligman offers the example of a family that loves each other dearly but has been disrupted by some sort of conflict. In this context, it is important for the family to act as if they love each other before they sincerely do (Seligman et al. 2008).

Giving primacy to active practice, rather than cognitive belief, opens this shared world for different individuals. In the practice of ritual, that is, through the ritual act, different individuals construct a shared world: "Sharing the act, they both point to or index the shared world that is their relationship" (Seligman et al. 2008). Difference among the individuals does not collapse into a single consciousness in the ritual act. Instead, the ritual act serves as the way in which individuals are able to enter this shared, subjunctive, 'as-if' world. This subjunctive world, nonetheless, exists in direct tension with and in response to the reality lived outside of the ritual. Specifically, Seligman demonstrates that "the subjunctive world created by ritual is always doomed ultimately to fail—the ordered world of flawless repetition can never fully replace the broken world of experience" (Seligman et al. 2008). Essentially, because ritual creates a shared world of order amongst participants, the ritual is not a reflection of some sort of (sincerely conceived) harmonious world. The human work of ritual is ongoing, as its participants strive to create harmony amidst reality's discordance. This tragic sense of the world is precisely why the work of ritual is important for human existence. By participating in a ritual, individuals are able to enter into a constructed world of order, which then allows them to live as if the subjunctive world of ritual is the world of reality. This phenomenon is not a result of actively thinking about the disjunction between the ritual world and lived experience. Instead, participants are living into this 'as-if' world through the act itself (Seligman et al. 2008). There is great responsibility among humans to enact ceaselessly these rituals in response to the chaotic lived experience in order to create an ordered subjunctive 'as-if' world.

In making their case for ritual's priority over sincerity, Seligman and his colleagues draw primarily from a fourth-century BCE Chinese document asserting that humans are to "build patterns of relationships out of this fractured world and thereby create an ordered way of life" (Seligman et al. 2008). The text further maintains that it is proper for humans to have a fixed purpose, attained through repeated study. Such study does not mean transcending a context, it means "refining one's responses to situations" (Seligman et al. 2008). One of the ways that humans participate in this repeated study is enacting rituals and practices from the past. Seligman explains:

> These rituals, then, arose from the dispositions themselves: they were simply actions taken in response to certain situations in the past. But the later-born sages deemed some of these actions exemplary, and as such defined them as part of a ritual canon that people in general should enact. The goal of such an enactment would be to refine one's own dispositions: by reenacting exemplary actions from the past, one trains one's responses so that one can achieve propriety. (Seligman et al. 2008, pp. 33–34)

Ritual, then, becomes a set of relations that is in tension with the world of lived experience, prompting the question of how participants are to act outside of the world of ritual. Again, working from Confucian writings, Seligman demonstrates that one of the goals of ritual is to continue into this subjunctive 'as-if' world, even outside of the ritualization (Seligman et al. 2008). He writes that "if one spends one's life doing rituals properly, then one gains a sense of how the subjunctive world constructed out of these rituals could be constructed in situations without ritual precedent" (Seligman et al. 2008). This way of framing the relation between the ritual world and the world of lived experience highlights the efficacy of ritualized acts, as opposed to acts governed solely by sincerity. Specifically, through the repeated "study" by ritual, one is able to live in the midst of the chaotic world by living as if one is in the subjunctive, ordered world of ritual instead of relying on the sincere, abstracted world of ideas.

Because practicing rituals can serve as a way for participants to navigate the world of chaos outside of the ritualization, ritual also provides a different understanding of autonomy. Seligman contrasts ritual's sense of autonomy with that of sincerity's, which calls for individuals to be uninhibited by anything other than the self (the individual's inward examination to determine authenticity) (Seligman et al. 2008). In ritual, autonomy is precisely the result of a person who is able to act without "ritual precedent" (Seligman et al. 2008). Seligman turns to the Jewish rabbinic tradition, wherein the goal of becoming a rabbi "is to be achieved through a submission to ritual" such that "[t]he inner comes to reflect the outer, and not the other way around" (Seligman et al. 2008). This means that autonomy comes about through relations with others, with traditions being comprised of the voices and practices of people from the past. In contrast, working within a sincere mode puts an intense amount of responsibility upon the individual, since it is only through that single individual's search for an authentic self that the individual determines action. Consequently, there is no shared world among individuals and no practices by which individuals can enter a shared world. Seligman explains, "The establishment of a stable and unquestionable *as is*, rather than a common *as if*, becomes the projected basis for the intersubjective world" (Seligman et al. 2008). Therefore, the individual self becomes the only point of reference for autonomy, as opposed to the community conditioned by the tradition of ritual.

This ritual-based understanding of autonomy is evident in the way that ritual accepts authoritative procedures within the world created it creates. Sincerity views such authority structures as mere convention and, thus, unauthentic. Ritual, in contrast, sees them as a formative force in creating a subjunctive world, providing order to the lived experience of chaos. Seligman depicts this difference by distinguishing how community love is accomplished in Confucian and Mohist arguments. The Mohist relied on the inward transformation of individuals, whereas the Confucian emphasis on ritual argued that "social peace would come through ... the constraints of ritual repetition" (Seligman et al. 2008). In the ritual, both the future and the will are circumscribed through the repetition. In regard to the future, Seligman argues that in revisiting the past through the ritual, the unlimited future possibilities are placed in a frame of already known (i.e., past) experiences. Ritual constrains through prescribed gestures and words and creates a community thereby able to embrace both the past and the future (Seligman et al. 2008). Likewise, this same repetition circumscribes the individual will by placing "the individual actor in a very particular relation to a body of practices (or even modes of speech and addresses), a way of being, which imposes obligations" (Seligman et al. 2008). This repetition makes the past present again. By way of Kierkegaard, Seligman demonstrates that a modern sense of repetition is like the ancient Greek understanding of recollection, except performed in the opposite direction. Specifically, repetition is a way of recollecting forward. He argues that repetition "stamps a shape onto the formlessness and chaos of existence" (Seligman et al. 2008). In this way, then, Seligman and his colleagues show that the practices of ritual form a community through sharing a common past, creating a subjunctive world, and orienting toward a shared future formed by the repetition of that past, all of which comes about in the very practice of the ritual, rather than the sincere search for inward authenticity among individuals.

The theoretical work of Seligman and his colleagues provides some clarity as to how Zizioulas's communal ontology, as substantiated by Morrill and McFarland, is practiced in the Eucharist. One of the key elements of Seligman's theory is the way in which ritual provides a sense of order to a world that is experienced as chaotic. Zizioulas provides a Christian theological rendering of this notion by asserting both that God created the world *ex nihilo* and that Original Sin comprises a (chaos-inducing) refusal of communion between the world and God. In his essay, "Proprietors or Priests of Creation," Zizioulas argues that because God created the world from nothing, it will return to nothingness unless it is brought into communion with God. That communion can only come about through the agency of humans, who occupy the unique position in creation as priests due to their ability to transcend createdness through their freedom as persons in communion (Zizioulas 2011). Because we are living in the context of Original Sin, we experience the world as chaotic precisely because humans refuse communion with other creatures and God and refer creation back to ourselves instead of God.[4]

The ritualization of the Eucharist is the practice by which Christians construct and provide a sense of order in the face of this chaos. The first way that this ordering takes place is in the gathering of the baptized. As Zizioulas argues, through baptism, Christians are resurrected into the community of Christ and come into an ecclesial hypostasis. Consequently, the gathering of baptized Christians for the Eucharist is an ordering of human creatures in community who can freely love one another

---

[4]   This understanding of the world is distinct from the Jewish and Confucian sources with which Seligman is dialoging, because this Christian understanding of the world sees the world as a created order that only becomes chaotic after humans refuse to maintain the communion between God and the world, which is precisely why ritual is necessary after Original Sin. Conversely, the Jewish and Confucian sources used by Seligman see the world as inherently chaotic from the beginning. See (Seligman et al. 2008).

without the constraints of biological necessity. Then, the gathered community ritually brings together the rest of creation through developing nature, as seen in the preparation of the bread and the wine. As stated above, the human labor of making bread and wine is the relation of various creatures from wheat, water, salt, yeast, grapes, and the process of fermentation. The ritual preparation and offering in the Eucharist comprise a performance of these very different creatures relating to one another in an ordered manner, as opposed to a relation defined by chaos.

Additionally, the way in which ritual is an index by which participants enter into a subjunctive 'as-if' world that exists in tension with the world of lived experience is crucial to Seligman's theory of ritual. The Eucharist creates a world that reorients creaturely relationships, eliminating a sense of competition among different creatures. Rather, as McFarland's notion of creaturely movement demonstrates, these creatures come together into a subjunctive world created by the ritualization of the Eucharist in which they contribute to their collective movement toward perfection and communion with God. Zizioulas is, likewise, quite clear in acknowledging that the biological aspects of humans do not disappear in the practice of the Eucharist. In fact, there is a tension between what he calls the biological hypostasis and the ecclesial hypostasis. Specifically, Zizioulas argues that though humans live in this ecclesial hypostasis during the ritualization, the body is not denied in the ritual act of the Eucharist. There is always the tension and possibility that humans could direct creation toward themselves instead of God. This acknowledgment is precisely why Seligman and his colleagues carefully demonstrate that ritual is the ongoing practice and work of getting the ritual correct. It is not a matter of first establishing the correct ideas and then moving into the practice. Rather, through continuously practicing the Eucharist and creating this subjunctive 'as-if' world in which creatures relate to one another in an orderly way, Christians live into the ecclesial hypostasis, while simultaneously living in the inherent tension between the world constructed by the ritualization and the world of lived experience.

The tension between the subjunctive world and the world of lived experience is precisely the tension between the fallen world and the eschatological reality in which Christians now live in hope for its full realization in the future eschaton. Zizioulas argues that in the ritualization of the Eucharist humans live into the eschatological reality brought by the Spirit through the epiclectic and anamnestic character of the ritual (Zizioulas 2002). As discussed above, Morrill provides the necessary nuance to this notion by showing that in early Christian communities, anamnesis is the remembrance of God's past action in Christ, as well as an interruption of the eschatological reality of redeemed creation in the fallen world, calling Christians into kenotic service to the world. Seligman and his colleagues' theory of the ritual's circumscribing character of both the future and human will is also at play here. Specifically, in practicing the Eucharistic ritual, Christians remember God's past acts in history in and through Christ. In doing so, participants circumscribe the limitless possibilities of the future, which Zizioulas terms "remembering the future". Through the ritualization of the Eucharist, Christians enter into the eschatological reality and live as if the world is redeemed, with God fully realizing this redemption in the future eschaton. Also, in the same act, the traditional character of the ritual circumscribes the participants' wills through their enacting particular gestures from the Christian tradition. For example, offering the bread and wine in community, as Zizioulas demonstrates, is a practice of transcending all of humanly forged boundaries: The assembled people act as ecclesial hypostases offering creation to God as the priests of creation. In this practice, humans accept communion as necessary for being in a manner that includes all of creation, and, through gathering, developing, and recapitulating creation back to God, human persons live in service to the world.

Seligman's ritual theory demonstrates the power and flexibility of a ritual mode of being in the world because it has consequences beyond the ritual world, into the world of lived experience. This insight is important for recognizing the ways in which the subjunctive world created by the ritual can be a distinct reality only inhabited by the participants during the act of ritualization. As I noted above, Zizioulas' communal ontology is prone to this problem. Morrill's critique of Schmemann's overly realized eschatology applies here: If the eschaton is fully realized in the ritual, then there is no need for persons to live in service to the world outside of the act of ritualization. However, enlisting Seligman's theory shows that in continually practicing the ritual, participants are preparing themselves to act in situations and contexts beyond the ritual. Indeed, this is one of ritual's very goals. Turning to a communal ontology that takes creaturely movement and anamnesis seriously, we perceive the Eucharistic ritual shaping participants to accept communion as essential to being and to living itself. This is, moreover, a communion among all of creation. Christians thus can live within the chaotic world as if they are living in the subjunctive world created by the Eucharist—and act accordingly. The communal ontology Zizioulas conceives is, therefore, necessarily understood as practiced in an embodied way. Formed by the ritual, the participants can live into the kenotic service to the world outside their enactments of the Eucharist.

5. Conclusions

This project has arisen from a deep concern for living in a context defined by global climate change, and it serves as the beginning work of interrogating the ways in which Christian ritualization can be a transformative force in confronting ecologically degrading practices. In the United States, most Americans approach global climate change through sincere means. If we consider the problem at all, we do so by cognitively considering the ways we can individually address the issue. We bring reusable bags to the grocery store, purchase "green" products, or drive (alone) in a hybrid vehicle. However, this sincere approach leaves formative practices in place that substantiate divisions between humans and other creatures creating the chaotic world of rising sea levels, increased migration, spreading vector-borne illnesses, and permanent soil loss. We exist in what political theorist and bioethicist Bruce Jennings calls a consumptive social contract (Jennings 2016).[5] We mindlessly consume without regard for each other or the inherent limits of our consumption's foundation, namely, the closed ecological system that makes life and creaturely flourishing possible. In other words, our current way of being rests on limiting non-human creaturely movement for the sake of our own individualized consumption. We live in the truth of being, rather than the truth of communion, and we do so at total creaturely peril.

The Eucharistic practice, as I have described it here, interrupts the foundations of this consumptive social contract, creating the subjunctive 'as-if' world of the redeemed creation. Through the Eucharistic practice, diverse creatures intentionally gather together and relate through interdependence, rather than desire for independent gain and consumption. The baker engages the limits of wheat, water, salt, and yeast to create creaturely abundance in bread. It is through this sort of relational interdependence that these creatures are able to move together toward creaturely perfection. However, the ritual does not end when the bread emerges from the oven and wine is poured from the cask. Human creatures come together in communion, gathering the diversity of creation and offering it to God in remembrance of God's redeeming work and the expectation of its full realization. This ritualization empowers practitioners to engage in kenotic service beyond the ritual, and it is this service that dangerously cracks the foundation of the consumptive social contract. The practice of baking and sharing bread invites the same careful attention in our relating to other creatures. In a world characterized by global climate change, the Eucharist asks us to live as we truly are: Creatures whose flourishing is only possible through the mutual engagement with one another and God. Intentionally gathering as a community to acknowledge our dependence on God is paramount for shunning the practices (and accompanying dispositions) that dangerously aver human independence from ecological realities. Innovative advances in theological education, such as Princeton Theological Seminary's agriculturally based theology and ecology curriculum, serve as examples of how Christian ritualization can thoughtfully and practically

---

5   Jennings states a social contract refers to "norms of common consent that provide social cohesion," and the consumptive social contract has informed ethics, governance, and politics during period of change that have led to market capitalism, liberalism, and representative democracy but relied on extractive use of finite ecological resources.

engage our ecological crisis.[6] Our practices and modes of being that valorize the autonomous individual are the very practices that undermine the systems that make our mutual flourishing possible. The Eucharist invites us to shun our mindless consumption and enter the rich communion of creation. Cooking shared meals together, engaging in alternative economic models such as community supported agriculture programs, and attending to the particularities of a place take the practice and truth of communion into everyday life. The subjunctive 'as-if' world continues at the dinner table where all creatures are welcome.

Funding: This research received no funding.

Conflicts of Interest: The author declares no conflicts of interest.

References

Groppe, Elizabeth T. 2005. Creation Ex Nihilo and Ex Amore: Ontological Freedom in the Theologies of John Zizioulas and Catherine Mowry LaCugna. *Modern Theology* 21: 463–96. [CrossRef]

Irwin, Kevin W. 2005. *Models of the Eucharist*. New York: Paulist Press.

Jennings, Bruce. 2016. *Ecological Governance: Toward a New Social Contract with the Earth*. Morgantown: West Virginia University Press.

McFarland, Ian A. 2014. *From Nothing: A Theology of Creation*. Louisville: Westminster John Knox Press.

Morrill, Bruce T. 2000. *Anamnesis as Dangerous Memory: Political and Liturgical Theology in Dialogue*. Collegeville: Liturgical Press.

Schmemann, Alexander. 1973. *For the Life of the World*. Crestwood: St. Vladimir's Seminary Press.

Seligman, Adam B., Robert P. Weller, Michael J. Puett, and Bennett Simon. 2008. *Ritual and Its Consequences: An Essay on the Limits of Sincerity*. New York: Oxford University Press.

Zizioulas, John D. 2002. *Being as Communion: Studies n Personhood and the Church*. Crestwood: St. Vladimir's Seminary Press.

Zizioulas, John D. 2011. Proprietors or Priests of Creation? In *The Eucharistic Communion and the World*. Edited by Luke Ben Tallon. New York: T&T Clark, pp. 133–41.

---

6 See https://www.ptsem.edu/discover/farminary/overview for more information about Princeton Theological Seminary's "Farminary" and Certificate in Theology, Ecology, and Faith Formation.

Article

The Epic of Evolution and a Theology of Sacramental Ecology

David C. McDuffie

Department of Religious Studies, The University of North Carolina at Greensboro, Greensboro, NC 27412, USA; dcmcduff@uncg.edu

Received: 23 January 2019; Accepted: 22 March 2019; Published: 1 April 2019

Abstract: The 'Epic of Evolution' is the scientific story that reveals that we live in an approximately 14-billion-year-old universe on a planet that is approximately 4.6 billion years old and that we are a part of the ongoing process of life that has existed on Earth for 3.5–4 billion years. This article focuses on the religious and ecological significance of the evolutionary epic in an effort to seamlessly connect the ecological value attributed as a part of an understanding of the evolutionary connectedness of life on earth with the Divine grace understood to be present in Christian sacramental worship. With a particular emphasis on the Eucharist, I argue that the sacramental perspective of grace being conveyed through material reality provides the potential for Christian sacramental tradition to make a significant contribution to protecting the threatened ecological communities of our planet. By incorporating William Temple's concept of a 'sacramental universe,' I propose that the grace that is understood to be present in the substances of the bread and wine of the Eucharist points outward so that it can also be witnessed in all of God's ongoing Creation. When the Eucharist is understood as taking place in a sacramental universe from which ecological grace flows; the incarnation can be recognized not as a one-time event but as an ongoing sacramental process through which God is revealed through the perpetual emergence of life. Consequently, as the primary form of sacramental worship in Christian tradition, the Eucharistic witness to the incarnation of God in Jesus and thanksgiving for life overcoming death provide Christians with a ritual orientation for recognizing the incarnational presence of God as an ever-present reality potentially witnessed in all that is. Therefore, the formal sacrament of the Eucharist is a part of a broader sacramental ecology of earthly life in which the presence of Divine grace can be witnessed in all aspects of the natural order. As a result, connecting Eucharistic grace with the value associated with an awareness of the ecological and genetic connectedness of all forms of life serves as a mutual enrichment of sacramental tradition and contemporary efforts to protect life on Earth.

Keywords: Epic of Evolution; sacramental theology; Eucharist; ecology; sacramental universe; ecological grace; E.O. Wilson

1. Introduction

There is grandeur in this view of life, with its several powers, having been originally breathed into a few forms or into one; and that whilst this planet has gone cycling on according to the fixed law of gravity, from so simple a beginning endless forms most beautiful and most wonderful have been, and are being, evolved.

These are the last lines from the 1859 first edition of Charles Darwin's *The Origin of Species* in which he developed his theory of evolution through natural selection (Darwin 2006, p. 760). The culmination of Darwin's work on speciation served to illuminate the realization that all living things are connected in one giant web or tree of life that spans millions of years of natural history on Earth. Ironically, Darwin had no understanding of the primary biological factor perpetuating this process. The emergence of the science of genetics unlocked this mystery, and in the more than 150 year interval since the publication of *Origin*, we have been provided with evidence that supports Darwin's brilliant insight. We now know that we are genetically related and ecologically connected to all living things from chimpanzees and bonobos, our closest living relatives with whom we share approximately 99% of our genetic information, to microscopic bacteria. In brief, all living things on our planet are related through our genetic codes, and it is probable that this genetic kinship can be traced back to the emergence of life's common ancestor, the first single-celled life on Earth. These developments in the biological sciences combined with the sciences of geology and cosmological physics have revealed to us that we live in an approximately 14-billion-year-old universe on a planet that is approximately 4.6 billion years old and that we are a part of the ongoing process of life that has existed on Earth for 3.5–4 billion years. This is the story of the natural history from which we emerged and of which we are inextricably a part, and it is a narrative that is added to on nearly a daily basis by ongoing scientific investigation.

According to biologist E.O. Wilson, a proper understanding and appreciation of this 'Epic of Evolution' is the key to attributing the ecological value that is necessary to protect the world's threatened biodiversity.[1] In *Biophilia*, he writes, "I will make the case that to explore and affiliate with life is a deep and complicated process in mental development. To an extent still undervalued in philosophy and religion, our existence depends on this propensity, our spirit is woven from it, hope rises on its currents." Further, he concludes: "to the degree that we come to understand other organisms, we will place a greater value on them, and on ourselves" (Wilson 1984, pp. 1–2). I agree with Wilson on this point, and in the following paper, I will address Wilson's reference to religion's undervaluation of our inextricable connectedness to Nature by exploring the relationship between the scientific narrative of the Epic of Evolution, ecological value, and the sacramental life of the Christian church.

More specifically, I will argue that the sacramental understanding of grace present in the Christian Eucharist can serve as an effective means to perpetuate ecological value for all of life and therefore serve as a valuable contribution to the conservation of the Earth's biodiversity.[2] By incorporating the concept of a 'sacramental universe' from Anglican sacramental theology, I propose that the grace that is understood to be present in the substances of the bread and wine of the Eucharist points outward so that it can also be witnessed in all of God's ongoing Creation.[3] Therefore, sacramental grace can potentially become a primary means for the Christian community to value, revere, and consequently care for the natural order.

Connecting the scientific narrative of the Epic of Evolution with a religious understanding of sacramental grace will seem to many to be a bit of a stretch, but I intend to show that not only are a sacramental understanding of Eucharistic grace and ecological value compatible, but also that a sacramental approach to ecology can potentially expand the scope and effectiveness of contemporary efforts to conserve biodiversity. Before moving into a discussion of how the idea of Eucharistic grace can perpetuate the ecological value that emerges from a proper understanding of the Epic of Evolution, let us first further examine the connections between scientific and religious narratives that have been recognized as present in the Epic itself.

---

[1]   Wilson is given credit for coining the term 'Epic of Evolution' in his Pulitzer Prize winning *On Human Nature*, first published in 1978 where he wrote that "the evolutionary epic is probably the best myth we will ever have" (Wilson 1978, p. 201).

[2]   For the purpose of this article, I will be focusing primarily on the relationship between the transformed Eucharistic substances of bread and wine and the material reality of the natural environment. However, it should be noted that Christian traditions have recognized several dimensions through which Christ's presence can be witnessed. For example, Bruce T. Morrill identifies the following three additional dimensions where the Eucharist contributes to an availability of divine presence: Christ hidden in the faithful, Christ witnessed through the proclamation of scripture, and Christ's leadership through those who minister to word and sacrament in the church. See (Morrill 2012).

[3]   William Temple referred to a "sacramental universe" in his Gifford Lectures. See (Temple 1951, Lecture 19).

2. A Naturalist's Revelation

I have to admit that I have always read E.O. Wilson as a deeply religious author. It is necessary to clarify that I am not claiming that Wilson identifies himself as such. Wilson certainly makes no such claims but is instead a self-professed secular humanist. In fact, in conversations concerning the relationship between religion and science, Wilson is quite frequently accused by religious critics of being overly reductionistic in his understanding of religion. There is certainly some truth to this criticism given Wilson's claim that religion, as well as ethics, are products of human evolutionary history that served as adaptive traits contributing to the survival of our *Homo Sapien* ancestors (Wilson 1999, pp. 260–90). Furthermore, he predicts that the "eventual result of the competition between the two worldviews [religion and science] ... will be the secularization of the human epic and of religion itself" (Wilson 1999, p. 290).

Yet, if one pays close enough attention, Wilson's criticism involves a rejection of a particular type of religious narrative, supernaturalistic religious narratives that contradict and claim to compete with the Epic of Evolution. However, he does not necessarily reject what might be called a religious or spiritual orientation. Recognizing the importance of storytelling in human culture, he writes, "People need a sacred narrative. They must have a sense of larger purpose, in one form or other, however intellectualized" (Wilson 1999, p. 289). For Wilson, the traditional orienting function of religious narratives remains, but he wishes to substitute a new, naturalistic narrative that will better orient humans toward a proper understanding of our kinship with all of life.[4] The awe, beauty, and wonder traditionally associated with religious devotion is maintained but is inspired not by the supernatural but instead by a naturalistic account of the Earth's ecology (Wilson 2012, p. 266).

Therefore, in this sense, the Epic of Evolution, as understood by Wilson, is connected to the function of traditional religious narratives of origin and orientation and is the most proper narrative to help us address the issue of the protection of the threatened biodiversity in our contemporary context.[5] In his Pulitzer-Prize-winning *On Human Nature*, first published in 1978, he writes that "the evolutionary epic is probably the best myth we will ever have. It can be adjusted until it comes as close to truth as the human mind is constructed to judge the truth" (Wilson 1978, p. 201). Elsewhere, in describing the religious function of the Epic of Evolution, Wilson writes: "If the sacred narrative cannot be in the form of a religious cosmology, it will be taken from the material history of the universe and the human species. That trend is in no way debasing. The true evolutionary epic, retold as poetry, is as intrinsically ennobling as any religious epic. Material reality discovered by science already possesses more content and grandeur than all religious cosmologies combined" (Wilson 1999, p. 289). We see here, once again, that Wilson's interpretation of the Epic represents both a rejection of and a connection to the function of traditional religious narratives.

However, I believe that the religious significance of Wilson's work is deeper than simply serving as a contemporary scientific alternative for the function of traditional religious narratives. I say this because there is evidence in aspects of Wilson's writings of a clear and profound respect for human spirituality. Furthermore, there are also indications that his work to establish a conservation ethic based on the Epic of Evolution is a continuation, albeit a reinterpretation, of the religiosity of his childhood acculturation. Describing his journey in young adulthood from supernatural theism to a complete devotion to natural history, he states: "I had no desire to purge religious feelings. They were bred in me; they suffused the wellsprings of my creative life" (Wilson 1999, p. 6). In an even more revealing

---

[4] See (Wilson 2012, pp. 287–97).
[5] According to Wilson, we have now entered the world's sixth great extinction event, the fifth being the event that led to the extinction of the dinosaurs 65 million years ago, where, if conditions remain the same, half the Earth's known species could either be extinct or seriously threatened by the mid-21st century. With this in mind, Wilson claims that the scientific narrative of evolutionary history is the story that can most effectively achieve the protection of the Earth's biodiversity from the factors that currently threaten it. See (Wilson 2007, pp. 4–5). The causes of this human-induced biological destruction are summarized by Wilson with the acronym HIPPO representing the following ecologically destructive forces: *Habitat Destruction, Invasive Species, Pollution, Population, Overharvesting*. See (Wilson 2002, p. 50).

passage from his autobiography, *Naturalist*, he describes the process by which he drifted away from the Southern Baptist faith of his acculturation and his consequent reinterpretation of grace and its relation to the attribution of value:

> The still faithful might say I never truly knew grace, never had it; but they would be wrong. The truth is that I found it and abandoned it. In the years following I drifted away from the church, and my attendance became desultory. My heart continued to believe in the light and the way, but increasingly in the abstract, and I looked for grace in some other setting. By the time I entered college at the age of seventeen, I was absorbed in natural history almost to the exclusion of everything else. I was enchanted with science as a means of explaining the physical world, which increasingly seemed to me to be the complete world. In essence, I still longed for grace, but rooted solidly on Earth. (Wilson 2006, pp. 43–44)

It is in this sense that I feel comfortable referring to Wilson as a deeply religious author. His goal is not to explain away the importance of a religious/spiritual impetus in human culture but to urge that human spirituality should be expressed in a way that recognizes Nature as "vital to our physical and spiritual well-being" and that the "spiritual roots of *Homo Sapiens* extend deep into the natural world through still mostly hidden channels of mental development" (Wilson 2007, pp. 26, 12). Value or grace, to use his term, emerges from material reality. For Wilson, what emerges from the scientific narrative is a unique form of valuation that results from understanding the complex and intricately connected life on Earth. In his words, "[t]o know this world is to gain proprietary attachment to it. To know it well is to love and take responsibility for it" (Wilson 2002, p. 131). I think it is justifiable to classify such a response as sacramental. It is to this topic that I will now turn.

3. A Sacramental Ecology of the Eucharist

The Book of Common Prayer defines the sacraments as "outward and visible signs of inward and spiritual grace, given by Christ as sure and certain means by which we can receive that grace" (2007, p. 857). This definition tells us two things. First, it tells us that the Christian sacramental system is inextricably linked with the life, ministry, and sacramental significance of Jesus. It also tells us quite clearly that, sacramentally, we experience God's grace through material reality. In the Eucharist, this grace is conveyed through the substances of water, bread, and wine. It does not take much of an imagination to expand the understanding of grace conveyed in these material substances to an acceptance that Divine grace is constantly present to us in the natural environment.

In fact, such an expansion of sacramental grace is quite clearly encouraged in the Book of Common Prayer: "God does not limit God's self to these rites; they are patterns of countless ways by which God uses material things to reach out to us" (2007, p. 861). In other words, when we receive the Eucharist as a part of Christian sacramental liturgy, it is not intended as an escape from the world but as spiritual nourishment so that we may be sent back into the world to recognize the grace that is potentially present in all of God's ongoing Creation. We are released from the Eucharistic rite to experience Divine grace in our day-to-day lives in our local environments, that is, in Nature. Consider the words from the post communion prayer in the Book of Common Prayer: "[Y]ou have fed us with spiritual food in the Sacrament of his Body and Blood. Send us now into the world in peace, and grant us strength and courage to love and serve you with gladness and singleness of heart; through Christ our Lord. Amen" (2007, p. 365). If we experience grace in the material substances of the bread, wine, and water present in the Christian sacraments, this grace is not confined within the boundaries of an individual liturgy or the walls of a church community but instead informs those who participate in these sacraments that God's grace can be revealed to us through anything or anyone we may encounter in our Earthly lives. Because value is necessarily applied to any means through which grace is potentially conveyed in the world, the implications of such a view for the attribution of ecological value are clear.

A prominent example of such a view can be found in William Temple's Gifford Lectures where he refers to the 'sacramental universe' in which we live out our lives.[6] In other words, if God is the source, center, and end of all material reality, then Divine grace is present to us in all that exists.[7] Again, Christian sacramentalism is grounded in material reality. According to Temple, Christianity "is the most avowedly materialist of all the great religions" (Temple 1951, p. 478). Therefore, a valuation of the material through the Christian commitment to an incarnational, sacramental view of Divine grace allows this valuation to be extended outward in a manner in which all that exists is potentially sacramental.

What we have here is a distinction between the unique sacraments of the Christian church and a more general form of sacramentality toward which they point. In *A Guide to the Sacraments*, John Macquarrie describes this extension of the sacramental system to a more generalized sacramentality: "Perhaps the goal of all sacramentality and sacramental theology is to make the things of this world so transparent that in them and through them we know God's presence and activity in our very midst, and so experience his grace." According to Macquarrie, this "general notion of sacramentality ... is not exclusively confined to Christianity but is found in many religions and philosophies" (Macquarrie 1997, p. 1). The significance of such an understanding of sacramentality for the attribution of ecological value is that the conveyers of sacramental grace are no longer seen as "'mere' things, but as bearers of meaning, value and potentiality, as messages from the ultimate mystery we call God" (Macquarrie 1997, p. vii). It is through the acceptance of the broader sacramentality of a sacramental universe that the Christian concept of sacramental grace is seamlessly brought into a relationship with the ecological value inspired though a proper interpretation of the evolutionary epic. In both understandings, what emerges from the inherent connectedness of ecological communities is greater than what can be predicated simply from a knowledge of the biological component parts of these communities.[8] Regardless of whether it is explicitly attributed with a connection with the Divine, the beautiful mystery of life on Earth inspires a sense of grace, and therefore value, for the natural order.

For Wilson, value emerges from material reality, through an understanding of the natural history of life from which we emerged, and is the source of our physical as well as our spiritual sustenance. This view is perfectly consistent with the broader notion of sacramentality that potentially flows from Christian sacramental tradition. However, if you will recall the Book of Common Prayer's definition of sacrament quoted above, there is also a tension between the uniqueness of a Christian sacramental rite, which is rooted in the history of Christian tradition, and the ecological value toward which it potentially points. This potential discontinuity requires a more careful articulation of the ecological significance of the Eucharistic rite. If one is going to assess the ecological significance of the Christian sacraments, the Eucharist is a good place to start. First, of the seven formal sacraments recognized in Christian tradition, the Eucharist is the one that is observed most frequently. As Macquarrie points out, the Eucharist is "the sacrament of maturity, which the communicant will continue to receive for the rest of his or her life and which will promote spiritual growth" (Macquarrie 1997, p. 102). I have mentioned how an understanding of Eucharistic grace in the substances of water, bread, and wine can be expanded to include a broader sacramentality for the entire natural environment. However, if Christian sacramental worship is going to make a significant contribution to the attribution of ecological value, the ecological value attributed must be considered inseparably related to the Christian tradition of which it is a part. As a result, we must move beyond simply focusing on the acceptance of the basic materiality of the substance of the Eucharist and examine, in a deeper way, the theological

---

[6] See (Temple 1951, Lecture 19).
[7] I am borrowing the language of God as the "source, center, and end" of all that exists from Dr. William L. Power, Professor Emeritus at the University of Georgia, with whom I studied from 2004 to 2008.
[8] Offering an ecological interpretation of the Aristotelian notion that "the whole is greater than the sum of its parts," Eugene P. Odum, the so-called father of modern Ecology, famously commented that "the ecosystem is greater than the sum of its parts."

and ritual significance of the sacrament itself. If a connection to the evolutionary epic is considered to be shoehorned into or simply a nice addendum to the sacramental tradition instead of emerging from the very heart of the tradition itself, it will not resonate and will therefore fall short of the potential I am claiming for it. In other words, if there are discontinuities between an understanding of the application of sacramental grace in the Eucharist and the attribution of ecological value, we need to stare them right in the face and not divert our attention for the sake of convenience or upholding an argument we hope to be true.

The Eucharist, perhaps more than any of the other sacraments of the church, represents the potential and tension between the formal sacraments of the church and the broader sacramentality that can potentially lead to a recognition of Divine grace in a sacramental universe. This is the case because the entire Christian theological narrative, the Alph, Chi, Omega of Christian tradition, is contained in the sacramental worship of the Eucharist. Our scriptural tradition begins with a poetic story of Divine Creation in which we are told that all of the created order is endowed with goodness as it is spoken into existence by the Spirit of God.[9] As Christians, we seek to understand the mystery of the incarnation of this Divine Word, the source of all life, through whom all things come into being.[10] And, we look forward in hope toward an eschatological fulfillment where Life will ultimately emerge from suffering and death.[11] These theological concepts lie at the heart of Christian sacramental tradition and undergird the Eucharistic liturgy.[12] They are also undeniably Ecological in nature. Therefore, the Eucharist orients its participants in the present while allowing us to simultaneously look inward, backward, and forward to discern how the theological concepts of creation, incarnation, and resurrection, which are inherent to the Eucharistic meal and integral to the eschatological hope of Christian tradition, project outward to correspond to the presence of Divine grace in all of material reality.[13]

In relation to the evolutionary epic, this naturalistic interpretation of the Eucharist can be seen as a narrative within a narrative. The Epic of Evolution as described by Wilson is a universal narrative that unites us all, genetically and ecologically, whether we choose to accept this or not. In our pluralistic cultural context, we must recognize that the Christian narrative as represented in the reiteration of the Eucharistic meal is not universal. It arose within the last two thousand years and is a part of a particular human history connected to the larger history of our species, *Homo sapiens*, that spans approximately 200,000 years. In other words, we can say that Nature is the source for all of the sacraments and therefore necessarily preceded any particular sacramental tradition.

However, there is also a deeper connection between Christian sacramental worship and the 14-billion-year cosmic history of our universe from which life emerged. Although the Eucharist is contained within the larger sacramental ecology of the history of life on Earth and the cosmic history of the universe, it is through participation in the Eucharistic liturgy that Christian worshipers can be ritually made aware of the grace that is present to be experienced in a sacramental universe. In other words, it is the reiteration of sacramental worship that has the greatest potential to point toward an awareness of and appreciation for a broader sense of sacramentality. While the Book of Common Prayer's definition of sacrament as an outward and visible sign of an inward and spiritual grace

---

[9] Genesis 1:1–2:3. Biblical references are taken from (*The Green Bible (New Revised Standard Version) 2008*) (The Green Bible 2008).

[10] John 1:3–4.

[11] In his *Worship as Theology: Foretaste of Glory Divine*, Don E. Saliers describes the emergence of the concept of true eschatology not simply as a discourse on the end times but "as a radical openness to the future." See (Saliers 1994, p. 51).

[12] The best way to gain an appreciation for this is to actually read through the prayers and rites of the Eucharistic liturgy. See (The 2007, pp. 316–409).

[13] While outsiders may scoff at the seeming supernatural character of religious doctrines such as the Creation, Incarnation, and Resurrection, they represent, particularly understood in relation to the context of the ancient cultures from which they emerged, profound affirmations of the natural order. The Incarnation, which is the ground and inspiration of our theological and sacramental tradition, is a radical statement that God's grace is revealed in physical form. William Temple was referring to the Incarnation when he wrote: "By the very nature of its central doctrine Christianity is committed to a belief in the ultimate significance of the historical process, and in the reality of matter and its place in the divine scheme." See (Temple 1951, p. 478).

supports a broader sacramentality, it is the unique sacraments of the church which point us outward to worship sacramentally in all of God's ongoing Creation.[14]

Furthermore, Christian tradition has a significant cosmic perspective through the theological understanding that God's grace is incarnate sacramentally through the creative action of the Divine Word in our sacramental universe. Therefore, the ecological value attributed through the Eucharist can be understood as inherent in, instead of extraneous to, the Christian tradition from which it emerges. The very meaning of tradition implies that our faith must be applied anew to shape us in the cultures we find ourselves in, in our contemporary context. Therefore, we need only to reenvision, as opposed to reinvent, our Eucharistic theology to seamlessly connect the concept of sacramental grace to the ecological value that emerges from a proper understanding of the evolutionary history of life on Earth.

4. Divine Presence and Mystery in Sacramental Grace and Ecological Value

With this in mind, I now want to turn to the concept of real divine presence in the Eucharist, a concept that undergirds all of the issues discussed in this paper. Real presence in the Eucharist has been interpreted rather broadly; however, for the purpose of this essay, I will focus on the understanding of real presence in the substances of the Eucharistic gifts of bread and wine, which entails an examination of the doctrine of transubstantiation.[15] I hold that the acceptance of the presence of Christ in the Eucharist, instead of a stumbling block, can be the key that opens to a broader sense of sacramentality wherein participation in the Eucharist can honestly address the issue of connections between sacramental grace and the ecological value related to the narrative of the Epic of Evolution. However, I want to begin with a point of discontinuity related to the doctrine of transubstantiation.

Transubstantiation has long been a stumbling block for Western Christianity, one that contributed to well-defined battle lines during the Reformation and one that is still often highly contentious in current theological discourse. This is due in large part to the fact that the doctrine of transubstantiation was the culmination of the increased emphasis, begun in the 9th century, on the understanding of the gifts of the Eucharistic bread and wine as being transformed into the sacrificial body and blood of Jesus as conveyers of divine grace.[16] The Fourth Lateran Council (1215) is the first instance of the terminology entering official church doctrine, and it has been continuously confirmed by the official teaching of the Catholic Church to the present. Contemporary criticism of transubstantiation frequently focuses on Thomas Aquinas' use of the Aristotelian categories of 'substance' and 'accident' in his development of the doctrine later in the 13th century to describe the change of substance from the gifts of bread and wine to the body and blood of Christ while retaining the 'accidental' properties of the former. In the space that I have here, I do not intend to provide either a justification for or refutation of the doctrine of transubstantiation or extensively outline the various ways in which contemporary theologians have attempted to mollify its interpretation with modified theologies of real presence.[17] Instead, I want to provide some perspective on what the doctrine of transubstantiation was intended to achieve and how an understanding of real presence in our contemporary context can be applicable

---

[14] In a discussion on Edward Schillibeeckx's reference to Christ as the 'primordial sacrament,' Macquarrie connects the overall sacramental system of the church with a broader sense of sacramentality as follows: "There is a kind of hierarchy here ... Christ is the sacrament of God; the church is the sacrament (body) of Christ; the seven sacraments are the sacraments of the church; the natural sacraments scattered around the world are, from a Christian point of view, approximations or pointers which find fulfillment in the sacraments of the gospel." See (Macquarrie 1997, p. 37).

[15] Concerning the broad understanding of Christ's presence in the Eucharist, Macquarrie writes the following: "The presence of Christ in the eucharist is a multiple presence. Since the eucharist always includes a reading from the Gospel, Christ is present in that word. Since it is Christ himself who presides at the eucharist, he is present also in the human minister, the priest, who rehearses the words and actions which Christ used at the Last Supper. Christ is present too in the eucharistic community, who are made one body with him, so that they dwell in him and he in them. And, of course, Christ is present in the bread and wine, over which have been said his words, 'This is my body', 'This is my blood.'" See (Macquarrie 1997, pp. 126–27).

[16] For a more extensive assessment of the debates related to the doctrine of the transubstantiation from the 9th to 13th centuries, see (Bradshaw and Johnson 2012, pp. 222–27).

[17] For a comment on some of these alternative theological perspectives to transubstantiation including "transignification" and "transfinalization," see (Bradshaw and Johnson 2012, p. 341).

to a theology of sacramental ecology that is necessarily predicated on a scientific perspective of the evolutionary and ecological connectedness of life on Earth.

Contemporary theologians widely criticize grounding belief in Christ's real presence in the eucharistic bread and wine in the Aristotelean metaphysics of transubstantiation as incongruous with how people today experience and reflect upon ritual and symbol in relation to the wider reality of their lives. However, to dismiss the reality of real presence in the Eucharist along with outdated metaphysical concepts associated with transubstantiation risks limiting a deeper understanding of the development of the concept of real presence in Christian history as well as the significance that such a doctrine potentially has when lived out in the world by the Christian community. For example, referencing the importance of recognizing the real presence of Christ in the Eucharist, David Brown defends Aquinas claiming that he "sought to defend that basic conception but in a way that excluded crude physical consumption" (Brown 2007, p. 410). Such a corrective defense was surely needed in Aquinas' time to counter the prevalence of a literalist interpretation of the consumption of the body and blood of Christ at the Eucharistic meal.[18] For Brown, what is essential is that we continue to identify with the bodily presence in the Eucharist since we encounter Eucharistic grace through material reality, both in terms of the substances of bread and wine but also in relation to our own bodies that take in these gifts with the faithful confidence that God's saving grace is mediated in some mysterious way through them. Our recognition of the bodily kinship that all life shares with Jesus is something that Brown fears we have failed to properly emphasize in our contemporary theological conversations. He writes:

> It is only really in the modern world that understanding of Christ's presence has moved primarily towards conceiving of it in terms of a presence within the gathered community or else as some sort of rarefied personal presence, essentially no different from the ubiquity of divinity. Transubstantiation is, admittedly, by any reckoning an implausible use of Aristotelian metaphysics. It did, however, have the merit that it thereby preserved some sense of it being important that we relate to Christ as having had and continuing to have a bodily identity like our own. (Brown 2007, p. 390)

Therefore, this is not simply a reiteration of the traditional doctrine of transubstantiation but a commitment to the significance of the real presence of Christ in the Eucharist in our current sacramental worship. The theological concept of transubstantiation is still useful, not in terms of defending its doctrinal formulation but in the sense, according to Macquarrie, that it "has come to stand for the view that there is in the eucharist a real abiding presence of Christ as against any view that denies this" (Macquarrie 1997, p. 131).

Brown's insistence that we recognize the bodily presence of Christ is important not only because it affirms the goodness of the natural order but also because it asserts that God relates to us immanently in a sacramental and incarnational way through material reality.[19] In this sense, the notion of real presence allows us to draw closer to God through our association with Jesus. According to Brown, the "divine nature in Christ renders his body incorruptible and so through association with that body our own too could achieve a similar status" (Brown 2007, p. 409). In a similar statement, he writes that "Christ's humanity is envisaged as coming close in order to create Christ-like beings in their own distinctive context" (Brown 2007, p. 419). By identifying with the body of Christ as real presence in the Eucharist, we can cultivate the understanding that God is still with us making the

---

[18] Concerning the continued widespread view of a literalist interpretation of the Eucharistic sacrifice of Christ, Macquarrie writes the following: "In spite of St. Thomas' attempt to construct a reasonable account of transubstantiation, one which should have put an end to the crudely materialistic interpretations that were going around, superstitious ideas continued to gain ground." See (Macquarrie 1997, p. 129).

[19] In brief, Brown argues for a broadened notion of sacramentality in which God is understood to be sacramentally present in all aspects of human culture and the entire natural world. For a description of the framework of his sacramental theology, see, in particular (Brown 2004, chp. 1).

divine presence known in the lives we are living in our necessarily ecological context. In brief, our imaginative association with Christ's bodily presence strengthens our sacramental connection to the loving grace of God that is ever available to us if we will only take the time to foster an awareness of its presence.[20]

Of course, locating the real divine presence in the Eucharist is not an empirical proposition. Instead, it is an orientation to life, a life that can be understood to be infused with value, meaning, and purpose in a sacramental universe. Brown describes this as follows:

> To state the obvious, whatever Christ's present body is like, it cannot be literally material, as though with sufficient progress in science we might one day be able to reach where it is now. Its nature has somehow to be reconciled with the fact that heaven, God's dwelling place, is a non-material reality and indeed omnipresent, just as God is . . . Yet none of this should be taken to indicate the abandonment of any notion of some degree of equivalence to material reality. (Brown 2007, p. 408)

Such an understanding is connected with the perspective that the grace conveyed through the Eucharist is, in fact, a mystery. Therefore, Brown's understanding of the bodily presence of Christ with which we identify in the Eucharist is not subject to empirical verification but is instead a mysterious presence that potentially points us toward an orientation that we, as embodied creatures, receive the grace of God through the substances of the world in which we exist and not through an ethereal or supernatural reality.

This may seem to place the understanding of real Eucharistic presence at odds with a scientific worldview. However, I would argue that the same sense of mystery that connects us to a larger presence of grace in the world through our participation in the Eucharist is the same sense that helps us value our kinship with all of life on Earth through an awareness of the Epic of Evolution. Consider Bruce Morrill's description of the place of mystery in the Eucharist:

> The word mystery . . . is not meant to hinder believers' use of reason and imagination as they seek a greater appreciation and joy in celebrating the Eucharist. Rather, to speak of the Eucharist as mystery is to acknowledge at the outset the complexity of our inquiry, and this not as a forbidding caution but a promising invitation. In fact, "mystery" was the preferred term of the earliest Christians for referring not only to the Eucharist and baptism but to all concrete ways in which they experienced God entering into and shaping their lives in Christ. (Morrill 2012, p. 1)

An acceptance of mystery of this kind is not a willful ignorance of scientific theory but is instead a profound respect for and faith in the source and sustenance of the lives we are blessed to live, a knowledge of which, we have to admit, is not completely known from our human perspective.

To further this point, it is instructive to compare this with the explanation of mystery from Bron Taylor who accepts the evolutionary and ecological history of life on Earth as the primary source of religious inspiration. Referencing environmentalist Loren Eiseley, he writes:

> With Loren Eiseley, I am convinced that the theory of evolution is the best explanation for the beauty, diversity, and fecundity of the biosphere. I also agree with him that nothing in the world fully explains the world. As he puts it, "I am an evolutionist . . . [but] in the world there is nothing to explain the world. Nothing to explain the necessity of life, nothing to explain the hunger of the elements to become life, nothing to explain why the stolid realm of rock and soil

---

[20] The use of the term 'imaginative' is a reference to Brown's *Tradition and Imagination: Revelation and Change* in which Brown uses 'imagination' as an interpretive term to argue that we should not separate revelation and tradition in theological discourse as if Biblical revelation holds a monopoly on definitive divine revelation. Furthermore, tradition is understood to be an ever-emergent process focused on interpreting the ongoing revelation of God in the world. See (Brown 1999).

and mineral should diversify itself into beauty, terror, and uncertainty." This humble admission captures, I think, the idea that the universe is a Great Mystery. (Taylor 2010, p. 220)

A willingness to accept a sense of mystery in life demonstrates a humility that is often lacking in both religious and scientific inquiry.[21] By accepting the real presence of the divine, incarnate in Christ in the Eucharist, we are, in a sense, opening ourselves to the broader mysteries of life that surround us, which, when properly understood, can also reflect to us the saving grace of God through an understanding of ecological grace in a sacramental universe.

5. Christ, the Primordial Sacrament in a Sacramental Universe

At this point, I want to take a closer look at how the mysterious bodily presence of Christ in the Eucharist can potentially connect the sacramental grace recognized in the formal ritual worship of the church with the larger sacramental universe in which it exists. I will begin with Edward Schillebeeckx's notion of Christ as the "primordial sacrament."

In the early 1960s, Schillebeeckx published *Christ, the Sacrament of the Encounter with God* in which he argues that "the sacraments are the properly human mode of encounter with God" and, furthermore, that "Jesus, as the personal visible realization of the divine grace of redemption, is *the* sacrament, the primordial sacrament" (Schillebeeckx 1963, pp. 6, 15). For Schillebeeckx, the sacraments continue the promise of the incarnation in that they serve as "the face of redemption turned visibly towards us, so that in them we are truly able to encounter the living Christ" (Schillebeeckx 1963, pp. 43–44). Consequently, because God is Emmanuel, "God with us" in an incarnational way through the sacraments, he claims that a "permanent sacramentality is thus an intrinsic requirement of the Christian religion" (Schillebeeckx 1963, p. 44).

The Eucharist, in particular, serves as the material expression of Christ's bodily presence in the world. Schillebeeckx describes the primordial sacrament of Christ as a stone thrown into a pond with the ripples flowing outward in concentric circles of grace from its central point of connection with the Eucharist serving as the central sacramental activity from which grace flows: "The sacrament of the Eucharist is situated at the heart of this central point—the Eucharist is the focal point of Christ's real presence among us. Around this focal point can be seen the first radiant lights—the other six sacraments" (Schillebeeckx 1963, p. 215). He adds that these "sacramental ripples ... continue to spread still further, though they gradually become less and less clearly defined—at this stage they are the sacramentals" (Schillebeeckx 1963, p. 215). In other words, the real presence of Christ in the Eucharist extends beyond the formal practice of the sacrament itself and into the world with an emanating grace that is the source of a broader sacramentality.[22]

In *Hymn of the Universe*, the Jesuit paleontologist Pierre Teilhard de Chardin offers a vivid demonstration of this idea. He relates a story in which, while observing the host, it began "gradually spreading out like a spot of oil but of course much more swiftly and luminously" (Teilhard de Chardin 1965, p. 47). Continuing, he states that "through the mysterious expansion of the host the whole world had become incandescent, had itself become like a single giant host" (Teilhard de Chardin 1965, p. 48). In this example, it is the host itself as the physical embodiment of

---

[21] As referenced at the beginning of this paper, E.O. Wilson is given credit with coining the term 'Epic of Evolution,' and it is worth noting that he implies a sense of mystery in the scientific understanding of life when he writes that the evolutionary epic "can be adjusted until it comes as close to truth as the human mind is constructed to judge the truth." See (Wilson 1978, p. 201).

[22] In discussing the extension of Eucharistic grace into a wider sacramental universe, we must not forget the understanding of the cosmic dimension of the Eucharist itself. While it points outward toward a broader sense of sacramentality, it also represents, in microcosm, the macrocosm of all of God's continuing creation. Take, for instance, the following statement from Alexander Schmemann: "In the eucharist, the *commemoration* is the gathering together of the entire experience of salvation, the entire fullness of that *reality* that is given us in the Church and that constitutes our life. It is the reality of the world as God's creation, the reality of the world as saved by Christ, the reality of the new heaven and the new earth, to which we ascend in the sacrament of ascension to the kingdom of God." See (Schmemann 1987, p. 221).

the presence of Christ on Earth that reaches out to touch the universe from which all life has emerged, bringing us with it into a greater realization of the immensity of divine creativity. Reflecting upon this experience, Teilhard de Chardin writes:

> [M]y mind awoke to a new and higher vision of things. I began to realize vaguely that the multiplicity of evolutions into which the world-process seems to us to be split up is in fact fundamentally the working out of one single great mystery; and this first glimpse of light caused me ... to tremble in the depths of my soul. But I was so accustomed to separating reality into different planes and categories of thought that I soon found myself lost in this spectacle, still new and strange to my tyro mind, of a cosmos in which the dimensions of divine reality, of spirit, and of matter were also intimately mingled. (Teilhard de Chardin 1965, p. 50)

In a similar, recent example, Catherine Vincie applies this extension of the real presence of the Eucharist to our expanding knowledge in the areas of ecological and evolutionary biology and cosmological physics that serve as the foundation of the Epic of Evolution as well as to our contemporary pluralistic context in which Christian sacramental life exists: "We must expand our imaginations to include in the communion of Christ those of other faith traditions and those who are not believers, as well as the community of Earth and the billions of galaxies that fill our skies. Christ is the Alpha of the universe; he is the new beginning, not the end" (Vincie 2014, p. 91). Vincie's placement of this conversation within the increasingly pluralistic cultures in which Christianity is practiced in many parts of the world is important since we must be cognizant of and humble enough to admit that Christian worship does not provide the exclusive means to access this sacramentality. As Sallie McFague points out, an ecological Christology should avoid falling into "Jesusolatry" by recognizing that "Jesus is the finger pointing to the moon" (McFague 2000, p. 34).

I would like to suggest that the Christian community can resist such exclusivist temptations when applying the Eucharist to an understanding that we live in a sacramental universe by recognizing that the presence of God that is revealed in a unique way in the life of Jesus is the same God who is still present with us, Christian and non-Christian, religious and non-religious. Stated in a slightly different way, the divine source of the universe and the life that has emerged and is still emerging from it is the same source of grace that was present in the life of Jesus. This sacramental grace can be experienced and embraced regardless of one's religious affiliation, and, I would argue even further, regardless of whether one is a theist or non-theist. I do not think that it is difficult to accept that the grace of God is present to all living things whether we realize it or not and also that this grace does not depend on human recognition for it to be efficacious. As Christians, we can acknowledge and accept the potential validity of other worldviews while maintaining the commitment that we are oriented to this presence sacramentally through our association with the bodily incarnation of God in Jesus. The historical centrality in Christian tradition of the life and revelation of God in Jesus connects Christian worshippers through Eucharistic practice to a potential encounter with the real presence of the divine in all things, a presence that binds everything that exists together in a vast interconnected divine embrace.

If we take such an understanding of the incarnation and its implications for a sacramental universe filled with ecological grace seriously, then everything is capable of having sacramental value. From a Christian perspective, this is not in addition to but as a result of our understanding that God became incarnate in the person of Jesus Christ. In his description of the host that expanded to include all of creation, Teilhard de Chardin adds that "in actual fact the immense host, having given life to everything and purified everything, *was now slowly contracting*; and the treasures it was drawing into itself were joyously pressed together within its living light" (Teilhard de Chardin 1965, p. 49). I think that Teilhard de Chardin's mystical vision is illustrative of how the sacramental worship of the Eucharist relates to the expanded sacramentality of a sacramental universe. Our experience of the real presence in the substances of the bread and wine received in the Eucharist expands our awareness of God's grace in all of the natural world. Yet, the Eucharist does not have an outward trajectory alone as it continuously draws us back in as a community of the faithful to glorify the gifts of creation in worship and to experience the mysterious presence of Christ so that we can be returned again and again into the wider world with the reminder that God is Emmanuel, "God with us," in order to emulate the self-giving sacrifice of Jesus in the lives we lead in our cultural and ecological communities.

Bernard Cooke relates the sacrifice of Christ in the Eucharist to the self-giving action of Jesus in which we are called to participate. In his words, this "means that the risen Christ is giving himself in new life to his friends. This self-giving by the risen Lord is his continuing action of 'offering sacrifice.' And the corollary of this is that Christians' action of 'offering sacrifice' consists in their loving self-gift to their fellow humans." Therefore, according to Cooke, "what the eucharist celebrates is that the entire life of these Christians, if lived out in loving concern for and genuine self-gift to their fellow humans, is a living sacrifice (Cooke 1994, pp. 112–13)." The mention here of self-giving and life is very important as it opens us up to a life of loving relationship with others, which, as Cooke points out, includes our fellow humans, but for the purpose of this essay, I would like to insist that this self-giving sacrifice can be extended to include all of God's ongoing Creation. This extension is implicit in Schillebeeckx's claim of a permanent sacramentality emanating outward from the Eucharist to the less-defined sacramentals of the wider world. It is also more explicitly evident in Brown's connection of incarnational presence, which is available in the Eucharist, to the concept of immanence: "So for God to impact on every aspect of us immanence must also be claimed: God involved in matter. Christians believe that this happened at the deepest and most profound level in the incarnation, but if there is to be a continuing effect this cannot have happened just once, but must relate to all material existence" (Brown 2004, pp. 81–82). The implication is that one's neighbors are not human alone but extend to the entire community of life an awareness of which can be sacramentally cultivated through participation in the thanksgiving of the Eucharistic meal.

6. Conclusions

Schubert Ogden maintains that all Christian theological claims must abide by the criteria of appropriateness and credibility (Ogden 1986, pp. 4–5). According to Ogden, Christian theology must be appropriate in the sense that it simultaneously accepts a connection to the tradition of which it is inextricably a part and to the contemporary context in which we live our lives. The Epic of Evolution compels us to look backward to our natural history for the purpose of understanding where we came from and who we are in our contemporary context so that we may value and protect the Earth's ecology as we go forward. The Eucharistic sacrament, while firmly rooted in Christian tradition, has the potential to significantly contribute to this backward and forward perspective by orienting us toward the recognition of sacramental grace present in the ongoing evolutionary epic. From this perspective, the Christian sacramental tradition can be understood as distinct but inseparably related to a broader understanding of sacramentality in which God's grace can be potentially witnessed, understood, and valued in all aspects of the natural world. As we come to the Eucharistic table, we humbly embrace life in all of its uncertainty, joy, sorrow, complexity, and beauty by fully immersing ourselves in sacramental worship so that we may come to reverence and protect God's ongoing Creation, what Wilson refers to as "Living Nature," the source of all grace and value.[23] Recognizing the power of religious and scientific narratives in our time, Wilson claims that, "[i]f religion and science could be united on the common ground of biological conservation, the problem would soon be solved" (Wilson 2007, p. 5). I propose that a deeper exploration of the ecological significance of sacramental theology is a step in the right direction.

Of course, there will be other interpretations of the Eucharist that continue to exist in Christian theological discourse, some of them more compatible with the scientific view of the Epic of Evolution and others less so. However, I would argue that a Eucharistic theology of ecological grace is an

---

[23] Wilson uses the theological language of "the Creation," defined by him as "living Nature," to bring science and religion together for the purpose of protecting biodiversity. See (Wilson 2007, p. 4).

appropriate and credible expression of Christian tradition. It maintains the perspective that the Eucharist serves as our primary orientation to sacramental grace without, on the one hand, distorting the tradition in order to cohere with the narrative of the Epic of Evolution or, on the other, allowing the tradition to distort a proper understanding of the ecological and evolutionary process of life from which we emerged and upon which we depend for our continued sustenance. Furthermore, a proper understanding of the tradition of Eucharistic practice makes it clear that the trajectory of the Eucharist is such that it can reach out to heal not only human communities but also to alleviate the degradation of all life on Earth.

It is my opinion that the very heart of Christian faith, worship, and theology is predicated on Jesus' claim in the Synoptic gospels that the greatest commandments are loving God and loving one's neighbor as oneself.[24] If one interprets these commandments sacramentally, then they are best understood not as separate commandments but instead as the second fulfilling the first. In other words, we love God by loving life which only exists for us in embodiment. Furthermore, the emphasis of Jesus' life and teaching as it has been passed down to us in tradition makes it clear that what constitutes our neighbor should be characterized by an ever-widening circle. It is not difficult to imagine that circle widening further to include, in the words of American environmentalist Aldo Leopold, "the integrity, stability, and beauty of the biotic community."[25] Therefore, the implications for loving God through love of neighbor in this manner are that all of life becomes a form of sacramental worship.

This greatest of all commandments intimately links us with the life of Jesus in being responsible, as humans, for offering our own self-giving sacrifice in the lives we lead for the fulfillment of the potential of God's ever-present grace in the evolving divine creation. Furthermore, our experience of the incarnation of Jesus embodied in the Eucharist can be lived out in Christian life by following Jesus' "way" of selfless love for God through love of neighbor. Morrill grounds the Eucharistic liturgy in the story of the road to Emmaus from the Gospel of Luke where the disciples only become aware of the identity of the risen Jesus following the breaking of bread in a ritual meal (Morrill 2012, pp. 9–11). He describes the significance of this foundational story as follows: "In light of the sacramental action, the full force of the word the Lord had proclaimed in their company sets their hearts blazing and their feet back on the road. Only now, however, they hit the road with purpose, the mission of bringing the message of Christ crucified to life for the world" (Morrill 2012, p. 10). This experience is available to us as well each time we approach the Eucharistic table to acknowledge the beautiful mystery that a real divine presence infuses all of life and that life continues to emerge from death as the evolutionary epic continues on, perpetuating ecological value through the loving grace of God in a sacramental universe. Embracing such a Eucharistic theology of ecological grace allows us to give thanks for this gift of life by glorifying God through the preservation of the evolving sacramental ecology from which all life emerges.

Funding: This research received no external funding.

Conflicts of Interest: The author declares no conflict of interest.

References

Book of Common Prayer. 2007. New York: Church Publishing Incorporated.
Bradshaw, Paul F., and Maxwell Johnson. 2012. *The Eucharistic Liturgies: Their Evolution and Interpretation*. Collegeville: Liturgical Press.
Brown, David. 1999. *Tradition and Imagination: Revelation and Change*. New York: Oxford University Press.
Brown, David. 2004. *God and Enchantment of Place: Reclaiming Human Experience*. New York: Oxford University Press.

---

[24] See Matthew 22:35–40, Mark 12:28–31, Luke 10:25–28.
[25] In his *A Sand County Almanac*, Aldo Leopold famously wrote that a "thing is right when it tends to preserve the integrity, stability, and beauty of the biotic community. It is wrong when it tends otherwise." See (Leopold 1968, pp. 224–25).

Brown, David. 2007. *God and Grace of Body: Sacrament in Ordinary*. New York: Oxford University Press.

Cooke, Bernard. 1994. *Sacraments and Sacramentality*. Mystic: Twenty-Third Publications.

Darwin, Charles. 2006. *From so Simple a Beginning: The Four Great Books of Charles Darwin*. New York: W. W. Norton & Company.

Leopold, Aldo. 1968. *A Sand County Almanac and Sketches Here and There*. New York: Oxford University Press.

Macquarrie, John. 1997. *A Guide to the Sacraments*. New York: Continuum.

McFague, Sallie. 2000. An Ecological Christology: Does Christianity Have it? In *Christianity and Ecology: Seeking the Well-Being of Earth and Humans*. Edited by Dieter T. Hessel and Rosemary Radford Ruether. Cambridge: Harvard University Press, pp. 29–45.

Morrill, Bruce T. 2012. *Encountering Christ in the Eucharist: The Paschal Mystery in People, Word, and Sacrament*. New York: Paulist Press.

Ogden, Schubert M. 1986. *On Theology*. San Francisco: Harper and Row Publishers.

Saliers, Don E. 1994. *Worship as Theology: Foretaste of Glory Divine*. Nashville: Abingdon Press.

Schillebeeckx, Edward. 1963. *Christ the Sacrament of the Encounter with God*. New York: Sheed and Ward.

Schmemann, Alexander. 1987. *The Eucharist: Sacrament of the Kingdom*. Crestwood: St. Vladimir's Seminary Press.

Taylor, Bron. 2010. *Dark Green Religion: Nature Spirituality and the Planetary Future*. Berkeley: University of California Press.

Teilhard de Chardin, Pierre. 1965. *Hymn of the Universe*. New York: Harper and Row, Publishers.

Temple, William. 1951. *Nature, Man, and God*. London: MacMillan and Company, Limited.

The Green Bible. 2008. *The Green Bible (New Revised Standard Version)*. New York: HarperCollins Publishers.

Vincie, Catherine. 2014. *Worship and the New Cosmology: Liturgical and Theological Challenges*. Collegeville: Liturgical Press.

Wilson, Edward O. 1978. *On Human Nature*. Cambridge: Harvard University Press.

Wilson, Edward O. 1984. *Biophilia*. Cambridge: Harvard University Press.

Wilson, Edward O. 1999. *Consilience: The Unity of Knowledge*. New York: Vintage Books.

Wilson, Edward O. 2002. *The Future of Life*. New York: Vintage Books.

Wilson, Edward O. 2006. *Naturalist*. Washington: Island Press.

Wilson, Edward O. 2007. *The Creation: An Appeal to Save Life on Earth*. New York: W. W. Norton & Company.

Wilson, Edward O. 2012. *The Social Conquest of Earth*. New York: W. W. Norton & Company.

Article

Sacramentality, Chaos Theory and Decoloniality

Edward Foley

Catholic Theological Union, 5416 South Cornell Avenue, Chicago, IL 60615, USA; foley@ctu.edu

Received: 6 June 2019; Accepted: 3 July 2019; Published: 5 July 2019

Abstract: This essay considers how an expanded understanding of sacramentality is enhanced by engagement with chaos theory and decolonial theory. These unique lenses enlarge traditional Roman Catholic frameworks for considering God's self-communication through sacramental action as well as the agency of ordinary believers and even non-believers in the sacramental enterprise.

Keywords: coloniality; decoloniality; chaos theory; sacrament; post-colonial theory; pandemonium tremendum

1. Introduction

It is well established doctrinally and empirically that sacramentality is core to Roman Catholic teaching and practice. A traditional expression of the doctrinal centrality of this belief is found in the "sacramental principle", that everything in the created world has the potential for revealing God (Himes 2014). The centrality of the sacraments and their liturgies to the self-understanding of the Roman Catholic church—especially the Eucharist—is magisterially epitomized in *Sacrosanctum Concilium*'s teaching that "the liturgy is the summit toward which the activity of the church is directed ... [and] the source from which all its power flows" (Sacrosanctum Concilium 1996, no. 10). From an empirical perspective, already in the 1990s sociologist Andrew Greeley (d. 2013) believed he could prove statistically that sacramentality was at the heart of the Roman Catholic imagination (Greeley 1991), a position he espoused throughout his lifetime (see Greeley 2001). This stance was supported by the work of other sociologists (e.g., Dinges et al. 1998) and theologians (e.g., Tracy 1998).

While the "catholic" imagination might be decidedly sacramental, data yet demonstrates that sacramental practice among Roman Catholics in the United States is in steady decline. According to recent figures from the Center for Applied Research in the Apostolate (CARA), over the past decade there has been a noticeable decrease in the number of infant baptisms, first communions, confirmations, and priestly ordinations, while the number of self-identified Roman Catholics in the U.S. is holding steady or showing a slight increase (CARA 2019).

Although some might suggest that this decline in engagement with the official sacraments of the Roman Catholic Church signals a waning of our sacramental imagination, another explanation seems more likely: Roman Catholic sacramental practices and their accompanying imaginations and spiritualities are becoming more liquid.

In 2000, Polish sociologist and philosopher Zygmunt Bauman christened the current era one of "liquid modernity" (Bauman 2000). While previous periods in history witnessed cycles of sometimes radical disintegration and renewal, Bauman argues that current modernity is different. Whereas the "solids" of a previous era (e.g., monarchy) were replaced by new solids (e.g., communism in Russia), in this modernity melting solids are not being displaced by new and improved solids. Rather, the state of commerce, relationships, education, society and even self-identity are characterized by liquidity, deregulation, liberalization and what Bauman calls "flexibilization": constantly poised for change (Bauman 2000, p. 3).

In a parallel vein, there are yet those who contend that we are witnessing liquid forms of religion and even an era of a liquid church. British theologian Pete Ward asserts that this liquid moment is an opportunity to promote a new way of being church within contemporary culture: more diffuse and less institutionalized (Ward 2002). Kees De Groot has a different image of liquid church that he believes takes the work of Bauman more seriously. His approach to "liquid *koinonia*" attempts to value momentary types of community in which people take part in various degrees (De Groot 2007, p. 189).

The ritual version of this phenomenon is what some have deemed "liquid ritualizing". Liquid ritualizing is characterized by an openness to ritual transfer, i.e., the reshaping of ritual to respond to a transformed context, including the borrowing of elements from other traditions (Arfman 2014, p. 23). According to Arfman, ideas freely seep, ooze and flow from one tradition to another. While not new, Arfman contends that there is an overabundance of ritual transfer today (Arfman 2014, p. 4). Decades earlier, in her discussion of "ritual invention", Catherine Bell agrees that while ritual invention is not a new phenomenon, the freedom people now feel "to eschew any claims for ritual antiquity may be relatively unprecedented" (Bell 1997, p. 225).

In my own work, I have espoused the need for the Roman Catholic Church to be more intentional in liquidizing our sacramentality in teaching and practice (Foley 2019). Previously, my proposals were rooted in the theological concept of *sensus fidelium*, i.e., "a basic means of understanding the faith and as such exercises a truth-finding and truth-attesting function that has as its special characteristic that it takes into account the faithful's experience in the world" (Rush 2009, p. 2; also, Rush 2017).

This exploration moves that discussion forward with two new dialogue partners: chaos theory and decolonial theory. These diverse yet complementary lenses provide unique optics for reimaging sacramentality in this liquid era. In particular, these offer singular avenues for expanding—maybe even exploding—the classic frameworks that honor both the mystery of God and the agency of human subjects in the sacramental interchange in fresh ways. The reason for engaging both of these concepts in this sacramental exploration is that chaos theory brings new frames for understanding God's action in the sacramental enterprise, and decolonial theory does the same for pondering people's action in this enterprise. If sacraments are actions requiring engagement—or as Edward Schillebeeckx would have it "encounter" (Schillebeeckx 1963)—of both God and people (cf. Sacrosanctum Concilium 1996, no. 7), then it seems both appropriate and necessary when expanding our sacramental imaginations to address both of these actors. Chaos theory provides a fresh optic for reimagining the nature of God's action in sacraments often framed through the theological shorthand *ex opera operato*, and decolonial theory an intriguing lens for reimagining people's action often framed as *ex opera operantis*. To that end, this essay will first examine the nature and contribution of chaos theory with particular attention to its theological ramifications concerning the gracious self-communication of God in the visible world. Next, we will turn to a consideration of decolonial theory and its contribution to a more liberated view of human subjects, especially but not exclusively the baptized, in sacramental practice. We will close with a brief conclusion.

2. Chaos Theory and the Mystery of God's Sacramental Self-Giving

It was the 1993 blockbuster *Jurassic Park* that introduced the concept of chaos theory to the masses through its character Ian Malcolm (Jeff Goldblum), a self-styled "chaotician." The language and foundational principles of chaos theory, however, had been around for decades before. The work of French mathematician Henri Poincaré (d. 1912) concerning the so called "*n*-body problem" (Poincaré 1890, 2017) about the predictability of planetary movements is often placed at the birth of this theory (Oestreicher 2007). Another key figure was the Soviet mathematician Andrey Nikolaevich Kolmogorov (d. 1987), particularly his studies of integrability and the unexpectedly complicated nature of simple deterministic equations (Livi et al. 2003, p. 4). The development of advanced computers in the mid-twentieth century provided the tool to challenge forever the prevailing deterministic theories rooted in the work of Isaac Newton (d. 1726). Pivotal was the work of meteorologist Edward Lorenz (d. 2008), sometimes called the "father of chaos theory" (Chang 2008). Lorenz was attempting to understand the chaotic behavior in weather and was encountering difficulties in creating a mathematical model that could accurate predict the weather. In running an experiment on weather modeling in 1961,

Lorenz discovered that even the divergence of one thousandth of a decimal point would render vastly different results (Lorenz 1963). His conclusion was "that any physical system that behaved nonperiodically would be unpredictable" (Gleick 1987, p. 18). His insight is sometimes referenced as the "butterfly effect." That moniker stems from a lecture Lorenz offered at the 1972 conferenced of the American Association for the Advancement of Science, entitled "Predictability: does the flap of a butterfly's wings in Brazil set off a tornado in Texas?" (Lorenz 1972). The actual term "chaos theory" was coined by mathematician James A. York and his student Tien-Yien Li in their 1975 article on the topic (Li and York 1975).

While multiple aspects of this relatively young theory continue to be debated, and consensus around a clear definition of chaos theory remains difficult to establish, its influence increasingly expands. Besides serious engagement in the previously noted fields of physics, mathematics and meteorology, the impact of chaos theory is also emerging in fields such as theoretical biology and engineering (Strogatz 2001), medicine and pharmacology (Kumar and Hedge 2012), and even theology.

Early on, this discussion in theological circles was broached from the perspective of "chance." The British statistician David Bartholomew (d. 2017), who published a groundbreaking work on the relationship between theology and chance (Bartholomew 1984), maps out some of this work in his article "God and Chance," though his later writings show a preference for the language of "unpredictability" rather than chance (Bartholomew 2016). Bartholomew does not ground his theological engagement with the topic of chance in the work of Lorenz, but more in quantum physics, biology and evolutionary theory. These fields and their penchant for stressing the unpredictability of nature provoked serious challenges to understanding Divine action and the nature of God's providence. In response, Bartholomew and others have argued that "since chance is such an integral part of creation, it must be part of God's plan . . . . [and] that everything which happens is ultimately God's responsibility" (Bartholomew 1984, p. 118). The theologian's task, therefore, is to muse respectfully about this divine mystery—at least unpredictable if not chaotic from a human perspective—while still charting a path for responsible living and believing.

One who does that deftly is James Huchingson in his theological reflection on what he calls the *pandemonium tremendum*, which is an apt analogy for chaos theory in theological mode. According to Huchingson, *pandemonium tremendum* "is the state antecedent to the creation, the comprehensive, unconditioned, and indeterminate source or ground of diversity among determinate things. It is the formless and the void of the *tohuwabohu* and the agitated deep of the *tehom*" (Huchingson 2001, p. 109). A former researcher for NASA, then associate professor of religious studies, Huchingson is attempting to develop "a model of God derived from an account of the primordial chaos" (Huchingson 2001, p. 222). Part of that project is embracing the Genesis revelation (1:2) of the abyss (תְּהוֹם) as a resource for holy inventiveness rather than some vat of useless or even demonic phenomena. As theologian An Yountae affirms, *tehom* is not merely raw chaos, but also "the womb of creative potential" (Yountae 2017, p. 11). Drawing upon communication theories and informed by the revolution in quantum mechanics, non-linear chaos theory, and the recent theory shattering accomplished through the use of computers (à la Lorenz), Huchingson is committed to this cosmological exploration in the hopes of generating a useful and credible metaphysic. A central theological dialogue partner for him is Paul Tillich.

What seems most useful about Huchingson's reflections is his contention that this *pandemonium tremendum* does not contradict any notion of an all-powerful God. Rather, he argues, that it is completely consonant with Tillich's understanding of "inexhaustible abundance", without which God could not be God (Huchingson 2002, p. 396). In this metaphysic, God does not police the chaos, but witnesses to it, bringing the divine will to bear upon it when necessary, and employing it as a virtually limitless storehouse for creation. His riff on God's question to Job, "Have you entered the storehouses of the snow" (Job 38:22) illustrates this point:

> Snow consists of delicate hexagonal flakes of ice, each with an intricate and novel geometrical design. As a deluge of countless exquisite flakes, a blizzard is an accurate and revealing

symbol for the infinite variety of the Pandemonium Tremendum. Snow is sent by God, but what is its origin? A scientifically innocent fantasy would imagine a storehouse for the snow, available to God to send upon the earth. In like manner, but placed in a metaphysical framework, the primordial chaos is the storehouse of variety that God likewise releases upon the earth to create, constitute, and sustain its integrity and order. If this image is accurate, God is necessary as the power that contains the primordial chaos, the one who "stores" it and places it "at hand" as a ready source of nurturing variety. (Huchingson 2002, p. 398)

Analogously, one could imagine the "sacramental principle," with its presupposition that everything in creation has the potential for revealing the divine, as positing its own form of *pandemonium tremendum*: or more aptly a *pandemonium sacramentum*. In this imaginary, sacramentality like snow is an inexhaustible resource upon which God draws in self-communicating to the world and shaping a sacramental people. God does not "police" this *pandemonium sacramentum* but is a witness to it as an inexhaustible and divinely willed invitation so that humanity might attend to God's manifestation in one of its infinite varieties, and respond in gratitude and gracious living.

Such a framework respects the ambiguous New Testament language of *musterion*, especially as it appears in the Pauline literature: much less concrete than its Latinization as *sacramentum*. Paul advances the concept of *musterion* as the mystery of God in Christ (Col. 2:2), prepared before the world existed (i.e., in the *pandemonium tremendum*, 1 Cor. 2:7), kept hidden in God (Eph 3:9), concealed from the rulers of this age (1 Cor 2:8), but which breaks into the world and human history (Rom 16:26).

Augustine (1954, d. 430) anticipates the blizzard of sacramentality in his wide-ranging use of the language of *sacramentum*, employing that term for over 300 ecclesial actions (Coutourier 1953). This expansiveness is echoed in his teaching that a sacrament is a kind of "visible word" (Augustine, *In Johannis evangelium tractatus*, 5.6 & 80.3). While Augustine's sacramental imagination seems bound by ecclesial frameworks, contemporary scholars have gone further. Alexander Schmemann (d. 1983) was a pioneer in his 1965 publication "The World as Sacrament" (Schmemann 1965a, 1979). Schmemann believed creation to be an essential means "both of the knowledge of God and communion with him" (Schmemann 1979, p. 220). As an "epiphany" of God, Schmemann contends that "the world was created as a matter of a sacrament" (Schmemann 1979, p. 223). Kristine Suna-Koro moves even further, contending that creation itself—not Christ, as in the Schillibeeckxean universe (Schillebeeckx 1963)—is the *Ursakrament* (Suna-Koro 2017). While he does not explicitly employ the language of sacramentality, Pope Francis seems to concur with this cosmic perspective. In his encyclical *Laudato Si'*, Francis (2015) speaks of the entire world as "a caress of God" (no. 84), considers the world a "divine manifestation" (no. 85) and hymns the "sacredness of the world" (no. 85) that not only manifests God but is actually a "locus of [God's] presence" (no. 88).

One of the startling ramifications of such a *pandemonium sacramentum* is that, even wider than Augustine could image, sacramentality thrives outside of Roman Catholicism and beyond Christianity. Thus, Herbert Vorgrimler, among others, can ponder the existence of "natural sacraments", i.e., expressions of sacramentality that existed before Judaeo-Christian revelation, or in non-Christian and non-Jewish humanity up to the present (Vorgrimler 1992, p. 16). Maybe even more unsettling is the possibility that sacramentality can thrive in the work of self-professed agnostics, apostates and atheists. Thus, Richard Kearney can posit a sacramental imagination in literary figures such as novelists Marcel Proust (d. 1922), James Joyce (d. 1941) and Virginia Woolf (d. 1941). Furthermore, Kearney argues that the "methodic suspension of confessional truth claims ... allows for a specific 'negative capability' regarding questions of doubt, proof, dogma or doctrine, so as to better appreciate the holy *thisness* and *thereness* of our flesh and blood existence ... allowing us to attend to the sacramental marvel of the everyday without the constraints of any particular confession" (Kearney 2009, pp. 245–46).

The empirical fact of unpredictability foundational to chaos theory provides a challenging but refreshing lens for reimaging sacramentality today. Edward Lorenz attempted to craft a theoretical model that would predict weather patterns with a significant degree of reliability. In the end, however, he came to understand that such was simply not practical. Analogously, Roman Catholicism has attempted to teach—sometimes impose—a theoretical model of sacramentality, still broadly influenced by scholastic thought, that presumes to explain the number, nature and effect of sacraments (e.g., Catechism of the Catholic Church 1993, nos. 1113ff). Given the unpredictability of the very mystery of God from a human standpoint, the fluid and pliant workings of the Holy Spirit, and the *pandemonium tremendum* that resources God's holy will, such ecclesial modeling is similarly impractical and brittle. In Jurassic Park, chaotician Ian Malcomb chided financier John Hammond for trying to control evolution. Malcomb summarizes his critique by noting "life will not be contained. Life breaks free, it expands to new territories and crashes through barriers, painfully, maybe even dangerously" (Koepp 1992). To paraphrase, sacramentality similarly will not be contained. It breaks free, it expands to new territories and crashes through barriers, painfully, maybe even dangerously.

3. Decoloniality and the Mystery of God's Sacramental People

While chaos theory can be a fresh framework for pondering God's self-giving in sacramental terms, decoloniality provides a different lens, useful in considering how human beings are agents of sacramentality.

Decoloniality is a form of critical theory emerging largely out of South America and gaining prominence over the past few decades. Coloniality is sometimes conflated with colonization, though theorists such as Walter Mignolo, Ramón Grosfoguel and others vigorously dispute such a conflation. Mignolo distinguishes these parallel but distinctive critical theories genealogically: with colonial theory lodged in French post-structuralism whereas coloniality is an epistemic shift away from European paradigms of rationality rooted in the "canonical jargon of the historiography of the Americas" (Mignolo 2011a, "Epistemic Disobedience", p. 47). Rather than genealogy, Grofoguel distinguishes colonialism from coloniality around the presence or absence of a colonial administration. Thus, colonialism references situations "enforced by the presence of a colonial administration." Coloniality, on the other hand, continues "in the present period in which colonial administrations have almost been eradicated from the capitalist world-system." For him, coloniality concerns both economic exploitation as well as the production of "subjectivities and knowledge" (Grosfoguel 2006).

Central to the decolonial turn is a fierce rejection of the "underlying logic of the foundation and unfolding of Western civilization from the Renaissance to today" (Mignolo 2011b, The Darker Side, p. 2). Such logic is epitomized in René Descartes' (d. 1650) *je pense, donc je suis*. This assertion created a new moment in western thought that placed "western man" as the foundation of a knowledge; in the process "Descartes was able to claim non-situated, universal, omniscient divine knowledge" (Grosfoguel 2006) that the decolonial turn systematically analyzes and voraciously rejects. Consequently, in large measure the decolonial turn is an "epistemic reconstruction" (Quijano 2007, p. 176), that in counter distinction to Eurocentrism honors border thinking, indigenous knowledge, and minority discourse.

Besides an epistemic venture, decoloniality is also political and economic. As an embodied enterprise it is about both thinking and doing (Mignolo 2011b, The Darker Side, p. xxiv). The incarnational side of the decolonial turn is manifest in concerns about the market place, labor, political structures, but also symbolization and the arts (Maldonado-Torres 2011). Decolonial pioneer Enrique Dussel recognizes that art is an ideology. Because of that, he argues that it is essential to study "the *aesthetic* production of works of art which express in their 'fidelity' to the face of the oppressed ... critical, prophetic and eschatological 'beauty'" (Dussel 1980, p. 50). While not explicitly a decolonial theorist, Alejandro García-Rivera's emphasis on a theological aesthetic that lifts up the lowly is a parallel confirmation of the critical role of prophetic modes of beauty (García-Rivera 1999).

One key mode of symbolization critical to our reflection here is ritual and its sub-genre of liturgy. From a political perspective, rituals of many forms have been used as tools of coloniality. Thus, in his reflection on the repressive role of images, symbolization and belief patterns in colonialism, Quijano notes,

> In the beginning colonialism was a product of a systematic repression ... of the specific beliefs, ideas, images, symbols or knowledge that were not useful to global colonial domination ... .

> The repression fell, above all, over the modes of knowing, of producing ... images and systems
> of images, symbols, modes of signification, over the resources, patterns, and instruments of
> formalized and objectivised expression, intellectual or visual. (Quijano 2007, p. 169)

Marc Ellis is pointed in his unmasking of liturgy as a technology of colonization and coloniality when he notes that "liturgy often pretends that its domain is primarily or only religious," and recognizes that many "experience the proclamation of liturgy's innocence as naïve" (Ellis 2015, p. 48). Kristine Suna-Koro contends that "liturgy has been part and parcel of the coloniality of being, power and knowledges. Many Christian liturgies ... are still permeated with unexamined imperialistic symbols, images of conquest, patriarchy, and racism" (Suna-Koro 2015, p. 250). For Sarah Kathleen Johnson, Christian ritual is not only an instrument of social control but can also be an instrumental of *cultural genocide* (Johnson 2018, p. 6).

Parallel to post-colonial theorists, scholars of coloniality recognize that the decolonial turn is essentially a rejection of the matrix of power controlling "authority, labor, sexuality and subjectivity—that is, the practical domains of political administration, production and exploitation, personal life and reproduction, and world-view and interpretive perspective" (Martinot 2008). Mignolo argues that the appropriate response to this Eurocentric matrix of power is what he calls "dewesternizing" through a process of "delinking": be that political, economic or epistemic delinking. As examples of political and economic delinking, Mignolo notes the need to end international dependency on institutions such as the International Monetary Fund and the World Bank. A critical arena for this work, according to Mignolo, is the World Public Form (WPF) "where 'delinking' is the norm, the method and the orientation" (Mignolo 2012).

In his discussion of delinking, Mignolo makes an explicit turn to Christianity. He notes:

> Another sphere of civil society in which dewesternization currently is being discussed is
> within a domain that I refer to as religious-political and epistemic delinking. The most visible,
> though certainly not the only line of thinking, has been advanced by Islamic scholarship ... .
> Related and parallel to Islamic dewesternization, there is a movement among Christians to
> "dewesternize the Gospels." If these tendencies persist it will facilitate a dialogue among
> civilizations that the WPF is seeking, and make visible that both Islam and Christianity
> are, in a way, forces of liberation that are captive within their own institutions and belief
> systems. To do so, Christians must delink from the imperial/colonial trap of Christianity
> in different ways and through different routes. Dewesternizing Christianity is a more
> complex phenomenon than Islamic dewesternization. Although Christianity was, originally,
> a non-Western religion, it became Westernized and imperial. (Mignolo 2012)

Key to that delinking for Roman Catholicism is a rethinking of the nature of sacramentality so central to its self-definition and theologies. Decoloniality is about returning agency in "thinking and doing" to indigenous peoples, local practices and contextual epistemologies. For Roman Catholics, a key route of this empowerment is returning and nourishing sacramental agency to the baptized. Whether one approves or not, increasing numbers of Roman Catholics are "delinking" from official church teaching and prescribed practices. They are engaging with new found freedom in the liquid ritualizing and reinvention noted above. Seldom, however, is such ritualizing honored as an authentic mode of sacramentalizing by leadership and, instead, is at best tolerated as acts of personal piety or dismissed as ritual deviance by unauthorized laity.

In our teaching and preaching, however, in our pastoral care and training of church ministers, the task of delinking sacramentality from clerical control and canonical imperatives is a critical route. Many baptized are incapable of recognizing or admitting a sacramental act without the presence of clergy. Even in the sacrament of marriage, in which the spouses are the acknowledged ministers and subjects with Christ of the sacrament (Belcher 2019, pp. 13–14), confusion about sacramental agency abounds, evidenced in the frequent query by an engaged couple to a priest: "Will you marry us, Father?".

Surprisingly, there are tremors of sacramental chaos even within official teaching and law: for example, allowing baptism to be administered by someone who is not Roman Catholic, Christian, or a believer of any stripe. Archetypic are nurses in neo-natal units in cities with a large Roman Catholic population such as Boston and Chicago, who are trained to baptize if an infant of Roman Catholic parents is deemed to be in danger of death. When a Hindu or Muslim or agnostic nurse alone in a neo-natal unit in such a situation baptizes, there is literally no "Christian" in the room, but "Christ is present" (Sacrosanctum Concilium 1996, no. 7).

Sacramental chaos in revelation and agency expands much further, however. In the incarnation, God chose to wed divinity with humanity, but not only in one time and place. As Anthony Kelly has aptly noted, Jesus resurrection and ascension did not result in an "excarnation". He elaborates:

> Though he is indeed "out of sight" as far as his physical, historical presence among us as Jesus of Nazareth is concerned, he is not so lost in the clouds ... as to be removed from all human communication and dematerialized into some other realm .... Rather, it is better to admit that we human beings are not yet fully embodied in the Body of Christ. From this viewpoint, the resurrection-ascension of Christ is an expanding bodily event, in according with God's continuing incarnational action in the world. (Kelly 2010, p. 803)

God continues to wed with humanity; every human being—not just the baptized—is created in the image of God (Genesis 1:27). That renders human beings not only capable of imbibing in the very sacramentality of creation and life but also, through a decolonial lens, renders every human being as potential agents of the same. Mignolo argued that delinking from the colonial power matrix would neither destroy it nor ignore. Rather, he posited a conflictual co-existence of rewesternization with dewesternization (Mignolo 2012). Delinking sacramentality from the hierarchical power matrix analogously will not necessarily destroy or displace hierarchy or official church. Rather, it will balance it—admittedly in a sometimes conflictual yet necessary co-existence—with the agency of human beings who are not simply *recipients* of sacraments but actually commissioned through holy invitation to be *agents* of sacramentality (Sacrosanctum Concilium 1996, no 7).

Here, the *pandemonium tremendum* that renders God as God, transformed into *pandemonium sacramentum* that honors the infinite ways in which God self-communicates to creatures and creation, transmutes into *pandemonium hominum*. It is no longer the storehouse of snow that dazzles in its abundance and diversity, but the storehouse of humanity, each human being analogous in particularity to each snowflake. The decolonial turn urges that this seven-billion-plus storehouse of incarnate particularity—grounded in untold forms of native knowing, contextual believing, and indigenous ritualizing—be honored and empowered as agents of sacramentality across the range of joys and sorrows, resurrections and crucifixions that shape the liturgies of their lives.

4. Conclusions

In the theological imagination of Alexander Schmemann, "the basic definition of man [sic] is that he is the *priest*. He stands at the centre of the world and unifies it in his act of blessing God, of both receiving the world from God and offering it to God" (Schmemann 1965b, p. 16). Schmemann also believes that after the Fall of humanity narrated in Genesis, human beings became less "priests" and more consumers", forgetting the sacramentality of the world.

There is no doubt that *homo adorans*, as Schmemann would have it, has become *homo consumens*. As Vincent Miller has incisively explained, religion itself has become one of those consumables (Miller 2003). Suggesting that all of humanity has forgotten the sacramentality of the world, however, seems to be an inappropriate, even simplistic binary. Sometimes it is not human beings or societies that have lapsed into forgetfulness, but organized religions such as Roman Catholicism that have forgotten to recognize the unpredictable self-communication of God in the cosmos, and similarly failed to recognize the unpredictable responses in the ritual inventiveness and liquid sacramentality that human beings instinctively practice.

Religions **2019**, *10*, 418

Katy Payne is a one-time musician turned zoologist who spent decades studying the sounds of whales, eventually credited along with colleague Linda Guinee for discovering the songs of humpback whales. Later in her career, she was visiting the Portland zoo, when she "felt" more than heard rumbling communication between two Asian elephants standing on opposite sides of a concrete wall. Enlisting the help of acoustic biologists, they discovered infrasonic communication, low frequency elephant discourse inaccessible to human ears. This led to the development of the Elephant Listening Project (http://elephantlisteningproject.org/). Published in *Silent Thunder*, her fascinating work documents how these goliaths developed a sophisticated communication system capable of broadcasting over many miles through African forests, but well below the auditory radar of humanoids (Payne 1998).

Just as Payne did not create this infrasonic communication between the world's largest land mammals, so tools such as chaos theory and decoloniality do not so much create new aspects of sacramentality as much as they help reveal in startling ways what is already at play. They pull back the veil on the mystery of God's abiding invitation for creaturely engagement in divine life, as well as our erratic yet enduring attempts to respond in all of our human particularity to the holy blizzard of that invitation. They supply tools, especially to church leaders, to apprehend the uncalibrated sacramentalizing constantly emanating along wavelengths that clerical training and colonialized ritually have unfortunately not prepared us to perceive. As the character Ian Malcolm reminds us: sacramentality will not be contained. It breaks free, it expands to new territories and crashes through barriers, painfully, maybe even dangerously.

Funding: This research received no external funding.

Conflicts of Interest: The author declares no conflict of interest.

References

Arfman, William. 2014. Liquid Ritualizing: Facing the Challenges of Late Modernity in an Emerging Ritual Field. *Journal of Religion in Europe* 7: 1–25. [CrossRef]

Augustine. 1954. *Johannis Evangelium Tractatus*. Edited by R. Willems, Corpus Christianorum and Series Latina. Turnhout: Brepols, vol. 36.

Bartholomew, David J. 1984. *God of Chance*. London: SCM.

Bartholomew, David J. 2016. God and Chance: Christian Perspectives. Available online: https://oxfordre.com/religion/view/10.1093/acrefore/9780199340378.001.0001/acrefore-9780199340378-e-23 (accessed on 2 April 2019).

Bauman, Zygmunt. 2000. *Liquid Modernity*. Cambridge: Polity.

Belcher, Kimberly. 2019. A Theology of Marriage. In *Catholic Marriage: A Pastoral and Liturgical Commentary*. Edited by Edward Foley. Chicago: Liturgy Training Publications, pp. 13–26.

Bell, Catherine. 1997. *Ritual: Perspectives and Dimensions*. New York: Oxford University Press.

CARA. 2019. Frequently Requested Church Statistics. Available online: https://cara.georgetown.edu/frequently-requested-church-statistics/ (accessed on 2 April 2019).

Catechism of the Catholic Church. 1993. Available online: http://www.vatican.va/archive/ENG0015/_INDEX.HTM#fonte (accessed on 30 June 2019).

Chang, Kenneth. 2008. The Father of Chaos Theory, Dies at 90. *New York Times*, April 17.

Coutourier, C. 1953. 'Sacramentum' et 'Mysterium' dans l'oeuvre de Saint Augustine. In *Etudes Augustiniennes*. Paris: Aubier, pp. 161–301.

De Groot, Kees. 2007. Rethinking Church in Liquid Modernity. In *Religion Inside and Outside Traditional Institutions*. Edited by Heinz Streib. Leiden-Boston: Brill, pp. 175–91.

Dinges, William, Dean R. Hoge, Mary Johnson, and Juan L. Gonzales. 1998. A Faith Loosely Held: the institutional allegiance of Young Catholics. *Commonweal*, July 17.

Dussel, Enrique. 1980. Christian Art of the Oppressed in Latin America (Towards an Aesthetics of Liberation). In *Symbol and Art in Worship*. Edited by Noel Maldonado and David Power. New York: Seabury Press, pp. 40–52.

Ellis, Marc. 2015. After the Holocaust and Israel: On Liturgy and the Postcolonial (Jewish) Prophetic in the New Diaspora. In *Liturgy in Postcolonial Perspectives*. Edited by Cláudio Carvalhaes. New York: Palgrave Macmillan, pp. 45–67.

Foley, Edward. 2019. The Ooze of God's Spirit: Liquid Sacramentality for a Liquid Age. In *Reforming Practical Theology. The Politics of Body and Space*. Edited by Auli Vähäkangas, Sivert Angel and Kirstine Helboe Johansen. International Academy of Practical Theology Conference Series; vol. 1, pp. 153–59.

Francis, Pope. 2015. *Laudato Si'*. Available online: http://w2.vatican.va/content/francesco/en/encyclicals/documents/papa-francesco_20150524_enciclica-laudato-si.html (accessed on 2 April 2019).

García-Rivera, Alejandro. 1999. *The Community of the Beautiful: A Theological Aesthetics*. Collegeville: Liturgical Press.

Gleick, James. 1987. *Chaos: Making a New Science*. New York: Viking Penguin.

Greeley, Andrew. 1991. Sacraments keep Catholics high on the church. *National Catholic Reporter*, April 12.

Greeley, Andrew. 2001. *The Sacramental Imagination*. Berkeley and Los Angeles: University of California Press.

Grosfoguel, Ramón. 2006. La Descolonizacion de la Economia y los Estudios Postcoloniales: Transmodernidad, pensamiento fronterizo y colonialidad global. *Tabula Rasa* 48: 17–48. Available online: https://www.eurozine.com/transmodernity-border-thinking-and-global-coloniality/ (accessed on 2 April 2019). [CrossRef]

Himes, Michael J. 2014. Finding God in All Things: A Sacramental Worldview and Its Effects. In *Becoming Beholders: Cultivating Sacramental Imagination and Actions in College Classrooms*. Edited by Karen Eifler and Thomas Landy. Collegeville: Liturgical Press, pp. 3–17.

Huchingson, James. 2001. *Pandemonium Tremendum: Chaos and Mystery in the Life of God*. Cleveland: Pilgrim Press.

Huchingson, James. 2002. Chaos, Communications Theory and God's Abundance. *Zygon* 37: 395–414. [CrossRef]

Johnson, Sarah Kathleen. 2018. On our Knees: Christian Ritual in Residential Schools and the Truth and Reconciliation Commission of Canada. *Studies in Religion/Sciences Religieuses* 41: 3–24. [CrossRef]

Kearney, Richard. 2009. Sacramental Imagination: Eucharists of the Ordinary Universe. *Analecta Hermeneutica* 1: 240–88.

Kelly, Anthony J. 2010. "The Body of Christ: Amen!": The Expanding Incarnation. *Theological Studies* 71: 792–816. [CrossRef]

Koepp, David. 1992. Jurassic Park: Screenplay. Available online: http://www.dailyscript.com/scripts/jurassicpark_script_final_12_92.html (accessed on 2 April 2019).

Kumar, Arunachalam, and B. M. Hedge. 2012. Chaos Theory: Impact on and Applications in Medicine. *Nite University Journal of Health Sciences* 2: 93–99. Available online: https://pdfs.semanticscholar.org/950a/c54e3494fce8d775efc7ebf094e7f5f85b3d.pdf (accessed on 2 April 2019).

Li, Tien-Yien, and James A. York. 1975. Period Three Implies Chaos. *American Mathematical Monthly* 82: 985–92. [CrossRef]

Livi, Robert, Stefan Ruffo, and Dima Shepelyansky. 2003. Kolmogorov Pathways from Integrability to Chaos and Beyond. In *The Kolmogorov Legacy in Physics*. Edited by Angelo Vulpiani and Roberto Livi. Berlin, Heidelberg and New York: Springer, pp. 3–32.

Lorenz, Edward. 1963. Deterministic Nonperiodic Flow. *Journal of the Atmospheric Sciences* 20: 130–48. [CrossRef]

Lorenz, Edward. 1972. Predictability: does the flap of a butterfly's wings in Brazil set off a tornado in Texas? Presentation at the American Association for the Advancement of Sciences. Available online: http://static.gymportalen.dk/sites/lru.dk/files/lru/132_kap6_lorenz_artikel_the_butterfly_effect.pdf (accessed on 2 April 2019).

Maldonado-Torres, Nelson. 2011. Thinking through the Decolonial Turn: Post-continental Interventions in Theory, Philosophy, and Critique—An Introduction. *Transmodernity: Journal of Peripheral Cultural Production of the Luso-Hispanic World* 1. Available online: https://escholarship.org/uc/item/59w8j02x (accessed on 2 April 2019).

Martinot, Steve. 2008. The Coloniality of Power: Notes towards De-Colonization. Available online: http//www.ocf.berkeley.edu/~{}marto/coloniiality.htm (accessed on 2 April 2019).

Mignolo, Walter. 2011a. Epistemic Disobedience and the Decolonial Option. *Transmodernity* 1: 3–23.

Mignolo, Walter. 2011b. *The Darker Side of Western Modernity: Global Futures, Decolonial Options*. Durham: Duke University Press.

Mignolo, Walter. 2012. Delinking, Decoloniality & Dewesternization: Interview with Walter Mignolo (Part II). Available online: http://criticallegalthinking.com/2012/05/02/delinking-decoloniality-dewesternization-interview-with-walter-mignolo-part-ii/ (accessed on 2 April 2019).

Miller, Vincent. 2003. *Consuming Religion: Christian Faith and Practice in a Consumer Culture.* New York: Continuum.

Oestreicher, Christian. 2007. A History of Chaos Theory. *Dialogues in Clinical Neuroscience* 9: 279–79. Available online: https://www.ncbi.nlm.nih.gov/pmc/articles/PMC3202497/ (accessed on 11 November 2918). [PubMed]

Payne, Katy. 1998. *Silent Thunder.* New York: Simon & Schuster.

Poincaré, Jules Henri. 1890. Sur le problème des trois corps et les équations de la dynamique. *Divergence des séries de M. Lindstedt. Acta Mathematica* 13: 1–270.

Poincaré, Jules Henri. 2017. *The Three-Body Problem and the Equations of Dynamics: Poincaré's Foundational Work on Dynamical Systems Theory.* Translated by Bruce D. Popp. Cham: Springer International Publishing.

Quijano, Aníbal. 2007. Coloniality and Modernity/Rationality. *Cultural Studies* 21: 168–78. [CrossRef]

Rush, Ormond. 2009. *The Eyes of Faith: The Sense of the Faithful and the Church's Reception of Revelation.* Washington, D.C.: Catholic University of America Press.

Rush, Ormond. 2017. Inverting the Pyramid: The *Sensus Fidelium* in a Synodal Church. *Theological Studies* 78: 299–325. [CrossRef]

Sacrosanctum Concilium. 1996. *Vatican Council II: The Basic Sixteen Documents.* Edited by Austin Flannery. Northport: Costello Publishing. First published 1963.

Schillebeeckx, Edward. 1963. *Christ, the Sacrament of the Encounter with God.* New York: Sheed & Ward.

Schmemann, Alexander. 1965a. The World as Sacrament. In *The Cosmic Piety: Modern Man and the Meaning of the Universe.* Edited by Christopher Derrick. New York: P. J. Kennedy and Sons, pp. 119–30.

Schmemann, Alexander. 1965b. *Sacraments and Orthodoxy.* New York: Herder and Herder.

Schmemann, Alexander. 1979. The World as Sacrament. In *Church, World, Mission.* Edited by Alexander Schmemann. Crestwood: St. Vladimir's Seminary Press, pp. 217–27.

Strogatz, Steven H. 2001. *Nonlinear Dynamics and Chaos: With Applications to Physics, Biology, Chemistry and Engineering.* New York: Perseus Books.

Suna-Koro, Kristine. 2015. Puzzling over Postcolonial Liturgical Heteroglossia: In search of Liturgical Decoloniality and dialogic Orthodoxy. In *Liturgy in Postcolonial Perspectives.* Edited by Cláudio Carvalhaes. New York: Palgrave Macmillan, pp. 241–53.

Suna-Koro, Kristine. 2017. *Counterpoint: Diaspora, Postcoloniality, and Sacramental Theology.* Eugene: Pickwick.

Tracy, David. 1998. *The Analogical Imagination: Christian Theology and the Culture of Pluralism.* New York: Crossroad Publishing.

Vorgrimler, Herbert. 1992. *Sacramental Theology.* Translated by Linda Maloney. Collegeville: Liturgical Press.

Ward, Pete. 2002. *Liquid Church.* Peabody: Henrickson.

Yountae, An. 2017. *The Decolonial Abyss: Mysticism and Cosmopolitics from the Ruins.* New York: Fordham University Press.

Article

Pansacramentalism, Interreligious Theology, and Lived Religion

Hans Gustafson

College of Arts and Sciences, University of St. Thomas, 2115 Summit Avenue, Mail 57P, St. Paul, MN 55105, USA; hsgustafson@stthomas.edu

Received: 21 May 2019; Accepted: 26 June 2019; Published: 28 June 2019

Abstract: Opening with a philosophical definition of sacrament(ality) as a mediator (mediation) of the sacred in the concrete world, this article offers pansacramentalism as a promising worldview—especially for those rooted in or emerging from the Christian traditions (since, for them, the language of sacramentality may have a stronger resonance)—for bringing together interreligious theology and data mined by Lived Religion approaches to the study of religion. After articulating the concept of pansacramentalism and emphasizing interreligious theology as an emerging model for doing theology, growing trends and changing sensibilities among young people's religious and spiritual lives (e.g., the "Nones") is considered insofar as such trends remain relevant for making contemporary theology accessible to the next generation. The article then considers the intersection of pansacramentalism and interreligious theology, especially the issue of determining sacramental authenticity. To explain how this challenge might be met, Abraham Heschel's theology of theomorphism is offered as but one example as a nuanced means for determining sacramental authenticity of the sacred in the world. Turning to "Lived Religion" approaches, rationale is offered for why pansacramentalism and interreligious theology ought to be taken seriously in the contemporary world, especially considering recent data about the nature of contemporary religious identities among young people living in the West.

Keywords: pansacramentalism; sacramentality; interreligious; lived religion; interreligious studies

1. Introduction

Opening with a philosophical definition of sacrament(ality) as a mediator (mediation) of the sacred in the concrete world, this article offers pansacramentalism as a promising worldview—especially for those rooted in or emerging from the Christian traditions (since, for them, the language of sacramentality may have a stronger resonance)—for bringing together interreligious theology and data mined by Lived Religion approaches to the study of religion. Perry Schmidt-Leukel's vision of interreligious theology is utilized, given its contemporary relevance, the depth with which it has been presented (earning a multi-lecture platform on the prestigious Gifford Lectures) (Schmidt-Leukel 2015), its resonance with pansacramentalism, and for its potential appeal to the growing trends and changing sensibilities among younger people today in the Western world (i.e., the so-called "Nones" and religiously unaffiliated who make-up the fastest growing religious identity in the West).

After articulating the concept of pansacramentalism and emphasizing interreligious theology as an emerging model for doing theology, this article accounts for the growing trends and changing sensibilities among young people today (e.g., the "Nones"). No doubt, such an exercise remains fruitful for any contemporary theological proposal, especially those that strive to remain grounded in traditional language and concepts such as sacramentality. The religious and spiritual lives among the next generation are worth considering here, especially insofar as the implications of pansacramentalism extend to this rapidly emerging group in the Western world.

Turning to the intersection of pansacramentalism and interreligious theology, the issue of determining sacramental authenticity is raised. To explain how this challenge might be met, an example is provided by employing Abraham Heschel's theology of theomorphism as a nuanced means for determining sacramental authenticity of the sacred in the world. However, ultimately, it is argued, that such criteria ought to be generated by religious traditions, communities, and individuals themselves. The example of Heschel's theology might be one such approach for those who assent to his theological vision and categories. Though Heschel comes out of the Jewish tradition, such an approach (and indeed the pansacramentalism and interreligious theology, for that matter) certainly need not be considered an Abrahamic pursuit. In fact, it might be argued that these approaches are more naturally at home among non-Abrahamic traditions.

Finally, turning to "Lived Religion" approaches to the study of religion and religious identity, rationale is given for why pansacramentalism and interreligious theology ought to be taken seriously in the contemporary world. In other words, it is hardly surprising that a pansacramental worldview, which maintains all things as potentially sacramental, coupled with the doing of theology interreligiously, resonates with recent data about the nature of contemporary religious identities, especially among young people living in the West, as reported by scholars of Lived Religion.

2. Sacramental Functionality and Pansacramentalism

In order to properly address pansacramentalism and interreligious theology in the greater scope of this special issue on sacramental theology, this article commences with a preliminary word about the term "sacrament." To most ears (especially in the Western world, and especially to non-Catholics), the term sacrament often connotes Catholicism. Of course, the term is used well beyond Catholicism (in most Protestant traditions), and beyond Christianity at that. In fact, it even predates Christianity tracing its roots to two pre-Christian era terms: *sacramentum* (Latin) and *mysterion* (Greek).[1] At the turn of the third century, Tertullian applied *sacramentum* to Christian rituals in order to articulate their sacredness (e.g., Baptism). Later, it gained popularity to reference any sacred symbol or ceremony, prior to which it was mostly only used to consecrate legal and financial pledges made in the Roman temple or the swearing oaths in legal, religious, or military contexts (Martos 2001, p. 4; Gustafson 2016a, p. 54; 2019). In the New Testament, Paul employs *mysterion* to refer to Baptism and the Lord's Supper. However, in the greater Greek context, the term was regularly used to denote secret sacred rituals understood to symbolically reveal hidden knowledge. This is, of course, in reference to the Greek gnostic mystery cults, in which the rituals were interpreted to instantly reveal a mystery. As such, *mysteria* unveil ultimate reality. Drawing on both terms, *sacramentum* and *mysterion*, the dominant Christian understanding, which later emerged, made prominent an understanding of sacrament that refers to both the communal dimension of *sacramentum* (e.g., swearing of an oath between persons) and the individual dimension of *mysterion* (i.e., the instant unveiling of hidden knowledge of sacred significance) (Gustafson 2016a, p. 54; 2019).

A fundamental function of sacraments is that they serve as symbols (mediators) of ultimate (or religious) significance. Symbols mediate between things: between the particular and the universal (that is, they make the universal particular, but they also make the particular universal). Symbols, understood this way, bring into the present that which they symbolize. Sacraments are religious symbols or symbols of ultimacy. This is to say that sacraments symbolize, or bring into the present, the sacred (however one might construe it). Below is a three-fold understanding of sacraments as religious symbols of ultimate significance:

---

[1]   Joseph Martos writes: "There were sacraments in the Greek and Roman religious world of early Christianity. There were the formal sacraments of the official state religion: oaths and offerings, oracles and auguries, public festivals and family devotions. There were also the sacraments of the mystery religions: symbolic rituals that dramatized deeper religious meanings for those who sought them" (Martos 2001, p. 23; also quoted in Gustafson 2019).

1. Sacraments are not just signs. This is to say that sacraments, like signs, point beyond themselves to something sacred or ultimate, but they also point inward (unlike signs). More accurately, sacraments make present, via self-expression, that which they symbolize.

2. Sacraments concretize the sacred. Employing corporeal material worldly elements, sacraments make present (concretize) the sacred in the present world. Pansacramentalism, as discussed below, maintains the potential for all things to function as sacraments insofar as they facilitate the concretization (the making present) of the sacred in the contemporary world. As such, a sacrament makes something that is particular (material element) universally relevant by revealing a hidden depth. Put another way, sacraments universalize the significance of particular material elements by using them to reveal something of sacred ultimate significance.

3. Sacraments invite participation. They hold the potential to draw people into their depths by revealing something ultimate and transformative. For instance, art (e.g., music, film, literature) and nature provide some of the most obvious examples of sacramental experience, in which there exists the potential to move people to realize something about the world, themselves, and/or their relation to the sacred in an ultimate and transformative way. Such experiences, when unpacked, are often understood to have unveiled something hidden or mysterious (*mysterion*) to a particular person or community, and as such, prompt the making of an oath or pledge (*sacramentum*) to chart a new path in one's life accordingly.[2]

With this basic framework of sacramental functionality in mind, I turn to the concept of pansacramentalism, a concept I first encountered in the work of Martin Buber. He employs the term 'pansacramentalism' to illuminate various distinct features of Hasidic sacramentality (Buber 1966, p. 178). I am unaware of any earlier usage, although Christian theological echoes exist in Karl Rahner's influential sacramental vision and Christopher C. Knight's "pansacramental naturalism" (Knight 2001), not to mention conceptual analogs that most certainly exist in non-Abrahamic traditions (e.g., Hindu-Brahmanic visions of God-world relatedness). Pansacramentalism is suggested here due to the Christian—or perhaps Abrahamic—origins of this special issue, which focuses on sacramental theology. However, an argument might be made that there is nothing intrinsic to the term, and other terms might be better suited for the task (see note 28).

The context of panentheism (or Panentheistic Pansacramentality[3]) is relevant for pansacramentalism. It is a concept that has pushed philosophical theologians and philosophers of religion to wrestle with similar enduring questions and challenges, especially the question of how the sacred and world are related. The term panentheism came into popular German (*Allingottlehre*) usage in 1829 by Karl Krause and was first used in English by William Ralph Inge's in 1899 (Inge 1948, p. 121; cf. Brierley 2004), however, the concept it refers to is hardly novel with antecedents found from Plato, Plotinus, Ramanuja to the present day in several traditions. Panentheism literarily refers to the claim that all is in *theos* or the divine, yet the divine is not exhausted by all things. In simpler terms, although God is in the world and the world is in God, God remains more than, and thus transcends, the world as such. The *Oxford Dictionary of the Christian Church* defines it as "the belief that the Being of God includes and penetrates the whole universe so that every part of it exists in Him, but (as against pantheism) that His Being is

---

2 A popular example of this is in the Christian tradition is Henri Nouwen's reflection on seeing Rembrandt's "The Return of the Prodigal Son" for the first time. It moved Nouwen to question his vocation and place in life and, in Nouwen's words "set in motion a long spiritual adventure that brought me to a new understanding of my vocation and offered me new strength to live it" (Nouwen 1994, p. 3). "Natural wonders, and other people are examples of potential sacraments demanding others to participate with them. . . . Standing at the base of a mountain, sitting on the shore of the sea, listening to a powerful ballad, viewing a moving piece of art, or gazing into the depths of another's eyes are all potential sacramental moments that beckon the person inward to reflect on her place in the world. In this manner, sacraments provoke action, foster self-reflection, and invite self-transformation" (Gustafson 2019).

3 Variations of panentheistic pansacramentality, and what follows in this section, were first presented in (Gustafson 2013; 2016a, pp. 288–93), and (Gustafson 2019). Panentheism posits all things in the divine (*theos*), yet also usually declares the divine to be more than all things. As such, panentheists wrestle with the question of how the sacred dwells in all things, and how all things dwell in the sacred.

more than, and is not exhausted by, the universe" (Panentheism n.d.). Christian thinkers who endorse it, often praise its promise as an alternative to pantheism (all-is-God as such) and an acosmic classical theistic worldview that radically separates the divine and world.

Pansacramentalism might be understood as either a particular version of panentheism (since there are several) and/or an attempt to articulate panentheism's core claim that all things exist in God, yet God remains more than all things. To put it simply, pansacramentalism refers to a worldview that maintains all things (earthly, corporeal, spiritual, or otherwise) as holding the potential to function as mediators (symbols) of the sacred (e.g., the divine, God[s]), etc.). The value pansacramentalism holds over panentheism is its particular vision for how all things function as sacramental mediators of the divine in the world. Pansacramentalism, perhaps by avoiding some of the excess (and oft misunderstood) philosophical baggage that accompanies panentheism in its diverse usage, allows for an unapologetic (and hopefully appealing) valuing of particularities in the concrete world, which not only includes traditional religious rituals and practices, but also the less-often recognized mundane and everyday acts of spirituality and experiences of the sacred. Pansacramentalism articulates an understanding of the relations between the world, the sacred, and persons that rests on, what I refer to as, the "principle of panentheistic pansacramentality" (P^3, for shorthand). This principle maintains "all things *sacramentally* exist in the sacred, and the sacred *sacramentally* exists in all things" (Gustafson 2019). P^3 serves panentheism, I suppose, by providing a theological response to the question of how all things exist in the sacred by maintaining that they (all things) do so *sacramentally* (if the above framework for sacramental functionality is assumed). It is beyond the scope of this article to dwell too invasively on precisely how the pansacramental relationship between the sacred and the world (all things) ought to be understood in a panentheistic manner.[4] Rather, it is sufficient to posit the basic underlying assumption of pansacramentalism that all things serve as potential mediators of the divine in some manner.

3. The Emergence of Interreligious Theology

The proposal this chapter makes is that pansacramentalism provides a promising worldview for engaging interreligious theology. Interreligious theology, for the purposes of this article, presupposes, with Perry Schmidt-Leukel, a broad understanding of theology to include an intellectual reflection on both theistic and nontheistic traditions (Schmidt-Leukel 2017, p. 8), including discourse between, among, and within Abrahamic, Dharmic, and non-religious secular traditions. In fact, the bulk of Schmidt-Leukel's interreligious theology has been worked out in the context of the Buddhist and Christian traditions. Needless to say, interreligious theology is by no means an inter-Abrahamic enterprise, but extends well beyond it and perhaps is even more naturally at home within and between non-Abrahamic traditions.[5] The most precise working definition for interreligious theology comes from Schmidt-Leukel, a scholar doing some of the most serious and significant theoretical work in this area today. He defines interreligious theology as "the form that theology assumes when it takes religious truth claims seriously, those of one's own religious tradition and those of all others. Taking them seriously means to search for possible truth in all of the religious testimonies" (Schmidt-Leukel 2017, p. 13). Keith Ward, with his monumental five-volume series,[6] and Wilfred Cantwell Smith, might be considered forerunners to the interreligious theology espoused by Schmidt-Leukel and Ephraim Meir; all worth recognition here.

---

4   For a more exhaustive dissection of this pansacramental vision embedded in a panentheistic context, see metaphors of (a) the world as God's body in (Ward 2004); and (b) the relationship between art and artist (house and builder), and the relationship between child and parent (baby and mother) in (Gustafson 2019).

5   E.g., Certain theories of tantra/tantric traditions within Hinduism and Buddhism, which date back to the 5th century C.E., might be interpreted to articulate a spirit of interreligious theology and perhaps even pansacramentality. The word tantra is derived from Sanskrit and means to "weave" as in the interweaving of various traditions together.

6   (Ward 1994, 1996, 1998, 2000, 2008).

Wilfred Cantwell Smith's well-known "world theology", presented in his *Towards a World Theology* (Smith [1981] 1989), takes seriously the project of doing theology interreligiously (or transreligiously[7]) insofar as he urges the global community to recognize the time has come to recognize our shared religious story embedded in, what he refers to as, "faith" (a universal shared among all traditions but expressed through differing and particular "beliefs."[8] Smith's world theology points to the abandonment of particular religious theological designators such as "Christian" theology or "Islamic" theology. Rather, world theology serves as a model of theological inquiry that draws on all religious traditions in order to elucidate the universal character of "faith", despite the particular manifestations of the beliefs emanating out of the religious, worldview, and lifeway traditions of the globe, past and present. A "world" theology such as this, it seems, envisions a collaborative system of diverse beliefs that is "continually developed by people from around the world, and of all religious identifications, who remain consciously aware of the one history of universal faith that undergirds all separate religions (with their distinct particular beliefs)" (Gustafson 2016b, p. 249). If theological accounts are to be taken seriously at all, they must, at the very least, account for each other, Smith argues. Theology ought to remain in the continual state of revision in light of contemporary discovery. Notable instances include the emergence of Greek philosophy (e.g., Thomas Aquinas' Christian theology in light of and dialogue with Aristotelian metaphysical philosophy, categories, and language) the discovery of the modern scientific method. Just as these major worldly influences pushed theologians to sharpen and revise their thought (for the better), Smith argues "the time has come for the reality of religious plurality to encourage a similar constructive rethinking as well" (Gustafson 2016b, p. 249),[9] without which theology will die (or just be ignored).

Keith Ward envisions that,

> The great religious traditions are histories of developing reflection on the primal disclosures that constitute a tradition. In their meeting, the opportunity exists for conversations in which each tradition is modified by its greater empathy for the insights embodied in other traditions. It is in this way that diversity, and the freedom it requires, can be helpful to the discovery of the partiality in one's own views, and thus of a more expansive truth (Ward 2007, p. 198).[10]

This vision does not perhaps go as far as Smith's "world theology", which proposes a truly interreligious theology insofar as it seemingly reserves more space for the particularity, uniqueness, and separation of one's own religious tradition. Ward, a committed Christian, demonstrates a rigorous investigation of theological issues important to Christianity and the understanding of Jesus for Christians by entering into conversation with the religious traditions of the world. Unlike Smith's "world theology", Ward's is one of Christian theology, especially since he begins with categories important to the Christian tradition (e.g., revelation, creation, community). Ward's disposition towards the overarching nature and benefit of this approach is instructive here for our consideration of pansacramentality and interreligious theology. He professes that "once an understanding of faith as acceptance of exclusively correct propositions is given up, one can no longer simply say that the Christian faith has the only truth and that all others are wrong. If faith is a response to a disclosure of the divine in this community, then why should there not be different disclosures of the divine in other communities?" (Ward 2002, p. 51)[11] Such an attitude represents an approach towards doing theology interreligiously and to finding the sacred in all things including other religions.

---

7   See (Martin 2016); contributions from Wesley J. Wildman, John L. Thatamanil, Peter Feldmeier, J.R. Hustwit, Rory McEntee, Jon Paul Sydnor, Jeanine Diller, Hans Gustafson, Christopher Denny, Jonathan Weidenbaum, and Anthony J. Watson.
8   I am indebted to Jim Fredericks' examination of Wilfred Cantwell Smith's theology in Fredericks, 1999, pp. 79–89; also referenced in (Gustafson 2016b, pp. 248–49).
9   Citing (Smith 2001, pp. 47–48).
10 Also quoted in (Gustafson 2016b, p. 249) and (Gustafson 2016a, p. 176).
11 Also quoted in (Gustafson 2016b, p. 249).

Ephraim Meir and Perry Schmidt-Leukel represent perhaps the two most rigorous contemporary thinkers working to articulate a theory of interreligious theology. Meir defines interreligious theology as "the reflection on the conditions for a dialogue in which partners learn from each other and appreciate or criticize each other. Not only mutual enrichment, but also mutual change could be the result of the interreligious encounter" (Meir 2015, p. 178). An aspect of Meir's vision of particular interest to this article is his emphasis on the lived religious experience. His vision of interreligious theology "does less work with official representatives of religious institutions—which is frequently boring and without depth—than with learning in bookless moments from and with people who live and think differently" (Meir 2015, pp. 178–79). It "deals with religious diversity and is part of the reflection upon communities in which multiculturality is lived. ... It takes lived religiosity in a particular context as a basis" (Meir 2015, p. 179). As such, Meir's interreligious theology seeks out and grounds reflection in the messy complicated entanglements of religious and cultural identities that take place within, between, and among religious individuals and communities. He writes, "this new kind of theology does not work 'from above' with identities fixed once and for all, but 'from below' with an analysis of concrete situations in which there are all kinds of belonging" (e.g., dual-belonging, multiple religious belonging, religious hybridity, bricolage, assemblage, syncretism, etc.) (Meir 2015, p. 179).

"Interreligious Theology", then, as understood by Schmidt-Leukel and endorsed in this article, can be briefly summarized with four "principles" or "starting points" (Schmidt-Leukel 2017, p. 130). First, interreligious theology is only possible when it operates on the assumption that theological truth can be found beyond one's own tradition.[12] Second, the process of seeking theologically relevant truth must be "guided by the conviction that ultimately, all truth—wherever and in whatever form it might be found—must be compatible."[13] This eliminates exclusivist approaches from being interreligious theology because there is no real openness to the possibility of discovering truth or insights from other traditions. Third, interreligious theology must be done interreligiously; that is, an interreligious theologian seeks out encounter, engagement, and discourse with individuals and communities living out other religious traditions, worldviews, and lifeways.[14] Fourth and finally, interreligious theology is "an open process;" that is, it is never finished, always in process, and "it will, therefore, be impossible for any single person to produce something like a completed interreligious theology" (Schmidt-Leukel 2017, p. 128).[15]

In addition to these four starting points (principles), Schmidt-Leukel argues that interreligious theology ought to methodologically proceed as *perspectival*, *imaginative*, *comparative*, and *constructive*. The interreligious theologian's *perspective* is one of integration. She remains confessional in the sense of being committed, attached, rooted, somewhere, but remains open to and prepared to revise, change, and transform her perspective when called to do so. However, "the real challenge for an interreligious theology arises not from the question of how many other perspectives one may be able to understand, but from the peculiar nature of religious perspectives, that is, from the insight into the close interweaving of religious beliefs with confessional stances" (Schmidt-Leukel 2017, p. 141). Interreligious theology needs to be *imaginative* because in order to empathize with other views, to understand them, to walk a mile in another's shoes, or, as Wilfred Cantwell Smith was fond of saying, that in order to "understand Buddhists, we must not look at something called Buddhism but at the world so far as possible through Buddhist eyes" (Smith [1981] 1989, p. 82)[16] we must be able to imagine the other's view in order to understand the "reasons that motivate the other in his or her belief. It means to put oneself imaginatively into the other's shoes" (Schmidt-Leukel 2017, p. 142). Interreligious

---

[12] I.e., Schmidt-Leukel refers to this principle as "a theological credit of trust" (Schmidt-Leukel 2017, pp. 130–33).

[13] I.e., Schmidt-Leukel refers to this principle as "the unity of reality" (Schmidt-Leukel 2017, pp. 133–36).

[14] I.e., Schmidt-Leukel refers to this principle as "tied to interreligious discourse" (Schmidt-Leukel 2017, pp. 136–38).

[15] Schmidt-Leukel refers to this principle as the "processual, essential incomplete nature" of interreligious theology (Schmidt-Leukel 2017, pp. 138–39).

[16] Also quoted in (Schmidt-Leukel 2017, p. 143).

theology ought to take place *comparatively*; that is, the spirit of comparative theology (i.e., learning about one's own tradition in, and perhaps transformed by, engagement with and learning about other traditions)[17] ought to be utilized insofar as the interreligious theologian embraces the likelihood that her self-understanding and understanding of her own religious tradition "may change if it is seen in light of the religious other" (Schmidt-Leukel 2017, p. 143). Finally, interreligious theology proceeds via a *constructive* methodology in that it must come to terms with (i.e., get over the fear of) syncretism,[18] and therefore embrace the possibility (and probability) that "such revisions may often take the form of reinterpretation or reconstruction" (Schmidt-Leukel 2017, p. 144). With pansacramentalism and the contemporary method of interreligious theology proposed above, I now turn to the significant trend of the religiously unaffiliated in the West, especially insofar as they make up a growing segment of young people. Their presence remains relevant, and increasingly so, for looking to multiple traditions for theological insights and religious wisdom.

4. Young American Nones and Somes

Turning to recent trends in religious identities, especially in the West, the sociological data shows growth in multiple and dual religious identities, hybridity, and religious bricolage (especially among younger generations). A group of particular significance is the emergence of the religiously unaffiliated (or the so-called "nones"), which today make up approximately one-third of all young adults (born between 1981 and 1996) in the United States. Accounting for the growing trends and changing sensibilities among younger people today is fruitful for any contemporary theological proposal, especially those that strive to ground their projects in traditional language and concepts (e.g., sacramentality). Therefore, it is worth considering what the implications of pansacramentalism are for the fastest growing religious identity in the West.

Elizabeth Drescher's recent study (Drescher 2016) on the spiritual lives of this group in the United States reveals that they reside equally throughout all regions of the country (with slightly fewer in the southeast) and are relatively equally represented among men and women. Drescher's data construct the stereotypical profile of an American None as someone "who is younger, urban, white, a bit more likely to be male than female, slightly more than most Americans to have had at least some college education, but no more likely to have completed college or graduate school" (Drescher 2016, p. 20). The most significant stereotype (worth considering) is that Nones are usually under 35 years of age.

However, even though America has followed many Western European nations in continuing its trajectory of becoming more secular and less religious, since the 1960s, it is not the case that the American non-religious have become more anti-religious and anti-spiritual, and it is certainly not the case that this significant young group of religiously unaffiliated are monolithic. Rather, they represent a diverse group of people with tendencies towards religion and spirituality also found in young Americans who do identify with a particular religious tradition. The recent work of sociologist Richard Flory is helpful here (Flory 2017). He stresses the internal diversity of this group, which is often overlooked (as it is with most religious groups). Some have parsed the religiously unaffiliated into atheists, agnostics, "no religious preference", "nothing", "spiritual but not religious", and others. However, Flory argues these subcategories remain too simplified. More importantly, and for this article,

---

[17] The "the term 'Comparative Theology' has been used in various ways, or applied to different types of engagement with religious plurality" by different thinkers in different contexts since 1700 (Cornille 2019, p. 9). Proper assessments of comparative theology include the recently published important works by Hedges (2017a) and Cornille (2019). As it particularly relates to this article on interreligious theology, and Schmidt-Leukel's interreligious theology vis-à-vis comparative theology and theology of religions, a clear discussion is offered by Hedges (2017a, pp. 5–23). For a poignant discussion on "the difference between comparative and interreligious theology", see (Leirvik 2018).

[18] Schmidt-Leukel writes, "I do not see any problems with syncretism as such. All great religions are, after all, the produce of syncretistic processes ... Currently one of the biggest obstacles to the idea of conscious interreligious borrowing seems to be the widespread fear of syncretism. Yet this fear ignores the syncretistic of all major religious traditions: They originated from and further developed under the influence of various other religions" (Schmidt-Leukel 2017, pp. 138, 144–45; 2009, pp. 67–89).

such categories do not always do justice to the Nones' complex relationships to the divine (God, Gods, or the transcendent) and religious institutions. Indeed, do not all people, regardless of their religious identity, have rather complex relations to God(s) and religious institutions? Thus, the same might be said for many young Americans who do identify with religion. Yes, for some Nones "religion has no place in their lives; others may be marginally interested in religion but rarely if ever attend services" (Flory 2017). However, the group overall still claims that religion does indeed have relevance in their lives, with many who attend religious services, pray and mediate, and believe in God(s).[19] Perhaps this is one driver behind the rise in the category of "Spiritual But Not Religions" (SBNR), which allows one to leave room for religiosity in their lives yet provides some distance from institutional affiliation.

Unlike their Western European counterparts, the young religiously unaffiliated in America are still on the whole religious, if "being religious" here refers to a belief in God, attending religious services, and praying. In fact, by these standards, American "nones" are more religious than Western European Christians (see Figure 1) (Pew Research Center 2018). In other words, SBNRs and the religiously unaffiliated in the United States are often misunderstood.[20] Interestingly, Drescher situates the Nones (which includes SBNRs) in relation to "Somes", the religiously affiliated. This is relevant for this article because she discovered that the "spiritualities of Nones are hardly distinct or isolated from the spiritualities of Somes with whom they share much of their everyday lives" (Drescher 2016, p. 8). For instance, those who share similar demographic characteristics as Nones, but are Somes (that is, those who do religiously identify), are becoming more likely to identify, practice, participate or belong to more than one tradition. In other words, it is becoming slightly more common in the West, especially among young people, to have multiple religious belongings, practices, and/or identities (e.g., dual belonging, religious hybridity, bricolage, etc.). This comports with my experience in the classroom as students seem to be more comfortable with confronting the complexity of their identity, especially their religious identity as being multiple and attracted to multiple traditions, or, at the very least, attracted to practices from various traditions.[21]

This brief detour into the sociological trends of young American Nones and Somes shows the horizon towards which young people seem to be moving when it comes to interfacing with the growing religious diversity of their world and the manifold ways to religiously identify that stem from it. Perhaps, and needless to say, Schmidt-Leukel's prediction that "it seems rather likely that future theology to a large extent [will] take the form of 'interreligious theology'" (Schmidt-Leukel 2017, p. 129) and the emphasis in this article on the category of pansacramentalism, may turn out to be rather appealing for young people who have, at the very least, some interest in the categories of theology and sacramentality (both of which have some Christian, or at least Abrahamic, roots).

---

[19] Note: there are, of course, those who continue to pray, meditate, and attend religious services not due to belief in these activities "as having any particular religious or spiritual content" (Flory 2017), rather they might understand these things to be healthy habits that lead to a more fulfilling life akin to attending a community gathering, being social, exercising, or eating a healthy diet.

[20] Drescher argues that Nones are often misunderstood, sometimes labeled "superficial, uncommitted, narcissistic" (Drescher 2016, p. 48; see also p. 5).

[21] This latter phenomenon, engaging in varying religious practices from several religions at different times to meet a variety of needs, is what Paul Hedges refers to as "Strategic Religious Participation in a Shared Religious Landscape." Less scandalous in Chinese and Asian contexts, it provides more space for participants to make suitable choices that are meaningful for them within their regional religious landscape (or "religious ecology"). It is understood by its residents as a "Shared Religious Landscape" in which traditions are "not composed of hermetically sealed borders of mutually exclusive religious belief-based territories" (Hedges 2017b, pp. 63, 51).

Compared with U.S. adults, relatively few Western European Christians and religiously unaffiliated people are religiously observant

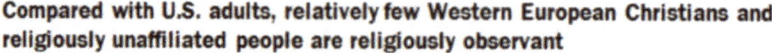

Compared with U.S. adults, relatively few Western European Christians and religiously unaffiliated people are religiously observant

% who ...

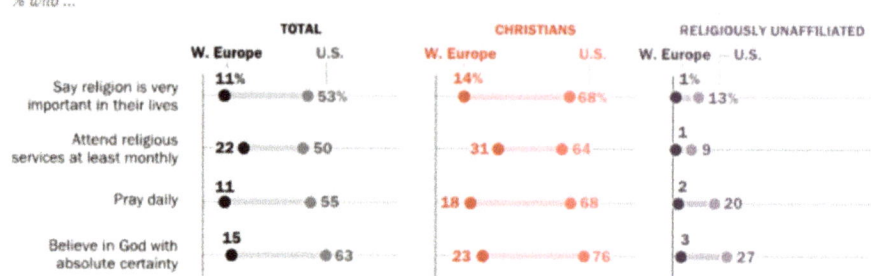

	TOTAL		CHRISTIANS		RELIGIOUSLY UNAFFILIATED	
	W. Europe	U.S.	W. Europe	U.S.	W. Europe	U.S.
Say religion is very important in their lives	11%	53%	14%	68%	1%	13%
Attend religious services at least monthly	22	50	31	64	1 / 9	
Pray daily	11	55	18	68	2	20
Believe in God with absolute certainty	15	63	23	76	3	27

Source: Survey conducted April–August 2017 in 15 countries. See Methodology for details. U.S. data from 2014 Religious Landscape Study "Being Christian in Western Europe"

PEW RESEARCH CENTER

Figure 1. Religious observance among Christians and the Unaffiliated in Western Europe and the U.S. (Sahgal 2018).

5. Pansacramentalism and Interreligious Theology

The contemporary method of interreligious theology and its predecessors described above, and the brief insight into trends among young Nones and Somes, is sufficient for the purposes of this article in making the case for why pansacramentalism, in particular for those who identify with, in some manner, a Christian tradition, serves as a promising starting point for embracing interreligious theology. This section turns to the question of determining sacramental authenticity for interreligious truth-seeking, and to the rationale for incorporating a Lived Religion approach to the encounter with, and study of, the religious other (i.e., for the doing of interreligious theology).

If all things are potentially sacramental, as pansacramentalism espouses, then how ought one to determine whether something is sacramental? Are there limits to pansacramentality? Can suffering be sacramental? If so, can all suffering be sacramental? Was Auschwitz sacramental? The claim of pansacramentalism is not that all things are actually sacramental, but rather all things are potential mediators of the divine in some manner; perhaps something might be interpreted as sacramental in a manner that reveals the terrifying limitations or God (e.g., Auschwitz perhaps exposes the limitations of God to intervene in horrendous human events carried out in the world).[22] How ought one to construct a criterion or set of criteria upon which something might be determined sacramental? No hard-and-fast answer is offered here, but rather religious traditions ought to look inward to their resources, wisdom, and communities, for meaningful criteria. Thus, no unified agreement will be reached on sacramental authenticity. To provide a sense of what this might mean, I offer an example by drawing on Abraham

---

[22] E.g., one might extract God's limitations (including suffering and pathos) from the powerful witness account Elie Wiesel narrates in his well-known book *Night* about being imprisoned at Auschwitz: "The SS hanged two Jewish men and a youth in front of the whole camp. The men died quickly, but the death throes of the youth lasted for half an hour. 'Where is God? Where is he?' someone asked behind me. As the youth still hung in torment in the noose after a long time, I heard the man call again, 'Where is God now?' And I heard a voice in myself answer: 'Where is he? He is here. He is hanging there on the gallows'" (Wiesel 1969, p. 75; also quoted in Moltmann 1993, p. 274; also quoted in Gustafson 2016a, p. 284).

Joshua Heschel's theology of divine pathos, theomorphism, and anthropomorphism. Keep in mind, this is but one example of how sacramental authenticity might be gauged. Ultimately such criteria will have to come from within religious traditions, communities, and individuals themselves. Heschel comes out of the Jewish tradition, but the criteria certainly need not come from only Abrahamic traditions. For instance, some might draw on Hinduism's Advaita Vedanta, Buddhism's doctrine of anattā (no-self), Shinto affirmations, Christian virtues, and so on. The idea here is that a criterion or some set of criteria will be useful for determining the sacredness of a thing if all things are deemed potentially sacred. Moreover, when we consider interreligious theology and the increasing comfort of young people to blend multiple traditions, the range from which a community or individual might certainly expand (e.g., hence a Christian might be inspirited by Heschel's Jewish theology of theomorphism, or Jew might be inspired by the Buddhist doctrine of no-self).

In *The Prophets*, Heschel offers the biblical vision of a God full of pathos. God "does not simply command and expect obedience; He is also moved and affected by what happens in the world, and reacts accordingly" (Heschel 2001, p. 288). Heschel's Biblical God, as full of pathos, is susceptible to being moved and affected by emotion. John Merkle points out that, "While Heschel's philosophical argument for the pathos of God challenges the tradition of classical metaphysical theology … it is not meant to challenge traditional Jewish understanding" (Merkle 2009, p. 4). By promoting a biblical concept of a God moved by and affected by emotion and suffering, unsurprisingly Heschel has sometimes been accused of anthropomorphizing God due to his alleged casting of human qualities (suffering, emotion, passibility) onto God. Heschel turns this charge on its head by raising the category of theomorphism, which is the casting of Godly qualities onto humans.

In Heschel's view, the prophets of ancient Israel, in proclaiming a God full of pathos, do not anthropomorphize God; rather, they theomorphize humans.[23] The prophets did not cast imperfect humanly qualities onto a perfect God, but cast perfect Godly qualities onto imperfect humans. For Heschel, virtues such as love, compassion, empathy, and pathos are not first and foremost human qualities, they are first and foremost Godly qualities. Hence, when the prophets speak of God as absolutely selfless and loving,

> absolute selflessness and mysteriously undeserved love are more akin to the divine than to the human. And if these are characteristics of human nature, then man is endowed with attributes of the divine. God's unconditional concern for justice is not an anthropomorphism. Rather, man's concern for justice is a theomorphism … The language of the prophets employed to describe that supreme concern was an anthropomorphism to end all anthropomorphism (Heschel 2001, p. 349).[24]

Heschel defends against the charge of anthropomorphizing God by pointing to the prophets' use of metaphorical theomorphic language. He writes, "to speak about God as if He were a person does not necessarily mean to personify Him, to stamp Him in the image of a person … The idea of the divine pathos is not a personification of God but an exemplification of divine reality … It does not represent a substance, but an act or a relationship" (Heschel 2001, pp. 350–51). Heschel's biblical vision of God allows for a mutual interrelation between God and persons. It yields a concept of the sacred (in this case "God") that is dynamic and in relation to people[25] (i.e., God is capable of change, but God's nature remains immutable). Heschel states: "The divine pathos which the prophets tried to express in many ways was not a name for His essence but rather for the modes of His reaction to Israel's conduct which would change if Israel modified its ways" (Heschel 1951, p. 245).

---

[23] The paragraphs that follow on Heschel's theology of theomorphism are adapted from (Gustafson 2016a, pp. 274, 281–82, 296–97).

[24] Also quoted in (Merkle 1985, p. 99).

[25] Though Heschel preserves God's immutable nature by positing that just because God is capable of change (in relations to the world and to people) does not entail that God's nature changes. God's nature remains immutable.

Theomorphism exposes the connection between the sacred as such and the sacred found within the individual person. Given pansacramentalism's vision to find the sacred in all things in a sacramental fashion, the challenge surfaces as to how to determine whether a "thing" is sacramental. Christians might (and perhaps Jews for that matter given Heschel's rigorous Jewish vision of God), as I have argued, employ Heschel's theology of theomorphism as a foundation for the "sacramental robustness" of a particular thing (person, action, experience, etc.). Sacraments communicate the sacred by virtue of the sacred being present within them, and Heschel's theology provides a foundation for thinking about how the sacred is present. Does a thing reflect the sacred, theomorphically or otherwise, in a manner consistent with one's religious tradition (however that might be perceived)? Heschel's theomorphism, and his defense against the charge of anthropomorphism serves as a model for interpreting theomorphic qualities found not just in persons, but in the world. Heschel writes,

> The idea of the divine pathos combining absolute selflessness with supreme concern for the poor and the exploited can hardly be regarded as the attribution of human characteristics. Where is the man who is endowed with such characteristics? Nowhere in the Bible is man characterized as merciful, gracious, slow to anger, abundant in love and truth, keeping love to the thousandth generation ... if these are characteristics of human nature, then man is endowed with attributes of the divine. (Heschel 2001, pp. 348–49)

Utilizing theomorphism to determine the "sacramental robustness" of a thing has the advantage of taking the relation between *external* sanctity and *intrasubjective* sanctity seriously. Inspired by Perry Schmidt-Leukel's fractal interpretation of religious diversity, I argue that one's *intrasubjective* sanctity (the sacredness within an individual person) mirrors the sacred itself and the sanctity of the cosmos (Gustafson 2019). Consider a person that works to promote justice, alleviate suffering in the world, and is simply the "sort of person who epitomizes what it means to be a saint" (Campbell and Putnam 2012, p. 620). In so doing, she exhibits theomorphic qualities, or God-formed qualities, in the world. Pansacramentalism posits that she makes the sacred present in the world. Political scientists David E. Campbell and Robert D. Putnam famously refer to this type of person as our "Aunt Susan." They claim that "We all have an Aunt Susan in our lives, the sort of person who epitomizes what it means to be a saint" (Campbell and Putnam 2012, p. 620). They develop their well-known "Aunt Susan Principle on this scenario, and in their formula, Susan's "religious background is different from our own", although for the present argument it need not be. Maybe Susan shares your religious tradition, or perhaps "Aunt Susan is not religious at all. But whatever her religious background (or lack thereof), you know that Aunt Susan is destined for heaven" (Campbell and Putnam 2012, p. 620). The more theomorphic Susan's actions and qualities, I suppose, then the more God-like, and thus the more sacramental, she is. In such a view, Aunt Susan, one might argue, is very theomorphic, or sacramental, in that she exhibits a combination of "absolute selflessness with supreme concern for the poor and the exploited" (Heschel 2001, pp. 348–49). In other words, a useful criterion for determining the sacramental robustness of a thing (in this case, a person's life or actions) is a theomorphic principle that states wherever qualities of the sacred (God-like traits) manifest in the world (e.g., person, action, etc.), the more sacramental that thing is.

An implication of this view is that there can be degrees of sacramentality. Therefore, a "next step" is to determine—rather, it is for religious traditions, communities, and individuals to determine—what qualifies as qualities of the sacred. Perhaps this is where the religions themselves, and their practitioners, offer wisdom. Jews might look to the Hebrew Bible (as Heschel has done), Christians to Jesus, and Muslims to the Qur'an, to determine what qualifies as qualities of the sacred (e.g., compassion, justice, virtue, mercy, love, honesty, courage, wisdom, discernment, etc.). However, given the emergence of interreligious theology, the data for determining the sacramental robustness of a thing can be expanded beyond one's own religious tradition. It is in this respect that the value of Lived Religion surfaces, not only as a frequently employed approach to the academic study of religion and theology but also as a fruitful method for the everyday religious and interreligious experience. For Christians in particular, the category of "sacramentality" might serve as a welcoming gateway to consider seeking truth, authenticity, and wisdom in traditions other than their own. If Christians can accept that all things hold the potential to manifest the sacred in some fashion, this unlocks non-Christian traditions as potential avenues for religious truth and experience not previously considered. As such, identifying non-Christian "things" as having some sacramental robustness provides the opportunity—or perhaps mandates—that they be considered in the doing of theology. Hence, such a pansacramental Christian theology then becomes an interreligious theology.[26]

6. Lived Religion's Contribution to Pansacramental Interreligious Theology

It is hardly surprising that a pansacramental worldview, which maintains that all things hold the potential to manifest the sacred in some manner, coupled with the doing of theology interreligiously,[27] resonates with recent data about the nature of contemporary religious identities and is enhanced by the recent trend in the study of religion to emphasize "Lived Religion" (LR) approaches.

LR is about "what people actually believe and do" and is, therefore, "real, particular, and often messy—a far cry from safe or neat accounts contained in textbooks" (Gregg and Scholefield 2015, p. 7) on world religions. This approach, which privileges religion-as-lived over religion-as-preached, investigates religion at the "on the ground" (e.g., in the trenches, on the streets, in homes, offices, and places in between). Such an approach proceeds by examining the various ways communities and individuals demonstrably manifest their religious, spiritual, and secular worldviews and lifeways in their concrete daily lives including the mundane and ordinary. As Meredith McGuire asserts, this approach claims that "individual religious commitment is evidenced less by avowed commitment to and participation in the activities of religious organizations than by the way each person expresses and experiences his or her faith and practice in ordinary places and in everyday moments" (McGuire 2008, p. 213). Furthermore, it rests on the premise that to more fully understand "modern religious lives, we need to try to grasp the complexity, diversity, and fluidity of real individuals' religion-as-practiced, in the context of their everyday lives" (McGuire 2008, p. 213).

In short, LR is the study of religion in the everyday (including family, workplace, and social entanglement), but of course, it includes the examination of religious communities (synagogue, church, mosque, etc.) (Stringer 2015, p. 4). Scholars on the leading edge and formation of LR emphasize the hyper-locality and particularity of "religioning" (the doing of religion). Robert Orsi grounds LR on the principle that religion "cannot be neatly separated from the other practices of everyday life, from the ways that human beings work on the landscape, for example, or dispose of corpses, or arrange for the security of their offspring" (Orsi 1997, pp. 6–7). In a similar fashion, Nancy Ammerman adds that "finding religion in everyday life means looking wherever and however we find people invoking a sacred presence" (Ammerman 2014, pp. 190–91). To be sure, as McGuire sagely counsels, although "studies of religious organizations and movements are still relevant, they cannot capture the quality of people's everyday religious lives. As messy as these lives may be in practice, individuals' lived religions are what really matters to them" (McGuire 2008, p. 213).

---

[26] I have suggested the merit for the consideration of adjusting the universal claims of pansacramentalism to employ non-Christian-centric language to something more neutral, if possible; especially given how imbued the language of sacramentality is with Christianity (and especially Catholicism). Thus, I have suggested the consideration of other terms such as Eliade's "hierophany", "theophany", or perhaps it is best to simply use "sacred." "In this case, pansacramentality might be better labeled as pan-hierophanism or pan-theophanism. In fact, such language is more in keeping with the spirit of practicality, for Eliade used these terms to express his recognition of 'wide-ranging structural similarities across all religions' (Schmidt-Leukel 2017, p. 227). Eliade states, as quoted by Schmidt-Leukel, 'we are faced with a manifestation, vastly different obviously, of the sacred in a fragment of the universe' (Eliade [1939] 1996, p. 463; also quoted in Schmidt-Leukel 2017, p. 227; also quoted in Gustafson 2019).

[27] Oddbjørn Leirvik observes, "to be relevant, university theology must relate critically and constructively to the lived diversity of beliefs and practices among European Muslims, and their multifaith surroundings. At first glance, the cues of 'university theology' and 'lived religion' might seem to point in different directions—academic and theoretical versus popular and practical. But just as academic theology may relate dynamically to lived religion, lived religion may have theological implications and even ambitions to influence the way in which theology is done in the academy. This interactive understanding of theology also applies to interreligious ways of doing theology" (Leirvik 2018).

As noted above, it certainly takes no stretch of the imagination to envision why the spirit of pansacramentalism might easily find common ground with an LR approach. They both emphasize the idea that all places and spaces humans occupy, all experiences humans report, and all practices humans engage not only become fertile ground for genuine sacramental experience, but also serve as the primary object of study for the LR approach in its quest to investigate how people concretely live out their religious identities in the complicated and messiness of the here and now. So, LR serves pansacramentalism by taking seriously the everydayness of lived religious experience and thusly provides potential "data" for sacramental experience. Likewise, interreligious theology, a theological sub-discipline that takes seriously the value of claims from multiple traditions, finds a valuable ally in LR and an avenue through which to receive claims of religious experience worthy of theological digestion.

(Pan)sacramentality correlates with the quest for sacred in the particular and LR is almost hyper-focused on the particular manifestations of religion as carried out by individual people and communities. LR helps to remind the pansacramental theologian to seek beyond neatly sealed or traditional religious boundaries for sacramental experience. It calls forth the sacramental potential of all things. Again, McGuire is instructive by pointing out that "when we no longer assume that individuals' religions can be equated with their religious affiliation or encompassed by their membership in a religious organization, then we realize that we must ask different questions" (McGuire 2008, p. 213). For the theologian interested in pansacramentalism and particularity, these different questions include the potential sacred (sacramental) nature of all things, regardless of how mundane, ordinary, or boring they may appear.

Such emphasis on the everyday particularity and the lived religion of individuals help illuminate and sharpen the complexity of the growing trend, especially among younger people, to report complicated, mixed, multiple, dual, and hybrid religious identities. As noted above, there are several reasons that contribute to this trend, however, the role that LR and interreligious pansacramental theology might play is to take these religious identities seriously and ask what they might mean not only for understanding and the study of the category of "religion", but also for understanding how individual religious lives (especially experience) relate to traditions as historically preached and preserved. Might pansacramentalism, interreligious theology, and LR serve some liberative function not only to descandalize such complicated religious identities, but also to recognize how religious identities, especially in the construction of theological worldviews and ways of life, intersect with so-called non-religious influences on identity such as language, culture, age, class, gender, race, and so on. Above all, an overarching aim here is not only to achieve a more accurate and nuanced view of how people religiously (or non-religiously) identify, but to ever-strive for greater clarity of truth-seeking and knowledge generation in the academic fields of the study of religion, interreligious studies, and theological studies.

Of course, there are limits and challenges to the LR method, which remain present to pansacramental interreligious theology as well. There is the concern of over-normalizing the particular lived reality of religious experience to the determent of historical traditions and to the point of the latter withering away. How does religion-as-preached and religion as historically and institutionally founded retain a place of some authority in the study of LR? Another legitimate concern, as mentioned above, consists in determining genuine and authentic sacramental experience so as not to suggest that simply all things are of sacred significance (and perhaps understood as normatively "good").[28] Certainly, there ought to be room to call out harmful and oppressive experiences and actions as just that without deeming them sacred and therefore "good." The example from Heschel was but one attempt to draw on a particular tradition to determine a criterion upon which a tradition or an individual

---

[28] Make no mistake. The claim here is not that somehow, for example, Auschwitz was a divine good and ought to have happened. Of course not.

might employ in order to deem something as sacramental. Of course, others may look to their own tradition(s), histories, and experiences to generate such criteria for sacramental authenticity, or perhaps they will draw on several in the spirit of interreligious theology. Ultimately, perfect and unified criteria will not be agreed upon. However, that hardly seems problematic. Might we find some comfort in simply resting in the uncertainty that characterizes all of life? For such an attitude, we are already experts—especially those who have lived a little—for truly all of life is ultimately uncertain.

Funding: This research received no external funding.

Conflicts of Interest: The author declares no conflict of interest.

References

Ammerman, Nancy T. 2014. The 2013 Paul Hanly Furfey Lecture: Finding Religion in Everyday Life. *Sociology of Religion* 75: 189–207. [CrossRef]

Brierley, Michael W. 2004. Naming a Quiet Revolution: The Panentheistic Turn in Modern Theology. In *In Whom We Live and Move and Have Our Being: Panentheistic Reflections on God's Presence in a Scientific World*. Edited by Philip Clayton and Arthur Peacocke. Grand Rapids: Eerdmans, pp. 1–15.

Buber, Martin. 1966. Symbolic and Sacramental Existence. In *The Origin and Meaning of Hasidism*. Translated by Maurice Friedman. New York: Harper & Row.

Campbell, David E., and Robert D. Putnam. 2012. America's Grace: How a Tolerant Nation Bridges Its Religious Divides. *Political Science Quarterly* 126: 611–40. [CrossRef]

Cornille, Catherine. 2019. *Meaning and Method in Comparative Theology*. Hoboken: Wiley Blackwell.

Drescher, Elizabeth. 2016. *Choosing Our Religion: The Spiritual Lives of America's Nones*. New York: Oxford University Press.

Eliade, Mircea. 1996. *Patterns in Comparative Religion*. Lincoln: University of Nebraska Press. First published 1939.

Flory, Richard. 2017. The Changing Nature of America's Irreligious Explained. *The Conversation*. January 23. Available online: http://theconversation.com/the-changing-nature-of-americas-irreligious-explained-71066 (accessed on 16 May 2019).

Gregg, Stephen E., and Lynne Scholefield. 2015. *Engaging with Living Religion: A Guide to Fieldwork in the Study of Religion*. London: Routledge.

Gustafson, Hans. 2013. Pansacramentality as a New Model for the God-World Relationship in Panentheism. Paper presented at the Upper Midwest Regional Meeting of the American Academy of Religion, St. Paul, MN, USA, April 6.

Gustafson, Hans. 2016a. *Finding All Things in God: Pansacramentalism and Doing Theology Interreligiously*. Eugene: Pickwick.

Gustafson, Hans. 2016b. Is Transreligious Theology Unavoidable in Interreligious Theology and Dialogue? *Open Theology* 2: 248–60. [CrossRef]

Gustafson, Hans. 2019. The Silent Witness of Intuition: Pansacramentality, Interreligious Encounter, and a Fractal Interpretation of Religious Diversity. In *New Paths for Interreligious Theology: Perry Schmidt-Leukel's Fractal Interpretation of Religious Diversity*. Edited by Alan Race and Paul Knitter. Maryknoll: Orbis Books.

Hedges, Paul. 2017a. *Comparative Theology: A Critical and Methodological Perspective*. Leiden: Brill.

Hedges, Paul. 2017b. Multiple Religious Belonging after Religion: Theorising Strategic Religious Participation in a Shared Religious Landscape as a Chinese Model. *Open Theology* 3: 48–72. [CrossRef]

Heschel, Abraham Joshua. 1951. *Man Is Not Alone: A Philosophy of Religion*. New York: Farrar, Straus & Young.

Heschel, Abraham Joshua. 2001. *The Prophets*. New York: Perennial Classics.

Inge, William Ralph. 1948. *Christian Mysticism*. London: Methuen.

Knight, Christopher C. 2001. *Wrestling with the Divine: Religion, Science, and Revelation*. Minneapolis: Fortress Press.

Leirvik, Oddbjørn. 2018. Interreligious University Theologies, Christian/Islamic. *Islam and Christian-Muslim Relations* 29: 509–23. [CrossRef]

Martin, Jerry L. 2016. Is Transreligious Theology Possible? Special Issue. *Open Theology* 2.

Martos, Joseph. 2001. *Doors to the Sacred: A Historical Introduction to Sacraments in the Catholic Church*, Revised Edition. Liguori: Liguori/Triumph.

McGuire, Meredith B. 2008. *Lived Religion: Faith and Practice in Everyday Life*. New York: Oxford University Press.

Meir, Ephraim. 2015. *Interreligious Theology: Its Value and Mooring in Modern Jewish Philosophy*. Berlin: DeGruyter.

Merkle, John C. 1985. *The Genesis of Faith: The Depth Theology of Abraham Joshua Heschel*. New York: Macmillan.

Merkle, John C. 2009. *Approaching God: The Way of Abraham Joshua Heschel*. Collegeville: Liturgical Press.

Moltmann, Jürgen. 1993. *The Crucified God*. Minneapolis: Fortress.

Nouwen, Henri. 1994. *The Return of the Prodigal Son: A Story of Homecoming*. New York: Doubleday.

Orsi, Robert. 1997. Everyday Miracles: The Study of Lived Religion. In *Lived Religion in America: Toward a History of Practice*. Edited by David D. Hall. Princeton: Princeton University Press.

Panentheism. n.d. *The Oxford Dictionary of the Christian Church*. Edited by F. L. Cross and E. A. Livingstone. Oxford Reference Online. Oxford: Oxford University Press. Available online: https://www.oxfordreference.com/view/10.1093/oi/authority.20110803100303684 (accessed on 18 June 2019).

Pew Research Center. 2018. Being Christian in Western Europe. *Pew Research Center*, May 29. Available online: http://assets.pewresearch.org/wp-content/uploads/sites/11/2016/04/Religion-in-Everyday-Life-FINAL.pdf (accessed on 8 April 2019).

Sahgal, Neha. 2018. 10 Key Findings about Religion in Western Europe. *Pew Research Center*, May 29. Available online: https://www.pewresearch.org/fact-tank/2018/05/29/10-key-findings-about-religion-in-western-europe/ (accessed on 27 June 2019).

Schmidt-Leukel, Perry. 2009. *Transformation by Integration: How Inter-Faith Encounter Changes Christianity*. London: SCM Press.

Schmidt-Leukel, Perry. 2015. Interreligious Theology: The Future Shape of Theology. Paper presented at Five-Part Lecture Series Presented as the Gifford Lectures at the University of Glasgow, Glasgow, UK, October 13–21.

Schmidt-Leukel, Perry. 2017. *Religious Pluralism and Interreligious Theology: The Gifford Lectures—An Extended Edition*. Maryknoll: Orbis.

Smith, Wilfred Cantwell. 1989. *Towards a World Theology*. Maryknoll: Orbis. First published 1981.

Smith, Wilfred Cantwell. 2001. The Christian in a Religiously Plural World. In *Christianity and Other Religions*. Edited by John Hick and Brian Hebblethwaite. Oxford: Oneworld.

Stringer, Martin D. 2015. Lived Religion and Difficult Conversations. *Birmingham Conversations of the Faith, Neighbors, Changemakers Collaboration*. 4. Available online: http://www.fncbham.org.uk/wp-content/uploads/2015/05/Lived-Religion-and-Difficult-Conversations.pdf (accessed on 25 July 2018).

Ward, Keith. 1994. *Religion and Revelation: A Theology of Revelation in the World's Religions*. New York: Oxford University Press.

Ward, Keith. 1996. *Religion and Creation*. New York: Oxford University Press.

Ward, Keith. 1998. *Religion and Human Nature*. New York: Oxford University Press.

Ward, Keith. 2000. *Religion and Community*. Oxford: Clarendon Press.

Ward, Keith. 2002. The Importance of Liberal Theology. In *The Future of Liberal Theology*. Edited by Mark D. Chapman. Aldershot: Ashgate Press.

Ward, Keith. 2004. The World as the Body of God: A Panentheistic Metaphor. In *In Whom We Live and Move and Have Our Being*. Edited by Philip Clayton and Arthur Peacocke. Grand Rapids: Eerdmans, pp. 62–72.

Ward, Keith. 2007. Liberal Theology and the God of Love. In *The God of Love and Human Dignity: Essays in Honour of George M. Newlands*. Edited by Paul Middleton. London: T & T Clark.

Ward, Keith. 2008. *Religion and Human Fulfilment*. London: SCM Press.

Wiesel, Elie. 1969. *Night*. New York: Avon.

Article

Between the Center and the Margins: Young Catholics, "Sorta-Catholics," and Baptismal Identity

Rhodora Beaton

Department of Liturgical and Sacramental Theology, Aquinas Institute of Theology, Saint Louis, MO 63108, USA; beaton@ai.edu

Received: 1 August 2019; Accepted: 30 August 2019; Published: 3 September 2019

Abstract: Increased pastoral and theological attention to the vocational implications of baptism is sorely needed. As a small contribution to this conversation, this article will examine the insights of young Catholics and their self-described "former Catholic" peers (ages 15–29) regarding key aspects of the Christian life. These insights offer a foundation for evolving understandings of baptismal identity at both the center and the margins of the church. Two recent efforts to formally solicit the opinions of young people will be examined. They are the Pre-Synodal preparations for the 2018 Synod on Young People and the recent study, published by Saint Mary's Press in collaboration with the Center for Applied Research in the Apostolate (CARA) under the title *Going, Going Gone: The Dynamics of Disaffiliation in Young Catholics*. The responses from these young people, placed in conversation with recent theological work on baptism and the lay vocation, offer possibilities for consideration as Catholics ponder the changing demographics of the Church. The conclusion will argue for the urgent necessity of listening to these voices and will suggest that a mystagogical approach offers one helpful path towards a deeper understanding and practice of the baptismal vocation.

Keywords: baptism; vocation; Synod on the Youth; laity; mystagogy; disaffiliation; Second Vatican Council

---

1. Introduction

In the first decades of the twenty-first century, the number of lay Catholics celebrating the sacraments of initiation and matrimony has declined precipitously in the US. According to recent Center for Applied Research in the Apostolate (CARA) data, the number of Catholic marriages decreased from 261,626 in the year 2000 to 143,082 in 2017. Perhaps even more striking, 335,832 fewer infants were baptized in 2017 than in 2000. The number of adult baptisms also dropped by approximately 50%. By contrast, ordinations to the priesthood and diaconate have steadily increased, alongside a respectable increase in the number of lay ecclesial ministers, including vowed religious, in parish ministry[1] (CARA 2019). While the reasons for these shifts are both varied and beyond the scope of this paper, the patterns point to theological as well as pastoral challenges.

One of the challenges that has accompanied these shifts is the need for a more adequate understanding of the Christian vocation of the laity that has traditionally been rooted in baptism. While the lay vocation is commonly associated with baptism, the baptismal rites say nothing about "the laity," although they speak both literally and symbolically about the theological realities of Christian life. This focus is especially clear in the *Rite of Christian Initiation of Adults* in which pre- and post-baptismal formation are framed by liturgical reflection on the experience of the Christian "mysteries" of Scripture and the sacraments, as well as by works of charity (International Commission on English in the Liturgy

---

[1] Presbyteral ordinations, which hit a low point of 442 in 2000, have risen to 504 in 2017. The number of permanent deacons has also continued its steady increase from 12,378 in 2000 to 18,287 in 2017 CARA indicates that there were 29,146 lay ecclesial ministers in parish settings in 1995 and 39,651 in 2014. Data not available for 2000 or 2018 (CARA 2019).

[1988] 1990, nos. 75, 244). Magisterial texts that take an ecclesiological rather than liturgical focus, often reference baptism, but do not engage the ritual texts directly. Vatican II's *Decree on the Laity*, for example, mentions baptism only once, stating that "The laity derive the right and duty to the apostolate from their union with Christ the head; incorporated into Christ's Mystical Body through Baptism and strengthened by the power of the Holy Spirit through Confirmation, they are assigned to the apostolate by the Lord Himself" (*Apostolicam actuositatem* [1965] 1996, no. 3). *Lumen gentium* devotes nine paragraphs to the laity, although it does so most frequently in terms of the laity's relationship to the bishops. The text defines "laity" as "all the faithful except those in holy Orders and those who belong to a religious state approved by the church: all the faithful, that is, who by Baptism are incorporated into Christ, are constituted the people of God, who have been made sharers in their own way in the priestly, prophetic and kingly office of Christ and play their part in carrying out the mission of the whole Christian people in the church and in the world. To be secular is the special characteristic of the laity" (*Lumen gentium* [1964] 1996, no. 31.) It is this secular characteristic which will be emphasized both in the subsequent paragraphs of *Lumen gentium* and later in Pope John Paul II's Post-Synodal Apostolic Exhortation *Christifideles laici* (John Paul II 1988, nos. 15, 17, 22–23).

In the twenty-first century, an age in which both marriages and baptisms have declined, even as the number of disaffiliated Catholics has increased, the question of the Christian vocation rooted in baptism takes on greater urgency. Despite the post-Vatican II efforts of theologians, pastors, and campus ministers, the young people who contributed to the Final Document of the 2018 Pre-Synodal Meeting of Young People held at the Vatican, maintain that "the term 'vocation' has become synonymous with the priesthood and religious life in the culture of the Church" (Pre-Synodal Meeting of Young People 2018, no. 8). Exclusive even of marriage or consecrated life, such a viewpoint can seem to leave little theological guidance for the increasing number of young, and not-so-young, lay people who do not experience a call to any of these states of life. Pope Francis addresses this issue very briefly in his Post-Synodal Apostolic Exhortation *Christus vivit*, writing "For those who are not called to married or the consecrated life, it must always be remembered that the first and most important vocation is the vocation we have received in baptism. Those who are single, even if not by their own choice, can offer a particular witness to that vocation through their own path of personal growth" (Francis 2019, no. 267). The fact that even the pope directs his observation specifically towards those who are *not* called to marriage or consecrated life seems to undermine his point that "the most important vocation is the [one] that we receive in baptism." Do those who are called to marriage or the consecrated life not also need to remember this "most important vocation"? More than a sacrament that grounds the Christian vocation as a whole, in practice baptism is often treated like a pre-vocational sacrament that lays the groundwork for marriage, religious life or holy orders. Despite efforts to the contrary, this ingrained approach diminishes the significance of both the rites of baptism and the Christian vocation in the world.

Increased pastoral and theological attention to the vocational implications of baptism is sorely needed. As a small contribution to this conversation, this article will examine the insights of young Catholics and their self-described "former Catholic" peers (ages 15–29) regarding key aspects of the Christian life. These insights can offer a foundation for evolving understandings of baptismal identity at both the center and the margins of the church. We will first examine two recent efforts to formally solicit the opinions of young people. These venues are the Pre-Synodal preparations for 2018 Synod on Young People, the Faith, and Vocational Discernment and the recent study, published by Saint Mary's Press in collaboration with the Center for Applied Research in the Apostolate in September 2017 under the title *Going, Going Gone: The Dynamics of Disaffiliation in Young Catholics*. The responses from these young people, placed in conversation with recent theological work on baptism and the lay vocation, offer several avenues for consideration as Catholics[2] ponder the changing demographics of the Church and the changing needs of those among the baptized who, as the young people at the Pre-Synodal meeting put it, "see vocation as inclusive of life, love, aspiration, place in and contribution to the world, and way to make an impact" (Pre-Synodal Meeting of Young People 2018, no. 8). This paper will argue for the urgent necessity of listening to these voices. As a partial response, it will also suggest that a mystagogical approach, grounded in the liturgical experience of the rites can offer one path towards a deeper understanding and practice of the baptismal vocation. It is out of this liturgical experience that, as the Rite of Christian Initiation of Adults puts it, "belongs to Christians and increases as it is lived, ...new perceptions of the faith, of the Church, and of the world" might be derived (International Commission on English in the Liturgy [1988] 1990, no. 245), and a path towards a deeper understanding of the baptismal vocation might be found in community.

2. A Word about the Sources

The experiences and opinions of lay Roman Catholics are rarely formally solicited by national or international ecclesiastical structures. In the past decade however, due perhaps to the alarmingly declining number of lay people at liturgies, both the Vatican and a small Catholic publisher in the state of Minnesota sought to ask young Catholics directly about their experiences. While these approaches differed, in both cases, substantial feedback was forthcoming.

The Saint Mary's Press/CARA study focused specifically on "surveying and interviewing youth and young adults (ages 15–25) who once self-identified as Catholic, but no longer do so" (Saint Mary's Press of Minnesota and CARA 2017, p. 5). The study, which relied on both qualitative and quantitative data, isolated three distinct categories of the disaffiliated: the Injured, the Drifter, and the Dissenter. It was also clear that "often departure from the Catholic faith is rooted primarily in one of the three main categories, but rarely can disaffiliation be assigned to just one category or cause—and even all three may be involved" (Saint Mary's Press of Minnesota and CARA 2017, p. 13). The authors emphasize the importance of the qualitive data "to illuminate ... the reality that behind every life story is a 'name.'" These are names that, most likely, were given in baptism and recorded in parish record books. The authors of the study remind the reader that "each person who disaffiliates has a name, a story, and longings of the heart and mind" (Saint Mary's Press of Minnesota and CARA 2017, p. 7). As indicated in their responses, these baptized individuals continue to seek the good as they understand it but have chosen to do so outside of the Catholic community. They challenge the Church, the authors of the study indicate, to ask: "Can we prioritize families on the margins?...Can we provide religious formation that address the important issues and questions that young Catholics are thinking about at earlier and earlier ages?...How do we define what it means to 'be Catholic'?....How aware are we of the rise of the 'sorta-Catholic' or 'Catholic-ish' young people (and adults)—those with a tenuous relationship or connection to the Church? Do we fully embrace these young people as 'valid' Catholics, knowing they don't fully accept and embrace the fullness of the Church's teachings and practices?" (Saint Mary's Press of Minnesota and CARA 2017, p. 35). These Catholics "on the margins" may also have existed in the past, but their more visible absence today raises important questions about what the baptized but not practicing experience is like, as well as what can or should be expected from baptism and/or the baptized.

One might ask "why the margins?" Why not simply focus on the young people who have remained Catholic, some of whom offered their insights to the bishops of the synod, and hear from them about what has "worked"? Aside from an obvious concern for evangelization, or in some cases re-evangelization, the methodological emphasis on the "margins" has become important both

---

[2] Although the challenges of baptismal identify affect and are being addressed by many Christian denominations, this article will focus primarily on the Roman Catholic context. Given the limits of the Saint Mary's Press/CARA study, the focus is also necessarily reflective of the United States Catholic experience.

theologically and pastorally, particularly in the pontificate of Pope Francis. Richard Gaillardetz suggests that this emphasis has its foundations in the conciliar theology of Yves Congar (Gaillardetz 2014, p. 70), who points out that "most of the time, initiatives do not come from the center but from the periphery" (Congar [1967] 2011, p. 239). Congar observes that "the margin is closer to the periphery than to the center ... .the center, with its vocation to oversee *structure*, prefers something *defined* to something that is searching and striving for expression. Yet a spiritual organism is more likely to *grow* out of the elements searching and striving for expression" (Congar [1967] 2011, p. 240). The young people who were interviewed for the qualitative element of the Saint Mary's Press/CARA study were striving for expression. Some had wanted to tell their story but had not yet had the opportunity to do so (Saint Mary's Press of Minnesota and CARA 2017, p. 7). As Gaillardetz, Congar, and Pope Francis point out, the Church needs both the center and the margins. If the center maintains the structure, the margins offer a place for growth, even if that place becomes somewhat frayed or unruly.

The Synod on Young People, the Faith, and Vocational Discernment was held in Rome in October of 2018. In addition to the bishops with voting rights, ecumenical observers and young auditors also attended. The preparation for this meeting included the input of many young lay people. As the synod website puts it quite bluntly, "the will to speak to youths directly was something specifically new" (General Secretariat of the Synod of Bishops 2018b). The initiative to speak directly took several manifestations. The first of these took the form of an online questionnaire, accessible in a variety of languages and available from June–December 2017. The Vatican reports that "more than 200,000 made contact (with more than half who filled it out completely)" (General Secretariat of the Synod of Bishops 2018b). While participation in the questionnaire was both open and voluntary and much about the participants remains unverified, it was directed to people 16–29 years of age.[3] In addition to the survey, three hundred young people, including representatives from other religions, gathered in Rome for a pre-synodal meeting in March 2018. They were accompanied by an additional fifteen thousand virtual participants through social media. According to the synod website, "for one week, these participants exchanged views by elaborating their reflections which were merged into a document that expresses (with doubts, uncertainties, desires and hopes) the thoughts and experiences of young people in the 21st century" (General Secretariat of the Synod of Bishops 2018b). Among the delegates sent from the United States were a religious brother who teaches high school, a single man who serves as director of campus ministry at a Catholic university, and a married woman who is a mother and a youth minister (United States Conference of Catholic Bishops 2019).[4] As part of their work together, this group produced a document titled "Young People, The Faith and Vocational Discernment: Pre-Synodal Meeting Final Document," as a guide for the synod itself (Pre-Synodal Meeting of Young People 2018).

While the young and disaffiliated of the Saint Mary's Press/CARA study and the young people chosen by their bishops to represent their countries may seem entirely different from one another, their responses indicate that the connections between them remain relatively intact. For example, one subject of the Saint Mary's Press/CARA study observes that "most of my friends are still Catholic and maybe, like if I have somebody [in my life], I could return to the Catholic Church" (Saint Mary's Press

---

3   The full results of this study are available on the synod website. The English translation, entitled, "The World of New Generations According to the Online Questionnaire" begins on page 81 (General Secretariat of the Synod of Bishops 2018a).
4   The USCCB website describes the delegates chosen by the USCCB as follows: "Br. Javier Hansen, FSC, originally from northern California, is a Brother of the Christian Schools in the Lasallian District of San Francisco-New Orleans, currently serving as a religion teacher at Cathedral High School-El Paso, Texas; Nick López, originally from San Antonio, currently serves as the director of campus ministry for the University of Dallas. He is also a guest columnist for the Catholic News Service column, In Light of Faith, focused on millennials; [and] Katie Prejean McGrady, of the Diocese of Lake Charles in Louisiana, is a wife, new mother, youth minister, and a popular speaker who has been working with many youth and young adult communities across the country." It is also noted that "there will be other delegates at the Pre-Synod representing other groups (i.e., Eastern Rite Catholic Churches, various apostolates and movements) who live in the U.S." (United States Conference of Catholic Bishops 2019). Katie Prejean McGrady, who wrote about her experience in *America Magazine*, described the process as "an effort to help the bishops understand precisely what is going on with people of a certain age so that they can then better understand how to preach to, teach thoroughly and accompany youth and young adults" (McGrady 2018).

of Minnesota and CARA 2017, p. 24). The researchers themselves observe that many of the disaffiliated young people are not "closed to belief (or fuller belief)" (Saint Mary's Press of Minnesota and CARA 2017, p. 30). Similarly, the young people participating in the Pre-Synodal Meeting of Young People, including those of other religions, indicate that they are likewise in relationship with disaffiliated peers. They sought to represent not only themselves or other practicing Catholics, but also "lots of young people [who have] lost trust in institutions, have become disaffiliated with organized religion and would not see themselves as 'religious'" (Pre-Synodal Meeting of Young People 2018, no. 5). These groups are clearly distinct, yet it is also clear that they do not exist in isolation from one another; the "center" and the "margins" are not as distant as one might expect. As Paul Crowley has observed "contemporary Christians in the Western world inhabit the very same world as their atheist or agnostic friends and make many of the same basic assumptions about how reality is structured and functions . . . .Some have lost the ability to believe, not because they do not know what the church has proposed for belief, but because the doctrinal 'content' of faith has become intellectually incredible, as belonging to another world of meaning and reference and certainly not to the world of empirical demonstration" (Crowley 2015, p. 8). This world that contemporary Christians share with their atheist and agnostic friends is the context in which contemporary baptismal identity is lived out, strengthened, or rejected. The themes and struggles that emerge from the insights of these young baptized Christians therefore have much to say about the future of the Church in the contemporary world.

3. Baptism and the Christian Life: Implicit Expectations

The second half of the twentieth century witnessed the emergence of the sacrament of baptism from shadowy sacristies into the brightness of Sunday morning liturgies. New baptistries with fonts suitable for full-immersion were constructed and have become striking focal points for parish liturgy. With the revision of the Easter Triduum in the late 1950s and the increasingly normative theology of the Rite of Christian Initiation of Adults, this once private, family-oriented sacrament has reclaimed its public space in the Church and world. As a result, Catholics witness baptisms more frequently and at least some, quite reasonably, seem to expect that the sacrament ought to have a noticeable effect. Concerns about this effect are at the root of both challenges and possible developments in the search for a theology of the baptismal vocation to the Christian life. As might be expected, the document produced by the Pre-Synodal Meeting of Young People articulates the concerns of this generation in greater theological nuance than the individual survey responses and interviews of the Saint Mary's Press/CARA study. In both cases, despite the different outcomes in terms of relationship to the institutional church, it is clear that some of the key teachings of the Second Vatican Council, particularly those associated with baptism and the lay vocation have taken root. Among these are a deep concern and expectation for holiness as a mark of Christian life; a desire to read the signs of the times and address social issues with an appreciation for the human dignity of all people, particularly those on the margins; and finally, a desire for more substantial theological education. We will consider each of these issues raised in the responses of the young people in light of the documents of the Second Vatican Council and related scholarship in the contemporary Roman Catholic theological context.

In the minds of young Catholics at both the center and the margins, a concern with holiness, or in some cases, a deep concern with a perceived *lack* of holiness, takes center stage. In the category of "The Injured," the Saint Mary's Press/CARA study considered the role of the Church community in the experience of young Catholics who left the Church due to a negative experience. Although the word "holiness" did not necessarily come up directly, some former Catholics root their decision to disaffiliate in a perception of "the Church as inauthentic or hypocritical . . . This was especially true if a young person perceived a family member's everyday attitudes or behaviors as unethical or immoral, yet that same family member attended church on Sunday and otherwise professed belief in the Catholic faith" (Saint Mary's Press of Minnesota and CARA 2017, p. 15). As one individual put it, "it was just like the feeling of not feeling like you are part of something because sometimes you have these people that are extremely religious and then they become extremely hypocritical and they think they are better than everybody else. But they do these bad things and it's like, how could you be part of that?" (Saint Mary's Press of Minnesota and CARA 2017, p. 16). In these cases, it was the witness (or lack thereof) of other lay Catholics that disrupted the faith journey of a young and perhaps already marginal Catholic. The young people might have had high expectations of other Catholics in part because of the influence of *Lumen gentium's* teaching that the universal call to holiness is rooted in the sacrament of baptism. In light of the possible consequences of disaffiliation, the Council's exhortation that all the baptized "must therefore hold on to and perfect in their lives that holiness which they have received from God" takes on a sharper meaning: "All Christians ... are called ... to the perfection of charity and this holiness is conducive to a more human way of living even in society here on earth" (*Lumen gentium* [1964] 1996, no 40). When this vocational call to charity and holiness remains unanswered, or fails to be evident in Christian life, harm is done to the most vulnerable members of the community; they are pushed even farther to the margins.

The young people represented at the Pre-synodal Meeting express a similar sentiment. These generational peers of the disaffiliated observe that "young people are attracted to the joy which should be a hallmark of our faith. Young people express a desire to see a Church that is a living testimony to what it teaches and witnesses to authenticity on the path to holiness, which includes acknowledging mistakes and asking for forgiveness" (Pre-Synodal Meeting of Young People 2018, no. 9). In this case, the concern seems not to be so much with family members or classmates, but with "leaders of the Church—ordained, religious and lay." This authenticity becomes a form of inspiration on the path to holiness. The young people at the Pre-Synodal Meeting do not necessarily require the "perfection" that *Lumen gentium* exhorts, but they clearly call for a witness that is joyful, authentic, and willing to acknowledge failure in order to seek forgiveness.

In the contemporary context, similar issues regarding the relationship between baptism and the Christian life have been raised in the field of moral theology. Christian ethicist Katie Grimes, for example, has recently argued that "the vice of white supremacy pervades the church's corporate body and thereby permeates all of its practices, including those of baptism and Eucharist" (Grimes 2017a, p. 22). Due to practices such as forced baptisms, and the radical social inequality between enslaved peoples and white, Christian, masters, Grimes argues that the ritual symbols of baptism have been hopelessly corrupted and will not be efficacious again until the Church has worked to dismantle white supremacy in the world.[5] She writes: "Performed under conditions of antiblackness supremacy, baptism became perverse: it ushered slaves not out of bondage and into freedom, but from freedom and into bondage. It brought slaves not out of death and into life, but from life and into death, both social and physical" (Grimes 2017b, p. 195). Rejecting the work of previous scholars who have viewed baptism as a potential source of healing for the injustices of the world, Grimes regards it as something that *should* be holy, but is currently perverse in its corruption.

Young Catholics associate holiness and authenticity. If someone or something is expected to be holy, then it *ought to be* holy. As the Pre-synodal group recognizes, failure, repentance, and forgiveness can be experienced along "the path to holiness" as a model of authenticity and Christian vulnerability. As the disaffiliated youth and Grimes point out, it is too often the case that baptized Christians fail (or refuse) to recognize the harm that they have done and therefore do not progress along the path to repentance and forgiveness. Individually or collectively, they may veer from the path of holiness, leaving scandal rather than sanctification in their wake. When baptism is celebrated as an isolated ritual, public as it may be, the disconnect between liturgical celebration and Christian life can become a source of harm rather than a sacramental sign of the presence of Christ in the liturgy and in the world.

If Vatican II's emphasis on holiness, especially to be found in *Lumen gentium*, has helped to shape the thinking of a generation, it is also the case that *Gaudium et spes's* emphases on the importance

---

5 See also (Grimes 2017b, pp. 189–204). See also, for example Christiana Zenner's *Just Water: Theology Ethics and Fresh Water Crises* in which she asks, "if the water of the Jordan River is polluted, pea-green, and degraded, is it really so holy?" (Zenner 2018, p. 188).

of engagement in the modern world and the dignity of the human person has struck an important chord. Massimo Faggioli has suggested that *"Gaudium et spes* is the real test for the council's impact on the church's theological tradition … .The church's historicity is not about looking back but about moving forward *ad extra"* (Faggioli 2012, p. 813). In both the disaffiliated group and in the group of young people at the Pre-Synodal Meeting, we see a resonance with and reception of the message of the preface to *Gaudium et spes.* It is clear that "the joys and hopes, the grief and anguish of the people of our time, especially of those who are poor or afflicted, are the joys and hopes, the grief and anguish of" many of the young people involved. They seem to believe that the Church does indeed carry "the responsibility of reading the signs of the times and of interpreting them in the light of the Gospel" (*Gaudium et spes* [1965] 1996, no. 4) even though they admit to disagreement regarding the proper tack to take moving forward. The young people involved in the Saint Mary's Press and CARA study express concerns about "LGBT people being stigmatized," about healing for the sick and the elderly, and about a lack of solidarity with or even tolerance for those whom they perceived to be suffering or excluded due to the actions of local Catholic communities (Saint Mary's Press of Minnesota and CARA 2017, pp. 15, 17, 57). Mostly in the study's category of "the Injured," these young people seem to be less concerned with doctrinal issues and more concerned with the outward practices of Christian living in their communities. The anguish of those who are suffering has become their anguish (or anger) as baptized members of the Church, and yet they do not see that the same anguish is shared by those who are in authority.

The Pre-Synodal text also takes up issues of the Church *ad extra.* "The young Church also looks outward; young people have a passion for political, civil and humanitarian activities. They want to act as Catholics in the public sphere for the betterment of society as a whole. In all aspects of Church life, young people wish to be accompanied and to be taken seriously as fully responsible members of the Church" (Pre-Synodal Meeting of Young People 2018, no. 12). These young people have embraced the message of *Gaudium et spes,* and, perhaps in light of the teachings of *Lumen gentium,* also understand themselves as "fully responsible members of the Church" who share in the experiences of "the people of our time." More specifically, they are "concerned about topics such as sexuality, addiction, failed marriages, broken families, as well as larger-scale social issues such as organized crime, human trafficking, violence, corruption, exploitation, femicide, all forms of persecution and the degradation of our natural environment. [They note that] these are of grave concern in vulnerable communities around the world" (Pre-Synodal Meeting of Young People 2018, no. 1). While some of these issues have also been taken up by the magisterium, it is clear that these young people wish to work personally and as a community to "address the social justice issues of our time" (Pre-Synodal Meeting of Young People 2018, no. 3). Although they do not necessarily agree with each other or with the magisterium on the best approach to these topics,[6] young people are aware of and engaged with the struggles of the modern world. They expect that the Church will play a productive role in addressing these challenges and they expect that their participation as "fully responsible members" will be welcomed. Some of them wish to be included in this effort as Catholics, while others no longer wish to be Catholic because they see Catholic identity as an impediment to the contribution that they wish to make.

---

[6] The Pre-Synodal document observes that "there is often great disagreement among young people, both within the Church and in the wider world, about some of her teachings which are especially controversial today … .What is important to note is that irrespective of their level of understanding of Church teaching, there is still disagreement and ongoing discussion among young people on … polemical issues [including] contraception, abortion, homosexuality, cohabitation, marriage, and how the priesthood is perceived in different realities of the Church" (Pre-Synodal Meeting of Young People 2018, no. 5). Similarly, the Saint Mary's Press/CARA study notes that "Dissenting young people who actively leave the Church express disagreement with Church teachings on many social issues, particularly same-sex marriage, abortion, and birth control, though the abortion issue seems nuanced in that there is often opposition to abortion, but support for an individual's right to choose that option" (Saint Mary's Press of Minnesota and CARA 2017, p. 21).

In a related way, we also see in both groups a concern for human dignity, the topic of the first chapter of *Gaudium et spes* and an overarching theme throughout the document. The Pre-synodal document takes up this topic in light of contemporary issues such as racism and the role of women in society observing that "racism at different levels affects young people in different parts of the world" (Pre-Synodal Meeting of Young People 2018, no. 2). In a related point, these young people lament that "there is still no binding consensus on the question of welcoming migrants and refugees, or on the issues which cause the phenomenon in the first place. This is despite the acknowledgment of the universal call to care for the dignity of every human person" (Pre-Synodal Meeting of Young People 2018, no. 2). Later in the document, they express a concern for the promotion of "the dignity of women, both in the Church and in wider society [noting that] today, there is a general problem in society that women are still not given an equal place. This is also true in the Church" (Pre-Synodal Meeting of Young People 2018, no. 5). Although there are no footnotes here, the echo of *Gaudium et spes*'s endorsement of the "equal dignity as persons" that is due to everyone regardless of "sex, race, color, social conditions, language, or religion" (*Gaudium et spes* [1965] 1996, no. 29) seems evident.

The Saint Mary's Press/CARA study of disaffiliated young people echoes some of these concerns and also considers the dignity that *Gaudium et spes* associates with religious freedom. According to the authors of the study one of the most common reasons for disaffiliation is the belief "that religion was forced on [an individual] and they are determined to not force religion/religious practice or a particular faith on their own children. Religion and religious practice ought to be a free choice, they argue" (Saint Mary's Press of Minnesota and CARA 2017, p. 27). A related, if significantly more mildly stated, sentiment can be found in the Pre-synodal text's description of the ideal mentor: "They should respect the freedom that comes with a young person's process of discernment and equip them with tools to do so well ... .A mentor should nurture the seeds of faith in young people, without expecting to immediately see the fruits of the work of the Holy Spirit" (Pre-Synodal Meeting of Young People 2018, no. 10). While this interpretation is perhaps not what the authors of *Gaudium et spes* had in mind, one can find here an echo of the Council's conviction that the dignity of human beings "requires them to act out of conscious and free choice as moved and drawn in a personal way from within, and not by their own blind impulses or by external constraint" (*Gaudium et spes* [1965] 1996, no. 17). One could certainly argue about the adequacy of conscience formation,[7] as well as about theological understandings of human freedom and parental obligations; however, these young people express a particular and emphatic respect for the dignity of their own children to act without external constraint especially in the realm of religious practice. Although some intend to teach their children about the existence of God, this subgroup is particularly adamant that it is both inappropriate and ineffective to force a child to participate in religious practices. As one young person put it, "I want her to have freedom of what she wants to do rather than it being forced upon her." Another observes "I do know that the more a person forced me back then and the harder, the more pushback I gave them. I think that would be the best advice I could give is just be open and don't be forceful and that will likely keep somebody in the same direction that they are going" (Saint Mary's Press of Minnesota and CARA 2017, pp. 27–29). These disaffiliated young people regard forced religious formation as both counter-productive and contrary to a child's dignity as a human person.

Finally, both groups articulate the need for more substantial theological formation. In some cases, this formation pertains to theological approaches to controversial social issues. In other cases, it has to do with as diverse topics as the perceived disconnect between science and religion, misunderstandings of the Catholic faith, and inadequate sacramental preparation. As the Pre-Synodal document puts it, young people "long for experiences that can deepen our relationship with Jesus in the real world" (Pre-Synodal Meeting of Young People 2018, no. 14). There is a sense here that both experiential and intellectual approaches are needed. In terms of their desire for experiential formation, the Pre-Synodal

---

[7]   For one analysis of these contemporary complications, see (Cox 2015, pp. 82–100).

group describe themselves as "more receptive to a 'literature of life' than an abstract theological discourse" (Pre-Synodal Meeting of Young People 2018, no. 5). The authors of the Saint Mary's Press/CARA study echo this self-reflection in their analysis, observing that "personal experience is the default mediator of meaning and truth for these young people" (Saint Mary's Press of Minnesota and CARA 2017, p. 24). As their approach to holiness indicates, the reality must reflect the description.

Despite, or perhaps because of, this emphasis on personal experience, young people "ask that our leaders speak in practical terms about controversial subjects such as homosexuality and gender issues, about which young people are already freely discussing without taboo" (Pre-Synodal Meeting of Young People 2018, no. 11). In these topics, the connection between experience and intellectual understanding becomes especially clear. We see a strong desire to engage the theological and ethical issues of the contemporary world in ways that are authentic and particular. "The young have many questions about the faith, but desire answers which are not watered-down, or which utilize pre-fabricated formulations" (Pre-Synodal Meeting of Young People 2018, no. 11). As one of the subjects of the Saint Mary's Press/CARA study put it more bluntly: "it didn't quite make much sense to me and I never felt like I was receiving satisfactory answers from my CCD teachers" (Saint Mary's Press of Minnesota and CARA 2017, p. 23). Some of these questions have to do with ethics, while others seem to span the theological disciplines regarding "fundamental questions about the beliefs of the catholic church and faith" (Saint Mary's Press of Minnesota and CARA 2017, p. 62). Another respondent said: "when I was 15 I read the bible, cover to cover … .The actual bible was wildly different and even more strict than what I knew to be true in my heart. After my reading I went to a priest at my church. His answers were extremely noncommittal and dismissive, maybe because I was young, but it was an extremely frustrating experience for me" (Saint Mary's Press of Minnesota and CARA 2017, 64). There is a frustration here both with the inadequacy of "pre-fabricated" answers and with a sense that serious theological questions are not being taken seriously. These young people seem to believe that their Christian vocation does indeed call them to that "spiritual formation...in theology, ethics and philosophy at least" which *Apostolicam actuositatem* considers "the foundation and condition of any fruitful apostolate" (*Apostolicam actuositatem* [1965] 1996, no. 29). Without this formation they become increasingly frustrated.

Both the pre-synod group and the subjects of the Saint Mary's Press/CARA study are also very concerned with the related issue of the relationship between faith and reason. The Pre-synodal text observes that "some perceive the Church to be 'anti-science' so its dialogue with the scientific community is also important, as science can illuminate the beauty of creation. In this context, the Church should also care for environmental issues, especially pollution" (Pre-Synodal Meeting of Young People 2018, no. 11). Several of the disaffiliated young people describe a similar difficulty: "as I started to enjoy math and science more, I just realized the discrepancy between science and religion. I guess that was another shaking point" (Saint Mary's Press of Minnesota and CARA 2017, p. 24). Another observed "there's a lot of contradictions that come with the bible and modern science. Also, I don't want to believe and worship a god who condemns them to hell for giving in to human nature" (Saint Mary's Press of Minnesota and CARA 2017, p. 62). In general, the CARA researchers observe that some who have disaffiliated "take issue with perceived Church teachings about the Bible, salvation, heaven, and life after death … [T]hough many in this group [the Dissenters] were involved in Catholic education, parish religious education, and youth ministry, they expressed deep disillusionment and frustration that their questions were never answered or they didn't have the opportunity to voice their questions in the first place" (Saint Mary's Press of Minnesota and CARA 2017, pp. 21–22). In at least some cases, the perceived teachings, as articulated by the individuals, are inaccurate (a belief that the Catholic Church teaches a literal interpretation of the Bible requiring belief that "someone was swallowed by a whale and then came out") or theologically uncertain and under-developed: "I'm sure I'll be fine in the afterlife as long as I'm a good person" (Saint Mary's Press of Minnesota and CARA 2017, pp. 26, 62).

The young people in these texts come from distinct subgroups within the same generation. One striking difference in their responses is the degree to which they indicate the influence of family and parents. The Pre-Synodal text mentions the importance of the family as a possible and privileged place for personality and vocational development (Pre-Synodal Meeting of Young People 2018, nos. 1, 9) and also makes a few references to experiencing the Church as a kind of family (Pre-Synodal Meeting of Young People 2018, no. 7). The subjects of the Saint Mary's Press/CARA study, particularly "the Drifters" make frequent mention of parents who changed denominations or stopped going to church altogether (Saint Mary's Press of Minnesota and CARA 2017, pp. 18–19, 58–59). While the Pre-Synodal group does not address particular parents at all, the disaffiliated young people indicate the specific influence of "sorta-Catholic" parents who, as the researchers observe "may sense the value of a faith community connection but may not be able to articulate their beliefs. [The researchers continue:] if parents feel inadequate to personally share their faith, or if they are also struggling to find genuine meaning in faith, then the family as a unit may be drifting" (Saint Mary's Press of Minnesota and CARA 2017, p. 19). The experiences of older generations also have a significant role to play. While families who play a stabilizing role in faith development seem almost taken for granted, families who are beginning to "drift" may point more strongly to the intergenerational influence of parents and family in faith development or disaffiliation.

Distinct as they may be, the young people whose voices are represented in these texts advocate for values that are in many ways in continuity with the teachings of the Second Vatican Council, albeit expressed in the key of twenty-first century cultures. As Edward Hahnenberg puts it, in the years since the Council, "what has changed ... is that what was once reserved for a few—namely, the quest for a deeper spiritual life—has now become the primary religious stance of most people" (Hahnenberg 2010, p. xii). These young people call for a Church that is both holy and authentic; they wish to be taken seriously as "full participants" who are capable of contributing on their own terms to the world that they inhabit, and they desire, or have in the past desired, theological conversations about doctrine and moral issues that respectfully address their own questions and experiences. These desires point to an understanding of baptismal identity that can contribute to the Church's evolving understanding and practice.

4. The Potential of a Mystagogical Framework

The challenges for an evolving understanding of baptismal identity abound in the twenty-first century Church. In addition to the issues addressed here, the relationship between marriage and baptism, ordination and baptism, and religious life and baptism continue to merit theological exploration. The question of the baptismal identity of the parents of these young people also looms large in the demographic analysis of twenty-first century Catholics. While the issues raised by the young people of the Pre-synodal Meeting and the Saint Mary's Press/CARA study contribute only a small section of the full picture, their frank insights offer a gift not only to the bishops at the synod but also to the broader Church.

This gift is a somewhat fragile one. Perhaps in recognition of that fragility, the responses of those who initiated the studies has been characterized by a tentative openness. In his Post-Synodal Apostolic Exhortation, *Christus vivit*, Pope Francis began by acknowledging that the process "raised issues that led me to ask new questions" (Francis 2019, no. 7). Similarly, the authors of the Saint Mary's Press/CARA study caution against "a rush to identify solutions or strategies that address the dynamics of disaffiliation" (Saint Mary's Press of Minnesota and CARA 2017, p. 32). They spend significant time, however, on "several initial questions they believe are important for pastoral ministry to address in light of the findings" (Saint Mary's Press of Minnesota and CARA 2017, p. 34). The topics that the researchers raise address key questions pertaining to operative understandings of Catholicity. They point to the need to "prioritize families on the margins" of Catholicism, those who are "sorta-Catholic" or "Catholic-ish" or who are baptized, but "don't fully accept and embrace the fullness of the Church's teachings and practices" (Saint Mary's Press of Minnesota and CARA 2017,

p. 35). These fragile margins encompass not only the individuals who responded, but their parents and families as well as other lay Catholics who are "staying," "have left," are worried about adult children who no longer attend liturgy or are wrestling with their own consciences regarding their response to the public scandals that have wracked the Church. These people are not often consulted by the magisterium, but when their insights are collected by sociologists, they offer a valuable resource to theologians and pastoral ministers.[8]

It is important to heed the advice of the researchers who remind us not to seek conclusions or solutions too quickly. In light of this, I offer one possible approach for consideration. This approach is not a comprehensive "fix," nor does it provide a solution to the steady stream of disaffiliation. Instead it builds on the insights of the young people to engage the strengths and weaknesses of the baptismal vocation as it is currently lived and might be lived in the future. It is an approach in which the Church as a community might be invited to deepen and strengthen its understanding of baptismal identity through a process of communal reflection that is rooted in sacramental practice; in other words, it is a mystagogical approach.

In her 2012 Madeleva Lecture *Becoming the Sign: Sacramental Living in a Post-Conciliar Church* in which she addresses what she calls the "laity shortage" (Hughes 2013, p. 3), Kathleen Hughes describes mystagogy as "the opening up of the mysteries for believers through reflection on actual experience" (Hughes 2013, p. 77). In keeping with the insights offered by the young people, it is a process that is centrally concerned with fostering holiness in Christian life, is rooted in individual and communal experience, provides a foundation for more intensely theological study, and can be adapted as a kind of ongoing formation in the Christian life. As a means for developing and strengthening baptismal identity it is also a method that relies thoroughly on the participation of communities of the baptized themselves. It is not an approach that can be applied and carried out by "professionals" but rather a process that takes the insights of participants seriously.

The study and application of mystagogy, traditionally associated with the post-baptismal Easter preaching of bishops in the fourth and fifth centuries, has begun to be retrieved. This retrieval is not only to be found in the final and somewhat neglected "Period of Postbaptismal Catechesis or Mystagogy" in the Rite of Christian Initiation of Adults, (International Commission on English in the Liturgy [1988] 1990, nos. 244–251) but also in the broader pastoral and theological realm.[9] Traditionally "the mysteries" which were opened up for new believers were the sacraments of initiation. The mystagogical preaching of bishops such as Cyril of Jerusalem, Theodore of Mopsuestia, John Chrysostom (Johnson 2007, pp. 120–34), and even Augustine of Hippo took place in the context of the Easter celebrations and involved a detailed spiritual and theological review of the liturgical rituals and their meanings. One example from the "Fifth Lecture on the Mysteries" by Cyril of Jerusalem is illustrative: "Next the deacon cries: 'Welcome one another,' and 'Let us kiss one another.' You must not suppose that this kiss is the kiss customarily exchanged in the streets by ordinary friends. This kiss is different, effecting as it does, a comingling of souls and mutually pledged forgiveness. The kiss, then, is a sign of true union of hearts, banishing every grudge. It was this that Christ had in view when He said: 'If, when you are bringing your gift to the altar, you suddenly remember that your brother has a grievance against you, leave your offering by the altar; first go and make your peace with your brother, and then come back to offer your gift'" (Cyril of Jerusalem 1970, no. 3). This excerpt from Cyril's preaching is characterized by a robust theological approach. First, Cyril is deeply grounded in the dialogue of the ritual text itself. In the course of his preaching, he takes the assembly through each liturgical phrase and gesture. Cyril moves from the ritual performance to a reference to everyday life; he is clear that although the meaning is different, the gestures of the liturgy are related to day-to-day

---

8   As Kathleen Hughes has recently pointed out: "People who care deeply about the church's sacramental life need to probe more deeply the implications of the Pew Forum and CARA studies and others like them" (Hughes 2013, p. 73).
9   In addition to the authors cited in this article, examples include, but are by no means limited to (Driscoll 2005; Elshof 2017; Mazza 1989; Ostdiek 2015; Rahner 1982; Vincie 2016).

experience. The meaning of the gesture, however, has to do with two key tenets of Christian life: unity and forgiveness. Cyril then adds an additional layer of Biblical interpretation. This addition would have the effect of exposing the new Christians to a potentially new passage of the Bible, while also cementing the understanding that, as Louis-Marie Chauvet would put it one and a half millennia later, Scripture, Sacraments and Ethics are the marks of Christian identity.[10]

A mystagogical method is thus characterized by its foundation in liturgical and day-to-day experience. The mystagogical preaching of the fourth and fifth century church is peppered with exhortations to "call to mind" specific elements of the rite along with copious advice about how to engage the liturgy even more deeply "next time." It is a preaching that is rooted in past experience but is oriented towards future experience. While baptism and Eucharist are the sacraments traditionally associated with mystagogy, this is an approach that is easily expanded. Bruce Morrill describes the potential for mystagogy among the elderly after a celebration of the Anointing of the Sick: "During one or two more gatherings, set in the context of liturgical prayer, people could ... share their reflections on the experience of the sacrament as well as their feelings as they face the future, whether in the short or long term" (Morrill 2009, p. 181). In this case, the mystagogy begins and is rooted in the ritual text but can also be expanded to invite reflection on the experience of Christian life in older age. Such discussion, Morrill suggests, has the potential to further illuminate the Paschal Mystery both for the elderly and for their families and communities. This rediscovery that, "mystagogy is lifelong" (Hughes 2007, p. 14) further opens up the possibilities for its application as an approach to deepening baptismal identity.

The communal practice of drawing on personal experience in the context of the sacramental life also has some potential to meet young Catholics where they are in terms of their emphasis on personal experience and their preference for a "'literature of life' [rather] than an abstract theological discourse." It also has the potential to address the concern that the Pre-synodal group raised about sacramental and intellectual formation. "Because of the lack of clear and attractive presentation as to what the Sacraments truly offer, some of us go through the process of receiving but undervaluing them (Pre-Synodal Meeting of Young People 2018, no. 14). Here, the theological explanation can be deployed specifically so that participants might engage the liturgy more deeply and live more fully according to authentic Christian tradition. For example, participants of all sorts might gather after the Easter baptisms or after a baptism at a Sunday liturgy to reflect on their experience of the ritual celebration. In light of this experience, the community could begin to develop for itself a deeper sense of what baptismal identity means both for the newly baptized and for other baptized members of the community.

Mystagogy today necessarily seeks to elicit frank conversation about individual experiences within the context of a communal sacramental experience. As Hughes puts it, "The key to mystagogical reflection is that it is subjective rather than objective; it is about *my* experience and *your* experience of an encounter with God through the sacramental celebration ... It relates experience and symbol and takes both utterly seriously" (Hughes 2007, p. 15). An authentic mystagogical experience must also be open to the sometimes negative experiences that accompany sacramental celebration. One particularly plaintive response from the Saint Mary's Press/CARA study to the question "What are the reasons that explain why you are no longer Catholic?" is as follows: "Because the church forgot about me during my 1st communion, & then our priest was arrest[ed] for sexual assault on a minor" (Saint Mary's Press of Minnesota and CARA 2017, p. 51). The experience of being forgotten during First Communion would necessarily color an individual's experiential understanding of Eucharist.

---

[10] While beyond the scope of this paper, Chauvet's understanding of the marks of the church can also provide a helpful conversation partner in terms of baptismal identity. Chauvet argues that the Church "has existence and meaning only because of its relationship to the *reign*, which in the world is wider than it ... .it is not the reign; it is only its sacrament. But that fact of being its sacrament ... demands that it be the sign of the reign, and therefore that it show the marks of the reign" (Chauvet 2001, p. 29).

In this context, the mystagogical reflection would have to be expanded to include not only the usual topics of Eucharistic theology, but also the pain of exclusion, and perhaps also betrayal in light of the community's experience of a predatory priest. "For mystagogy to be successful, we need to be able to identify and talk about our experience. That demands that we know what our experience is, that we are in touch with our inner world, and attentive to what we are doing when we gather for prayer" (Hughes 2007, p. 15). It might be added that successful mystatogy in our time may also demand work to restore the trust that has been lost in many communities. Mystagogy is a process of recognizing grace, and it also bears the potential for frank discussions of sin and reconciliation in the context of community. It should not become a forum for liturgical planning, however a deeper understanding of one another's experience, expressed in a prayerful context, can become a catalyst for liturgical development.

As Cyril of Jerusalem's preaching demonstrated, and Morrill's example illustrated, mystagogical practice can lead from the experience of the sacraments to an incorporation of the experience of Christian life. Paul Crowley argues, that in addition to communal liturgical reflection on the sacraments, it is also possible to use "the word 'mystagogy' in its root sense of guiding an initiate into the world of faith, into its depths as they are realized interpersonally in God" (Crowley 2015, p. 12). Crowley regards this as a useful approach for all Christians in the West, but particularly for those, both affiliated and disaffiliated, who struggle with belief. As the two texts that we have engaged indicate, both closely affiliated and disaffiliated young people share the same world. "Some have lost the ability to believe, not because they do not know what the church has proposed for belief, but because the doctrinal 'content' of faith has become intellectually incredible, as belonging to another world of meaning and reference and certainly not to the world of empirical demonstration" (Crowley 2015, p. 8). Even those who value their faith and *wish* to believe may run into difficulties when their meager, often exclusively catechetical rather than theological, education comes into contact with tens of undergraduate credits in STEM education. As one participant in the Saint Mary's Press/CARA study reported, s/he "stopped being religious because I began to learn more about the world. It became impossible to believe in the things taught by religion. No matter how hard I tried to believe in it, the knowledge I gained made it impossible" (Saint Mary's Press of Minnesota and CARA 2017, p. 56). A mystagogical framework is helpful in that it builds on experience and community to integrate Christian life in the context of a shared world. Grounded in the practice of ritual experience, it guards against the temptation to forget that "the transcendent has entered into the natural world and established it as the place of divine revelation" (Crowley 2015, p. 21).[11] It insists that humanity is not alone in the world, struggling against an unreasonable, uncaring, and disembodied God. Here the presence of God is to be discerned in one's own shared experience of sacramental liturgy and a Christian life "on the path to holiness" in relationship to the world. Guiding this process is the task of leaders, or perhaps "mentors" in today's language, who accompany others among the faithful as they "move from a vague awareness of the mystery dimension of their lives to a greater conception and affective clarity, and ... find a proper way to continue to allow experience and expression to inform one another" (Hughes 2007, p. 15).

In order for sound mystagogy, both of liturgy and of life, to take place however, those guiding the mystagogical process must have sufficient theological education. As Cyril of Jerusalem's example indicates, the person serving as guide to the mysteries must be theologically adept, profoundly familiar with the patterns of liturgy and life, and able to negotiate comfortably between liturgical, moral, and biblical theologies. These guides must be capable of sharing and eliciting theological insights that are

---

[11] "There is a sense in which the *saeculum* is established so that this revelation can take place: the locus of revelation is in fact the *saeculum*. The Word (*Logos*) creates the conditions of its very possibility of appearance within the created order." As Crowley cautions, "when Christian faith forgets this and separates itself in opposition to the very world that it otherwise hallows, it can degenerate into ideology. The secular world becomes the enemy, rather than the theater of lived religion that Christianity has otherwise hallowed. Believing becomes reduced to rational assent to culturally unintelligible propositions" (Crowley 2015, p. 21).

"not watered down, or … utiliz[ing] pre-fabricated formulations" (Pre-Synodal Meeting of Young People 2018, no. 11). They must be able to avoid falling into ideology, inadvertently reducing believing to what Crowley refers to as an attempt at "rational assent to culturally unintelligible propositions" (Crowley 2015, p. 21). To achieve this task, pastors, Catholic high school employees, CCD teachers, and youth ministers must be trained not only in catechesis and pedagogy suitable to various stages of human development, but they must also be theologically adept, and free from narrow catechetical curricula, in order to facilitate the serious theological discussions about science and religion, biblical hermeneutics, and thorny issues of eschatology for which young people are calling. They must not only know what the tradition says, but, as theologically informed ministers, also be able to apply it to the real theological questions that young people are asking. This need becomes increasingly urgent as Catholic colleges and universities in the US continue to slash theology and philosophy requirements (Hollerich 2018).

A mystagogical approach does not propose a solution to the many problems that the church faces, but it offers a structure in which communities can seek to deepen their understanding and practice of their baptismal identities through reflection on liturgical experience, sound theological engagement, and communal practice of the Christian life. It offers a space in which the kind of mentor that young people seek can continue to be formed as "a faithful Christian who engages with the Church and the world; someone who constantly seeks holiness; is a confidant without judgement; actively listens to the needs of young people and responds in kind; is deeply loving and self-aware; acknowledges their limits and knows the joys and sorrows of the spiritual journey" (Pre-Synodal Meeting of Young People 2018, no. 1). In this space, young and old can strengthen the bonds between the center and the margins in their conscious and self-reflective pursuit of holiness, their participation and encouragement of participation in the modern world, their respect for the human dignity of all, and their pursuit of the theological education that must necessarily ground Christian life in the world. In so doing, they will strengthen their own baptismal identity and become more equipped to mentor the generations that they hope will follow them.

5. Conclusions

As the number of baptisms decline and as young individuals disaffiliate from the church, in part because the practicing baptized have disappointed them, the need for a deeper understanding of what baptismal identity can and should be becomes increasingly urgent. These two groups of young people have articulated their need for a Church that is on the path to holiness, respectfully engaged with the modern world, and able to articulate the faith with clarity and authenticity in light of contemporary experience. Their consensus around these issues offers a starting point for others in the church to consider the baptismal vocation that is common to all the faithful. A mystagogical approach to the development of baptismal identity, while not an immediate solution to Christian challenges in any of these areas, can offer a framework that is both traditional and forward pointing, contemplative and active, sacramental and oriented *ad extra*. Grounded in the process of baptismal formation, it brings the lived experience of sacramental celebration into conversation with baptismal identity in the world, inviting all the faithful, young and old, lay and ordained, married and single, to deepen their participation in the liturgy and Christian life and in so doing to hold the inter-generational community of the baptized together in the larger context of the communion of saints. The young people of the Pre-synodal preparations and the Saint Mary's Press/CARA study are inviting the rest of the Church to ponder with them what it means to live a Christian life grounded in the baptismal vocation. In fact, they are inviting, if not begging, the church to *live* this baptismal identity in order fruitfully to "walk alongside them" as mentors and companions. Members of the baptized faithful ignore this urgent invitation at our peril.

Funding: This research received no external funding.

Conflicts of Interest: The author declares no conflict of interest.

References

Apostolicam actuositatem. 1996. *Vatican Council II: The Basic Sixteen Documents*. Edited by Austin Flannery. Northport: Costello Publishing. First published 1965.

CARA. 2019. Frequently Requested Church Statistics. Available online: https://cara.georgetown.edu/frequently-requested-church-statistics/ (accessed on 29 July 2019).

Chauvet, Louis-Marie. 2001. *The Sacraments: The Word of God at the Mercy of the Body*. Collegeville: Liturgical Press.

Congar, Yves. 2011. *True and False Reform in the Church*. Translated by Paul Philibert. Collegeville: Liturgical Press. First published 1967.

Cox, Kathryn Lilla. 2015. *Water Shaping Stone: Faith, Relationships, and Conscience Formation*. Collegeville: Liturgical Press.

Crowley, Paul. 2015. Mystagogy and Mission: The Challenge of Nonbelief and the Task of Theology. *Theological Studies* 76: 7–28. [CrossRef]

Cyril of Jerusalem. 1970. Fifth Lecture on the Mysteries. In *The Works of Saint Cyril of Jerusalem, vol 2*. Edited by Bernard M. Peebles. Washington, DC: Catholic University of America Press.

Driscoll, Michael. 2005. Musical Mystagogy: Catechizing Through the Sacred Arts. In *Music in Christian Worship: At the Service of the Liturgy*. Edited by Charlotte Kroeker. Collegeville: Liturgical Press, pp. 27–44.

Elshof, A. J. M. 2017. Mystagogy, religious education and lived catholic faith. *Journal of Religious Education* 64: 143–55. [CrossRef]

Faggioli, Massimo. 2012. Vatican II and the Church of the Margins. *Theological Studies* 72: 808–18.

Francis, Pope. 2019. *Christus vivit*. Available online: http://w2.vatican.va/content/francesco/en/apost_exhortations/documents/papa-francesco_esortazione-ap_20190325_christus-vivit.html (accessed on 29 July 2019).

Gaillardetz, Richard. 2014. The "Francis Moment": A New Kairos for Catholic Ecclesiology. *Catholic Theological Society of America Proceedings* 69: 63–80.

Gaudium et spes. 1996. *Vatican Council II: The Basic Sixteen Documents*. Edited by Austin Flannery. Northport: Costello Publishing. First published 1965.

General Secretariat of the Synod of Bishops. 2018a. *The World of New Generations According to the Online Questionnaire*. Rome: Libreria Editrice Vaticana, Available online: http://www.synod2018.va/content/dam/synod2018/documenti/Libri/libro%20mondo%20delle%20nuove%20generazioni.pdf (accessed on 29 July 2019).

General Secretariat of the Synod of Bishops. 2018b. Young People, The Faith and Vocational Discernment. Available online: http://www.synod.va/content/synod2018/en/news/book--the-world-of-new-generations-according-to-the-online-quest.html (accessed on 29 July 2019).

Grimes, Katie. 2017a. Breaking the Body of Christ: The Sacraments of Initiation in a Habitat of White Supremacy. *Political Theology* 18: 22–43. [CrossRef]

Grimes, Katie. 2017b. *Christ Divided: Antiblackness as Corporate Vice*. Minneapolis: Fortress Press.

Hahnenberg, Edward P. 2010. *Awakening Vocation: A Theology of Christian Call*. Collegeville: Liturgical Press.

Hollerich, Michael. 2018. Do Catholic Theology Departments Have a Future?: A Response to Massimo Faggioli. *Commonweal*. Available online: https://www.commonwealmagazine.org/do-catholic-theology-departments-have-future (accessed on 29 July 2019).

Hughes, Kathleen. 2007. *Saying Amen: A Mystagogy of the Sacraments*. Chicago: Liturgical Training Publications.

Hughes, Kathleen. 2013. *Becoming the Sign: Sacramental Living in a Post-Conciliar Church*. Mahwah: Paulist Press.

International Commission on English in the Liturgy. 1990. Rite of Christian Initiation of Adults. In *The Rites of the Catholic Church. vol. 1*. Collegeville: Liturgical Press. First published 1988.

John Paul, Pope, II. 1988. *Christifideles laici*. Available online: http://w2.vatican.va/content/john-paul-ii/en/apost_exhortations/documents/hf_jp-ii_exh_30121988_christifideles-laici.html (accessed on 29 July 2019).

Johnson, Maxwell. 2007. *The Rites of Christian Initiation: Their Evolution and Interpretation*. Revised and Expanded Edition. Collegeville: Liturgical Press.

Lumen gentium. 1996. *Vatican Council II: The Basic Sixteen Documents*. Edited by Austin Flannery. Northport: Costello Publishing. First published 1964.

Mazza, Enrico. 1989. *Mystagogy: A Theology of Liturgy in the Patristic Age*. Collegeville: Liturgical Press.

McGrady, Katie Prejean. 2018. The synod on young people needs to listen to all voices—Catholic or not. *America Magazine*. Available online: https://www.americamagazine.org/faith/2018/03/29/synod-young-people-needs-listen-all-voices-catholic-or-not (accessed on 29 July 2019).

Morrill, Bruce. 2009. *Divine Worship and Human Healing: Liturgical Theology at the Margins of Life and Death.* Collegeville: Liturgical Press.

Ostdiek, Gilbert. 2015. *Mystagogy of the Eucharist: A Resource for Faith Formation.* Collegeville: Liturgical Press.

Pre-Synodal Meeting of Young People. 2018. Final Document from the Pre-Synodal Meeting. Available online: http://www.synod.va/content/synod2018/en/news/final-document-from-the-pre-synodal-meeting.html (accessed on 29 July 2019).

Rahner, Karl. 1982. Reflections on Methodology in Theology. In *Confrontations. Theological Investigations.* Translated by David Bourke. New York: Crossroad, vol. 11, pp. 68–114.

Saint Mary's Press of Minnesota and CARA. 2017. *Going, Going, Gone: The Dynamics of Disaffiliation in Young Catholics.* Winona: Saint Mary's Press.

United States Conference of Catholic Bishops. 2019. Synod 2018: Information and FAQs. Available online: http://www.usccb.org/about/bishops-and-dioceses/synod-of-bishops/synod-2018/synod-2018-information-and-faqs.cfm (accessed on 29 July 2019).

Vincie, Catherine. 2016. Mystagogical Preaching. In *A Handbook for Catholic Preaching.* Edited by Edward Foley. Collegeville: Liturgical Press, pp. 134–45.

Zenner, Christiana. 2018. *Just Water: Theology, Ethics, and Fresh Water Crises,* rev. ed. Maryknoll: Orbis.

Article

Obedience as Belonging: Catholic Guilt and Frequent Confession in America

Jonathan Stotts

Christ the King Catholic Church, Nashville, TN 37212, USA; j.a.stotts@gmail.com

Received: 19 April 2019; Accepted: 1 June 2019; Published: 5 June 2019

Abstract: From the late 19th to the mid-20th century, the practice of private confession to a priest was a mainstay of Catholic parish life in the United States. By the 1970s, Catholics had largely abandoned the practice of private confession. One dominant narrative among Catholic theologians and clergy, identified chiefly with the papacy of John Paul II, attributes the decline in confession to the loss of healthy guilt that took place during the cultural upheaval of the 1960s. In conversation with the work of psychologist and philosopher Antoine Vergote, the present article challenges this narrative, arguing that a collective and unhealthy Catholic guilt existed among American Catholics well before the 1960s and in fact characterized the period in which private confession was practiced most frequently. I contend that obedience to moral prescriptions was not, for ordinary Catholics, part of an ethical program of self-reform but the condition for belonging to a church body that emphasized obedience. Finally, examining the relationship between weekly reception of communion and confession, I suggest that private confession emerged to support frequent communion, persisting only until the latter became standard practice among Catholics in the United States.

Keywords: sacramental theology; Roman Catholic Church; confession; sacrament of penance; Catholic guilt; psychoanalysis; moral theology; history of Catholicism in the United States; frequent communion; Antoine Vergote

1. Introduction

In a 1953 address to an international meeting of psychotherapists and psychologists, Pope Pius XII warned that curing a patient's guilt feelings does not necessarily remove the moral fault that produced them. Nonetheless, the pontiff allowed for a distinction between a "healthy guilt," a person's sensitive awareness of having violated what is known to be a law given by God for our own good, and what he describes as "an irrational and even morbid sense of guilt" (Pius XII 1953, nos. 34–37). In making this distinction, Pius XII recognized in the psychoanalytic sciences grounds for a certain autonomy from theology and church governance, provided that analysts and clinicians take responsibility for the moral implications of any counsels they might offer to their patients and recognize the limits of their interventions.

Therapists and clergy share a common concern for human guilt, but they often diverge on its origins, its usefulness, and its prognosis. What was surely on the mind of Pius XII was the likelihood of confusion about the role of the psychotherapist and the role of the priest as confessor. The Roman Catholic Church for centuries had taught that sins are forgiven through the celebration of the sacrament of penance, popularly called "confession."[1] This ritual exchange, which was understood to mediate God's forgiveness and healing, consisted of an exchange between the penitent, who made a verbal,

---

[1] In accord with the decrees of the 4th Lateran Council, the 16th century Council of Trent affirmed that priests and bishops alone have the power to absolve individuals of mortal sins, and that individual confession and absolution is the ordinary and necessary means by which God effectively forgives sins.

usually brief, confession of specific wrongdoings, and the priest, who responded by assigning a short "penance," commonly the recitation of familiar prayers like the Hail Mary or Our Father, and then by speaking a formula of absolution. According to Catholic teaching, the priest's absolution, together with the penitent's contrition, objectively removes the guilt that the penitent had incurred through sin.

With the growing popularization of psychotherapy and clinical psychology, Catholic clergy and theologians had to contend with an ambiguity between guilt feelings and the assurance of forgiveness. As Pius XII pointed out, to cure guilt feelings by means of psychotherapy does not mean that the sins of the patient are forgiven. Conversely, a priest's absolution of a penitent in the confessional leaves open the possibility that feelings of guilt might remain. The pope's tentative solution was to make a distinction between a "healthy"—that is, rational—guilt that presumably was removed by private confession to a priest, and an irrational and unhealthy guilt that the priest's absolution could not remove and which might become the object of psychotherapeutic intervention. Confession for healthy guilt, therapy for unhealthy guilt.

Thirty years later, Pope John Paul II repeated his predecessor's warnings about unhealthy guilt in *Reconciliation and Penance*, an apostolic exhortation written in order to reaffirm for Catholics throughout the world the importance, indeed the necessity, of private confession to a priest (John Paul II 1984). The occasion for this document's promulgation was a 1983 synod of bishops convened to discuss a dramatic and, to many, threatening trend: since the latter half of the 1960s, Catholics all over the world, who by all accounts had been going to confession frequently and habitually, had abruptly abandoned the practice. In his exhortation, meant to serve as summary response to the synod's findings, John Paul II attributes the decline in confession to the widespread disappearance of what he terms a "sense of sin" among the Catholic faithful. Echoing Pius XII, John Paul II distinguishes this "sense of sin" from a "morbid feeling of guilt," and also from awareness of "the mere transgression of legal norms and precepts" (John Paul II 1984, no. 16). Ignoring the warnings of Pius XII, the growing therapeutic movement had stepped beyond its proper role in the treatment of pathological feelings, and a widespread preference for therapy over religion had contributed to an epidemic of unhealthy guilt. Pathological forms of moral awareness subsumed the proper role of an authentic and legitimate sense of guilt, in part due to the rise of modern psychology, but also to deficiencies within educational systems, family life, and the mass media. This massive cultural decline, said the pope, had precipitated a crisis in confession by attacking the sense of sin that had motivated Catholics to frequent the confessional for generations.

John Paul II identified this rapid decline of private confession with a corresponding crisis of healthy Catholic guilt, and for decades bishops, priests, and Catholic lay apologists have taken up the chorus.[2] Other theological evaluations of the crisis were mixed.[3] For instance, like John Paul II, Monika Hellwig, a prolific theologian who took part in the Second Vatican Council, blamed an overly therapeutic and ego-driven culture for the loss of healthy guilt, but she was less pessimistic about the decline of private confession (Hellwig 1982). Liturgical theologian James Dallen celebrated the decline as a moral coming of age in which people are finally replacing a futile and moralistic sense of guilt with healthy communal bonds (Dallen 1986). Priest and theologian David Coffey more soberly attributes the crisis in confession to a pedagogical failure on the part of the church to communicate a coherent understanding of sin in light of changes in moral theological thinking (Coffey 2001). What these otherwise diverging theological evaluations of sacrament penance all share is a conviction that something crucial had shifted, and that the shift had dramatic implications on psychological, cultural, and religious levels.[4]

---

[2] For just a handful of recent examples from the Catholic hierarchy, see (Tartaglia 2015; Benedict XVI 2011; United States Conference of Catholic Bishops 2013; Francis 2019).
[3] The theological literature on penance during this time period is expansive. For a sampling, see (Collins et al. 1987; Dallen 1986; Hellwig 1982; Mitchell 1978). For a more recent treatment, see (Coffey 2001).
[4] Moreover, all of the texts cited above call for insights from other fields of study to clarify and critique open theological questions about the sacrament of penance, mainly by explicitly requesting aid from scholars in fields like psychology, sociology, and anthropology, but also in their own attempts to draw on insights from these fields.

Thus, in this article, I want to evaluate the narrative about the decline of confession embodied in texts like John Paul II's *Reconciliation and Penance* by examining the significance and role of private confession in the cultural and psychological matrices of American Catholic life before the Second Vatican Council.[5] Adopting an approach to the distinction between healthy and unhealthy guilt based on the work of philosopher and psychologist Antoine Vergote, I will appraise the "sense of sin" cultivated among the Catholic laity from the 18th to the early 20th centuries, the period in which frequent private confession emerged. A careful examination of the rise of frequent private confession in early American Catholicism cannot support the claim that a widespread and healthy sense of sin had declined in favor of its pathological alternatives. Rather, by examining the ritualization of these guilt feelings with attention to the growing practice of frequent communion, I argue that private confession appealed to ordinary Catholics who accepted guilt as condition of belonging to a church that expressed the tension between sinfulness and moral purity in simplistic and juridical terms. As the reception of communion emerged as a constitutive aspect of weekly parish life, frequent confession offered the laity a way to negotiate the tension between their sense of unworthiness and their desire to receive the eucharist by allowing the ritual manifestation of obedience to substitute for purity.

2. Healthy and Unhealthy Guilt in Religious Practice

By invoking a distinction between healthy and unhealthy forms of guilt, Catholic religious authorities like Pius XII and John Paul II drew attention to shifting boundaries between psychological and religious perspectives on health, and they directed the Catholic faithful to allow religious belief, ritual, and practice to inform their ideas about healthy and unhealthy guilt feelings. In so doing, the hierarchy attempted to safeguard a practice that it considered vital on both religious and psychological grounds. Indeed, despite his reservations about the modern social sciences, John Paul recognized that further progress in understanding and evaluating the current status of Catholic penitential practice requires the participation of other disciplinary methods of inquiry like psychology (John Paul II 1984, p. 17). Hence, an effective concrete implementation of the church's pastoral and catechetical ministry of reconciliation requires a synthesis of Biblical and theological principles with "elements of psychology, sociology and the other human sciences, which can serve to clarify situations, describe problems accurately and persuade listeners or readers to make concrete resolutions" (John Paul II 1984, p. 26).[6]

Writing only two years after the publication of John Paul's letter, Dallen echoed the need for such inquiry, noting, "Few scholars have tried to relate the development of its liturgy and discipline to sociocultural factors in the Church and society or to concurrent developments in the experience and understanding of the Church community, redemption, baptism, eucharist, sin, grace, and so on" (Dallen 1986, p. 356). He goes on to ask, "how are we to theologize about penance without studying how believers have experienced and celebrated it?" (Dallen 1986, p. 357). This is a crucial question. As John Paul, Dallen, and Hellwig all observed, theologians must draw on the insights of social scientific study of the relationship of the sacrament of penance to the more fundamental human processes that it ritualizes. In neglecting to clarify basic assumptions about what it means to be human by means of critical cultural and psychological methods of inquiry, theological treatments of penance are unable to connect theological explanations of the sacrament to the subjective experience of the Catholics who actually use—or refuse—it.

---

[5] Bernard Lonergan argues that theology is an ongoing, collaborative, and dynamic process that "mediates between a cultural matrix and the significance and role of a religion in that matrix." See (Lonergan 2007).

[6] Hellwig echoes this point, arguing that theologians "must understand the problem [of sacramental penance] from historical, psychological, and theological perspectives, with a sober but ruthlessly honest commitment to the Roman Catholic tradition" (Hellwig 1982, p. 1). See (Morrill 2014) for a candid and insightful comparison of Hellwig's book and John Paul II's encyclical.

2.1. Vergote's Cultural Psychological Perspective on Religious Guilt

Because the kinds of guilt feelings involved in the history of private confession are enmeshed in individual thoughts, desires, aggressive impulses, and fears—what Sigmund Freud called the world of the unconscious—investigating these guilt feelings in context requires the adoption of a psychological perspective that does not methodologically foreclose religious or theological modes of inquiry, but that can illuminate how people in a given religious context appropriate theological discourse and practices for personal, often unconscious purposes. Describing such an approach, cultural psychologist Jacob Belzen points out:

> Accepting that culture is a major shaping force in self-definition, conduct, and experience, requires a different kind of research than is usual in mainstream psychology of religion … it becomes necessary to study not the isolated individual, but also the beliefs, values and rules that are prevalent in a particular situation, together with the patterns of social relatedness and interaction that characterize that situation. (Belzen 2001, p. 48)

Antoine Vergote, a Belgian psychoanalyst and philosopher who taught psychology and educational science at the Catholic University of Leuven, embodies such attentiveness to the psychological dynamics of social relatedness. Vergote's interdisciplinary appreciation for the insights of cultural anthropology, sociology, psychoanalysis, and philosophy provides a helpful methodological approach that can "yield insight into the psychic processes that are involved in and determined by [a] culturally given religion" (Belzen 2001, p. 53).

Against making quick and casual judgments about the relationship between religion, rite, and emotion, Vergote writes that we can correctly interpret "religious attitudes and behaviors psychologically only when we understand them as a conflict-solving process" (Vergote 1993, p. 83). Such a process necessarily brings the subject's "desires, disillusionments, revolves, anxieties, identification with models, evolving experiences, and so on" in dialogue with the opportunities presented or prohibited by religious forms (Vergote 1993, p. 83). This dialogue constitutes how "the subjects produce their own religious representations and belief dispositions" (Vergote 1993, p. 83). Vergote supplements philosophy with a culturally informed psychology, avoiding reductionist ways of thinking about the relationship between religion, culture, and psychodynamic phenomena, showing how health and pathology can coexist in the same religious milieu.

Expanding on an idea popularly attributed to Freud—namely, that healthy persons should be able to work and to love—Vergote identifies four features of human living that are constitutive of mental health. First, the ability to work, or to meaningfully adapt to and transform one's surroundings for the benefit of oneself and others. Second, the ability to use language flexibly and creatively to present oneself to the world and others in it. Third, the ability to love, or to desire and pursue intersubjective union. And fourth, the ability to enjoy pleasure. These four criteria interpenetrate and affect one another, and the failure of one cannot help but impinge on the functioning of the others (Vergote 1988, pp. 16–21).

Given these criteria, psychic pathology can refer to any self-mutilating process that solves some emotional conflict by closing down possibilities for work, love, communication, and enjoyment. Though Vergote attributes these properly to individuals, he suggests that these criteria might be extended to the level of collective or cultural pathology. Any religious context that "diminishes its members' opportunity to realize their human potential and favors individual pathologies" can be described as pathological, if only in an analogical sense (Vergote 1988, p. 31). Indeed, we easily can envision cultural milieu, especially religious milieu, that win some imagined peace by dissuading their practitioners from seeking to transform the world, from concern for the other, from the labor of putting words to experience, or from accepting the pleasures of life. Thus, to return to the distinction between unhealthy and healthy religious guilt, we might begin by saying that healthy guilt does not prevent those who experience it from fulfilling the four functions outlined above, while unhealthy guilt causes some impediment to one or more of these functions. But before moving on to examining the role of guilt in United States Catholic culture, it will be helpful to define it more clearly.

2.2. Vergote's Retrieval of Freudian Guilt

As scholar of religion and mental health Hermann Westerink convincingly argues, Sigmund Freud's entire corpus can be interpreted profitably as an attempt to trace guilt from its numerous clinical expressions, through the structure of the psyche, all the way to the origins of human consciousness (Westerink 2009a).[7] The cost of living amongst others involves what Sigmund Freud termed a generalized sense of guilt, the feeling that "I" am being observed and measured by something "over me," such that I am caught between what I want and what I ought to do.[8] Because this perception is not a continuous feeling, Freud argued that this generalized sense of guilt can remain largely unconscious, except for moments when it awakens into specific feelings like remorse or guilt-feelings. Freud's archaeological exploration thus interweaves two different deployments of the term guilt. One pertains to the psychic tension between drives and social morality as constitutive of the human ego. This is a psychoanalytic and explanatory term. The other, usually translated in Freud's writings as the "sense of guilt" or "guilt feelings," refers to the experience of suffering experienced by a majority of Freud's patients, an experience thought by Freud to result from the theorized and largely unconscious psychic structure of guilt. Thus, guilt feelings are the result how psychic consciousness structures itself between desirous instinct and moralistic expectation.

In a retrieval of Freud that both learned from and challenged psychoanalyst Jacques Lacan's similar return, Vergote develops Freud's examination of guilt in light of the contributions of European phenomenological scholars like Martin Heidegger, Claude Levi-Strauss, and Maurice Merleau-Ponty. Beginning from the Freudian assumption that individual subjectivity is formed in a small social field constituted by multiple lines of force and appeal, Vergote argues that a subject's ongoing acceptance and rejection of these phenomena, together with the consequences of that subject's relationships (their acceptance or defense against the subject's decisions) create a psychic reality that already shapes the subject's future encounters (Vergote 1988, p. 23). For Vergote, the psychic dimensions of desire and debt are fundamental aspects of human subjectivity. By desire, he means, in my own loose terminology, the longing for satisfaction as it is structured and limited within language and culture. By debt, Vergote means the way that relational obligations shape how we understand what we should want and what we owe to others, constituting our dependence on the cultural and symbolic order for identity.[9]

Guilt is thus simultaneously culturally and psychologically constituted. As a psychological phenomenon, guilt signals the appraisal of one's subjective value according to some internalized way of evaluating the relationship of the self to some other or others.[10] The dynamic negotiation of relational and libidinal forces creates what we can somewhat more usefully term the moral conscience, which describes the person in the midst of weighing, sometimes discursively and sometimes intuitively, the possibilities afforded within the context of desires and obligations. As Vergote notes, "The moral conscience does not exist in anyone from the beginning, but is created in the acceptance of the necessity

---

[7] See also (Speziale-Bagliacca 2004). Speziale-Bagliacca writes, "Sigmund Freud never actually wrote a book dedicated entirely to guilt, but the various comments he made on the subject throughout his work make him the true initiator of the study of the sense of guilt and certainly the first person to approach the question systematically" (Speziale-Bagliacca 2004, p. 1).

[8] In his own words, "the perception which the ego has of being watched over in this way, the assessment of the tension between its own strivings and the demands of the super-ego." See (Freud 1962, p. 83).

[9] The influence of Jacques Lacan, under whom Vergote studied, is evident in his appeal to Lacan's distinction between the imaginary and symbolic orders as he makes his own interpretative return to Freud. For a discussion of Vergote's debt to Lacan, see (Westerink 2009b, pp. 213–45).

[10] Contemporary appraisal theories of emotion confirm this. One classic clinical psychological treatment of guilt as an emotional appraisal is (Tangney and Dearing 2004). See also (Tracy and Robins 2006). For a more psychoanalytic approach, see (Lewis 1971).

of the prohibition of desire" (Vergote et al. 1998, p. 82).[11] Conscience, as the source of persons' valuing and devaluing of themselves in context of bodily and relational embeddedness, describes the power of subjects to position themselves with respect to symbolic value, an interpersonal and meaning-laden judgment, and not simply with respect to satisfaction, the achievement of some pursued pleasure.[12] Feelings of guilt, then, do not signify the suffering that comes from the failure to attain a wished-for pleasure but rather the failure to uphold our obligations. We are unsatisfied with respect to our own desires, but we are guilty with respect to our ties to the other.

Thus, as a cultural phenomenon, guilt becomes possible when our perceived obligations to others are internalized as an authoritative standard for personal appraisal. These obligations can take many forms, like "What my father wants of me," or "What I am not allowed to have," and whether or not they are accurate approximations of what actual other people expect has little bearing on their psychological force. Moral standards are acquired largely by unconscious imitation as adaptive responses to real problems and to perceived expectations, and their ongoing influence is subject to the test of interpersonal experience. Guilt feelings are evidence of the internalization, or the felt sense, of the authoritative relationships that have become constitutive aspects of personal identity. Because of this, the emergence of healthy or pathological guilt must depend, in large part, on how our moral authorities support and nurture our ability to work, communicate, love, and appreciate pleasure.

In his psychoanalytic exploration of the structure of guilt, Vergote provides examples of what he calls a "religious neurosis of culpability," or religious guilt neurosis, a pattern of irrational behavior in which a person expresses an unconsciously held obsession over her or his own guilt by means of the religious symbols, rituals and discourse available (Vergote 1988, p. 48). Unable to resolve or even speak directly about a mostly hidden conflict, someone suffering from religious guilt neurosis can only recognize the threatening power of internalized guilt in images and practices that resonate with this power. Religious neurotics obsess about the requirements of ritual purity, about their own unworthiness, or about the dangerous closeness of an all-powerful, all-knowing divine power. None of these religious signifiers can directly articulate a neurotic person's actual conflict; rather, they maintain it in a careful equilibrium with the rest of life as a partially successful problem-solving mechanism.[13]

2.3. Collective Guilt and Religious Neurosis

Vergote reasons from the existence of individual religious guilt neurosis to the possibility of a cultural situation that, while not directly causing neurosis in all its subjects, nevertheless disposes them to suffer the general effects of a repressive or unhealthy sense of guilt. He terms this milieu a "collective neurosis," borrowing from Freud's use of the phrase to describe religion in general.[14] But while not all members of a collective neurosis become neurotic themselves, a repeated overemphasis on the significance of human sinfulness in the language and practice of a religious culture tends to inspire one of three possible responses: creative forms of subversion, total or partial withdrawal, or something of a capitulation to symptoms of obsessional neurosis.

Drawing our attention to a prime example of collective neurosis, Vergote reminds his readers of "the record of a religious education that holds sexuality in abeyance, represses all violence, and exalts

---

11   As Vergote goes on to insist, "Prohibition and judgment of condemnation are not synonymous" (Vergote et al. 1998, p. 82). To prohibit desires is not necessarily to identify them as radically evil but rather to identify the impossibility of their attaining anything of value of themselves. It is to recognize the emptiness of doing what one wants without any doubt or clarification or demand for reasonableness in the midst of others.

12   Cognitive psychologist Michael Lewis elaborates a developmental model that takes this distinction into account in (Lewis 2000). For a philosophical approach to the distinction between satisfaction and value, see (Lonergan 2007, pp. 31–32).

13   References to "scrupulosity" in traditional Catholic confessional theology share much in common with what Vergote describes as religious guilt neurosis.

14   Vergote employs the notion of "collective neurosis" in part to criticize Freud's interpretation of religion on the grounds that Freud elevated the pathological instances of religion, rather than its healthy manifestations, as his psychological paradigm for religious patients. While Freud gives a nod to the possibility of a healthy-minded religious outlook, he spends little time examining the conditions of healthy religion. See (Vergote et al. 1998, pp. 17–37). For a similar argument, see (Rizzuto 1979).

the idea of self-mastery," with specific references to the dangers of and risks associated with sexuality (Vergote et al. 1998, p. 73). He traces the troublesome effects of pre-Vatican II Catholic moral theological discourse and practice on the individual psyches of Catholics, whether they were specifically neurotic or merely diminished in their capacity for love, work, communication, or enjoyment by "a form of Christianity whose message becomes concentrated on the consciousness of sin and whose larger aims are reduced to the constant struggle against sin" (Vergote et al. 1998, p. 73). For inhabitants of this milieu, failures to uphold the standards of absolute purity in the realm of the imagination, to say nothing of the realm of human action, incurred the psychological equivalent of heavy taxation.

Vergote substantiated Freud's exploration of obsessive neurosis and confirmed the problematic status of the practice of private confession for individuals haunted by an aggravated sense of guilt. But Vergote disagreed that all who practice such rituals are necessarily neurotic. On the contrary, guilt belongs to human subjectivity itself: to be a human self is to be fundamentally and non-pathologically conflicted, torn between the push of desires and the pull of obligations. The question before us is whether the culture surrounding the practice of frequent confession was emblematic of a "healthy guilt," such that revisiting the practice of frequent confession might promote a religious culture predicated on and generally supportive of the harmonious interplay of a society of relatively healthy individuals. An affirmative answer to this question might justify the narrative about the decline of confession found in John Paul II's *Reconciliation and Penance*, while a negative answer will call into question the link between the decline and a corresponding loss of a healthy sense of sin.

Thus, in what follows, I want to evaluate the practice of frequent confession in 19th and early 20th century Catholicism in the United States by probing the relationship of its moral and cultural surroundings to just one of the four criteria outlined at the beginning of this section: namely, the ability of Catholics to express themselves creatively and authentically through the religious and moral discourse available to them through their participation in Catholic parish life. Within this milieu, Catholics made use of the various elements of their relio-cultural world, including a moral language centered on obedience and purity and the spiritual authority of an institutional priesthood, to renegotiate their place, their sense of agency, and their identity. By examining this culture in greater detail, we then will understand why it might have been helpful for ordinary Catholics to practice frequent confession. Furthermore, we will see also that the culture in which frequent confession became a popular practice severely inhibited the ability of Catholics to describe, accurately and honestly, their moral experiences in favor of a simplified moral discourse. Far from emerging as an effect of mid-20th century factors, unhealthy guilt was alive and well among Catholics before the cultural revolution of the 1960s.

3. The World of Catholic Guilt

The local parish was the heart of American Catholicism, the locus of the struggles of immigrant and American-born Catholics alike to forge an identity out the customs of their old country and the values of a predominantly northern European Protestantism. By the beginning of the nineteenth century, there were barely over a hundred Catholic parish churches in the United States (Dolan 2002, pp. 29–30). By 1860, churches full of Irish and German immigrants spread throughout New England, then south and west into Kentucky, Ohio, and Tennessee, with over three million Catholics making it the largest Christian denomination in the United States (Dolan 2002, p. 58). Despite their numbers, Catholics did not perceive themselves to be a particularly powerful social force. On the contrary, antebellum hostility for Catholic immigrants and their native counterparts spread throughout the country, prompting Roman Catholics to emphasize their differences and develop resources for maintaining their identity.[15]

---

[15] In a recent publication, historian Patrick W. Carey provides an exhaustive examination of the process by which American Catholic clergy and theologians sought to defend and explain the practice of sacramental confession in light of wider Protestant polemic. See (Carey 2018).

The rhetoric of Catholic preaching and teaching during the late 19th century testifies to what scholar of religions Ann Taves describes as the "creation of an enclosed Catholic subculture" designed to defend itself "as a beleaguered minority banding together to protect itself from the attacks of its enemies" (Taves 1986, p. 128). The parish and the subculture that surrounded it was, for many Catholics, a haven in the midst of a resentment that was as much religious as it was political. But the parish also served as a base from which American Catholicism could begin a long process of negotiation with the wider public that viewed it with suspicion and contempt.[16]

Forming the weekly core of parish practice was the celebration of the Mass, whose primary agent was the parish priest. Intoned in Latin with only a modicum of active responses from the participating laity, the Mass as a complex whole signified for many Catholics the mystery of a God who saves people by providing them with a redemptive ritual and men to offer it on their behalf, a ritual that required little comprehension on their part for it to be effective. Belonging to the church of the priests and maintaining the sense of such belonging throughout the vicissitudes of daily life was the key to pleasing God and enjoying the eventual rewards of heaven. Numerous and diverse devotional practices inside and outside the parish grounds—processions, praying the Rosary, novenas, to name just a few—fostered an integration of faith into daily life and strengthened Catholics' sense of identity (Taves 1986).

Communion, receiving from the priest the body and blood of Jesus under the appearance of bread and wine, was the fullest way of participating in the Mass. But for centuries reception of communion had been reserved in practice to the clergy, who were ritually obliged to receive, and to those in vowed religious life. The mystery and holiness ascribed to the sacrament coextended with a sense that only the worthiest might approach without fear. Most of the Catholic laity, encouraged to view themselves with suspicion and the reception of holy communion as reserved for the most pure, communed no more than once a year, an obligation laid down in 1215 by the Fourth Lateran Council. From a certain theological perspective, this arrangement was acceptable; according to the canons of the Council of Trent it was beneficial enough just to be in the presence of the sacrament with a living faith.[17] Those who did receive communion were expected to go to confession beforehand. As Catholics learned from grade school onward, no one conscious of a mortal sin dared, on pains of Hell, to receive communion, and only through the absolving powers of the priest in the confessional could one be freed of mortal sin.

The emphasis on mortal sin here is significant. The principle purpose of sacramental confession, according to Tridentine theology, is to restore the justifying grace lost through mortal sin, without which the sinner is cut off from church and God. The Council of Trent had ratified a distinction between two kinds of sin, venial and mortal. The damage done through venial sins, minor failures that do not entail a complete turning away from God, could be repaired through any number of satisfactory acts on the part of the Christian (prayer, going to church, giving alms, fasting). In contrast, mortal sins, whose seriousness merits the loss of God's indwelling grace given in baptism, required the mediation of the hierarchical ministry of the church. In other words, sacramental confession was the only means by which a Christian who had sinned mortally could be reunited to God.

Moreover, the Council of Trent insisted that sacramental confession is only valid if penitents confess *all* mortal sins of which they are conscious; this was termed "integral confession" (Coffey 2001, pp. 101–7).[18] In practice, the theological complexity of the distinction between mortal and venial

---

[16] Dolan describes the Catholic response as "a siege mentality" in the midst of "a nativist crusade" that "subjected Catholics to intense discrimination." See (Dolan 2002, p. 64).

[17] The Council of Trent distinguished three ways of receiving communion. Sinners (those without faith or those receiving in an unworthy state) received only "sacramental" communion, the consecrated host bereft of any positive spiritual effects. The lay faithful majority received "spiritual" communion by being in the presence of the sacrament with an attitude of faith and reverence. A third minority received it both spiritually and sacramentally. See (Council of Trent 1848, p. 81).

[18] My explanation here is cursory and skips over several important caveats and distinctions. For a basic treatment of the distinction between mortal and venial sin in the context of penance, see (Coffey 2001, pp. 9–14). For a more extended historical elaboration, see (Mahoney 1987).

sin, however valid such a distinction might be in its own right, made it difficult for lay persons to be completely certain which sins were venial and which sins were mortal, resulting in a pressure to confess them all, just to be safe. All the foregoing did much to support a climate of moral suspicion and scrupulosity throughout Roman Catholic parish life in Europe and, by extension, in the United States. It was assumed that the Catholic laity had to work tremendously hard to avoid committing a mortal sin, and because inevitably they would, local clergy made recourse to the sacrament of confession readily available.

3.1. Preoccupation with Sin as Disobedience

The dominant moral theology of the Catholic world, in the United States and elsewhere, was centered on the avoidance of personal sin. As moral theologian John Mahoney argues, the moral theology that evolved alongside and in support of private confession was "heavily responsible for increasing men's weakness and moral apprehension, with the strong sense of sin and guilt which it so thoroughly strove to inculcate or reinforce, and the humiliations and punishments with which it drove its message home" (Mahoney 1987, p. 28). Even while the number of Catholic going to confession was relatively low, the moral formation of the Catholic laity was an education in how to go to confession, just as the moral formation of the Catholic clergy centered on how to hear confessions.

In the emerging political arena of the European (and later, the American) nation-state, an understanding of sin in terms of law-breaking came to dominate Roman Catholic moral language (Mahoney 1987, p. 28). Drawing on the influence and meaningfulness of political institutions built on philosophical presuppositions about the necessity of law in the face of social chaos, a widespread understanding sin as law-breaking was embedded within compatible understandings of authority, power, and legal jurisdiction. Indeed, in a rejection of the medieval teleological tradition of moral reasoning that grounded reasons for acting in embodied human relationality, what counted as sin for Catholics in early modernity was determined not by the process of communal reasoning but by hearing the word of God and obeying.[19]

Sin language that appealed to the importance of law and order drew its rhetorical power from cultural and political upheaval, but embedded in this discourse are significant assumptions about the relationship of humans to one another and to God, assumptions that especially permeated the sacrament of confession. The embodiment of a moralistic and legalistic tradition in Catholic moral teaching and practice, above all in the formation of priests and the training of Catholics to go to confession, provided post-Tridentine Roman Catholicism with an understanding of the Christian life based almost entirely on notions of willpower, obedience, and clerical authority. Indeed, as Dolan argues, early American "enlightenment Catholicism," a generally optimistic and rationalist moral theology, was quickly displaced by the influences of first a French and later an Irish style of Catholicism that, despite their liturgical and devotional differences, were united by a common skepticism about human freedom and an emphasis on fear as a means of inciting moral obedience (Dolan 2002, pp. 39–40).

Catholic philosopher Charles Taylor's 2007 *A Secular Age*, a painstaking exploration of the relationship of religious identity to emerging forms of secularism, pays careful attention to the role of this kind of moral discourse in early modern Catholic culture (Taylor 2007). Taylor shows that despite maintaining a degree of separation from the Reformed and Puritan claims that Christians might achieve a positive assurance of their salvation, the pastoral ministries of the Roman Catholic church in North America and Europe tended nevertheless to emphasize certain clearly understandable

---

[19] The reasons for the gradual erosion of teleological ethics in the face of deontology are complicated. Mahoney locates it in the influence of the Spanish Jesuit theologian Francisco Suarez, whose emphasis on God's will as expressed specifically in the laws known through natural reasoning and divine revelation significantly shaped Catholic moral theology (Mahoney 1987, p. 226). An alternative, or perhaps complementary, explanation might be suggested by cultural historian Jean Delumeau's *Sin and Fear: The Emergence of a Western Guilt Culture*, which traces through sermon, art, and religious practice of Europe a growing internalization of the fear of death (Delumeau 1990). Philosopher Alasdair MacIntyre provides his own neo-Aristotelian interpretation of this shift in numerous places; in particular, see (MacIntyre 1984).

moral standards. These moral standards served not as "signs of election, but minimal conformity to the demands of God: the avoidance of mortal sin, or at least doing whatever is necessary to have these sins remitted" (Taylor 2007, p. 497). Sinning mortally placed one in a state of radical disobedience before God, such that one was assured of going to Hell were one to die before going to confession. Avoiding Hell as a penalty for mortal sin through obeying the moral law as communicated by the prescriptions of the church constituted the main vocation of Catholics, and it was an extraordinary layperson who sought a moral or spiritual world beyond minimal conformity to the church's ecclesial and ethical injunctions.[20]

3.2. Catholic Moral Reasoning

As I mentioned above, church law required penitents to make an "integral confession," the precise identification of each mortal sin of which one was conscious, noting its category and the number of times it was committed. Catholics were taught from childhood that to omit a single mortal sin had the effect of rendering the entire confession invalid, and so church pedagogy trained Catholics to categorize their actions according to a binary system of "grave" or "mortal" sins, which must be confessed, and "venial" sins, which might be confessed but did not have to be. But viewed in light of experience, the objective gravity of certain sins deemed by the church to be mortal often was somewhat confusing. Sins like murder or adultery were one thing, but to include missing Mass on a Sunday or failing to uphold the Friday fast in the church's list of mortal sins created for the laity a high degree of uncertainty around the distinction between mortal and venial sins. As Mahoney remarks, "in its attaching the element of sin so readily in the past to positive church laws on frequently trivial matters as a sanction to their observance, it has only helped to devalue the currency, and done little to engender and foster a healthy respect for real sin" (Mahoney 1987, p. 32). By emphasizing the danger of determining such complicated matters by oneself, confessional training encouraged Catholics simply to confess everything that might be sinful in the confident assurance that the priest's absolution would cover it all: when in doubt, confess it.

Furthermore, the content of Catholic moral codes tended to focus predominantly on the dangers of the misuse of human sexual faculties. Though he offers some speculation as to the causes of this focus, absent as it was for the most part throughout the pre-Reformation middle ages, Taylor limits himself to the objective observation that in comparison to other kinds of desire, sexual desire became for modern Catholics a special province of mortal sin:

> [Y]ou could go quite far in being unjust and hard-hearted in your dealings with subordinates and others, without incurring the automatic exclusion you incur by sexual license. Sexual deviation, and not listening to the church, seemed to be the major domains where automatic excluders lurked. Sexual purity, along with obedience, were therefore given extraordinary salience. (Taylor 2007, p. 498)

Taylor correctly identifies the explicitly sexual focus of the moral codes, made available to pastors through confessional manuals, which marked the Catholic moral theological discourses predominant in Europe and North America. Though we have very little data on the sexual lives of the Catholic laity themselves, evidence abounds for the clergy's suspicion of sexual pleasure during this time. While priests and bishops recognized that marital sex was good insofar as it was the means by which humanity participated in God's creation of new humans, the pleasure involved in procreation was viewed largely as a danger to the Christian moral life. Consecrated celibacy was recognized to be the purest state attainable in this life, and the closer that the laity could approximate this ideal, the

---

[20] Similarly, Mahoney observes, "As a consequence of this commitment to spiritual pathology, the discipline of moral theology was to relinquish almost all consideration of the good in man to other branches of theology, notably to what became known as spiritual theology" (Mahoney 1987, p. 27). This included all forms of pastoral care in parish contexts.

more holy they might become.[21] Indeed, it was often advised that married people abstain from sexual relations before receiving holy communion for fear that the remnants of sexual desire might pollute the sacrament. According to these assumptions, surveillance and control of sexual desire offered to Catholics the central battle for their souls, and because each and every offense constituted grave sin, the sacrament of confession provided the only opportunity for purification.[22]

As Taylor argues, the emphasis on sexuality likely contributed to the relative dearth of men in the confessional even during the period of frequent confession: the double presence of a celibate male authority and the necessity of speaking about "the most reserved and intimate facet of their lives" presented an almost insurmountable obstacle (Taylor 2007, p. 499). However, Catholic moral theology's suspicion of sexuality was but the most visible symptom of a much deeper suspicion of human instinctuality itself. Not only sexual desire but also impulses born of aggression fell under moral suspicion and censorship. Hence, Taylor single out both sexual disorder and refusal to listen to ecclesial authority as constitutive of an automatic exclusion from communion with the church. Moral purity and obedience to the church were assumed to flow from the same condition of soul.

Here we might see a certain parallel between the moral reasoning that Catholics employed in the confessional and what Lonergan has identified as a decadent Scholasticism governing Roman Catholic theological thought (Lonergan 2007, p. 80). However theologically correct the conclusions of the manuals used in seminary education, the transmission of their content to the faithful through popular literature and preaching was not intended to convey a style of theological reasoning but in establishing the correct truths to be believed and the correct precepts to be followed.[23] Even if the prescriptions of the moral manuals were the relatively trustworthy results of careful moral theological casuistry, Catholic morality as taught ordinary Catholics presented these prescriptions as though they were handed down in their present intelligible form by God, such that any difficulties in following them reflected solely the recipients' moral weakness. Hence, an attitude of obedience was deemed to be more trustworthy than a spirit of critical inquiry into the reasoning behind the church's moral law.

3.3. Catholic Guilt

In summary, Catholic culture in the United States during the 19th and 20th centuries fostered a suspicious view of human aggression and desire on the one hand and a carefully structured, rational system of moral guidelines and positivist principles on the other. Such an emphasis on obedience to the positive moral law as promulgated by the teaching authority of the church effectively cultivated and maintained in the Catholic faithful a division between reason, specifically the reasoning power of the church as divinely inspired, and desire, specifically understood in terms of concupiscence. For the laity, the ease with which it was possible to violate the positive laws of the church was evidence enough of the dubious legitimacy of their own everyday desires on moral theological grounds, and the opacity of these laws themselves demonstrated the failure of reason that made the faithful dependent on an infallible church for guidance. Catholic subjects were thus caught in a double bind, taught to trust neither their own reason, nor their desires, but to confirm their wills in obedience to the benevolent authority of the church.

Looking at the historical data, we thus can confirm that the culture of Roman Catholicism in the United States in the late 19th and early 20th centuries—the world of frequent confession—indeed manifested what Vergote calls a collective guilt neurosis, a phenomenon so well known that it has

---

[21] For historical analysis of this state of affairs, see (Tentler 2004, pp. 19–23). For instance, while priests preached and counseled from a generally positive view of marriage, they also encouraged married couples to abstain from sexual relations during significant periods of the church year, imitating those in clerical and religious life (Tentler 2004, p. 20).

[22] For an extensive theological and historical discussion of Catholic theology and sexual ethics during this time period, see (Curran 2008).

[23] On this point, see (Jordan 2006).

its own name: "Catholic guilt."[24] One of the primary symptoms of this culture was the inability of its participants to use its language in authentic and meaningful communication, particularly with reference to their desires and their obligations. The church as paternal authority provided conditions for purity based primarily on a suspicion of desire and an emphasis on obedience. By all accounts, the great majority of the Catholic faithful were not, in fact, neurotic. Though this culture's preoccupation with legalism, moral purity, and individual effort surely fostered Catholics suffering from guilt neurosis, its more general effect was to cultivate a wider malaise with respect to the very possibility of achieving and maintaining a high degree of moral purity. This work was left largely to priests, to those in religious life, and perhaps to the religiously inclined and pious laypersons. Those who did strive for moral purity had to deal with the vicissitudes of perfectionism and moral rigorism; whatever theoretical and objective status they attained was bought at the cost of significant psychological conflict.

4. Ritualizing Catholic Guilt During the Rise of Frequent Communion

Catholics inherited the culture of Catholic guilt and collaborated in its maintenance for centuries, passing its language and obligations on to their children, without, however, feeling the need to confess their sins frequently to priests. However, in the late 19th century, Catholics in the United States began to confess their sins at an unprecedented rate, a trend that continued until the late 1960s.[25] What changed? In the final section of this article, I will argue that the emergence of frequent reception of communion among the laity reconfigured their relationship to private confession. As the reception of communion became a viable and meaningful religious practice for the laity, it initially fostered the accompanying practice of frequent confession within a culture of collective guilt, only eventually to supplant it.

4.1. The Rise of Frequent Communion

As I indicated above, before the 20th century the Catholic laity in the United States and throughout the world rarely received communion at Mass. And as long as the reception of communion was portrayed as something for a spiritual elite, the number of Catholics who made use of either sacrament, communion or the confession that was expected to precede it, remained relatively small. But in the early 20th century, Pope Pius X challenged this longstanding practice as part of a series of liturgical reforms, encouraging the laity to receive communion weekly, or even daily, so long as they were free from mortal sin.[26] In an effort to implement the papal decree, as Joseph Dougherty painstakingly demonstrates in his landmark 2010 study, a long and ultimately successful campaign of Catholic church leaders, associations, and educators in the mid-19th century established weekly communion as the norm for the laity in the United States (Dougherty 2010, pp. 111–37). Catholics began to receive the Eucharist at the weekly Sunday Mass in great numbers. What did not change was the assumption that the laity needed to go to confession before they received communion. When the practice of receiving communion was rare, so was the need to confess. Frequent communion, however, required frequent confession, and priests in the United States began to hear confessions at an unprecedented rate (O'Toole 2004, pp. 134–48).

The success of the campaign for frequent communion promised the Catholic faithful a ritualized means acceptance in the eyes of God and church, and Catholics flocked to the confessional in order to gain access to the body of Christ. As we saw above, the confessional box normally was not the site of radical conversion, nor did it seem to be a particularly egregious source of suffering for those who

---

[24] Indeed, Catholic guilt even has its own Wikipedia page (Catholic Guilt 2019).
[25] Carey provides a detailed overview of the increase in confessions during this time period. See (Carey 2018, pp. 165–98).
[26] The 1905 decree Sacra Tridentina Synodus spells out Pius X's defense of frequent communion against a poisonous rigorism that, "under the pretext of showing due honor and reverence to the Eucharist, had infected the minds even of good men" (Sacred Congregation of the Council 1905). See (Dougherty 2010, pp. 81–110) for a careful analysis of this decree in the context of Pius X's papacy.

made use of it. Rather, it was a necessary, and in hindsight temporary, hurdle, allowing Catholics to demonstrate the obedience that made them worthy to receive communion.

As we saw above, the moral reasoning made available to ordinary Catholics in the United States tended to emphasize the importance of doubt, not as a mitigating factor, but as an indicator that one really ought to confess. Thus, in the mind of the American Catholic, going to confession before going to communion was understood to be absolutely necessary, for to do otherwise was to commit the sin of presumption. In this way, then, a logic developed according to which not going to confession became itself a sign of sin, perhaps the sign of sin in one's life, a refusal to submit one's desires to the power of the church. Put more simply, ordinary Catholics went to confession when the cost of not going to confession became too high, and only secondarily because they were overly concerned with having committed this or that sin.

The new possibility of weekly communion raised the stakes, so to speak, for what it meant to belong to the church. So long as the Catholic laity were content only to fulfill their Easter duty, a phrase used to describe the canonical requirement that all Catholics confess and commune once a year, there was little pressure to confess and, by extension, to have something to confess. But with the normalization of frequent communion and the assumed purity required to receive it, a Catholic's willingness to go to confession became itself a kind of moral barometer for one's worthiness to approach the communion rail. To refuse to go to confession, even if one was not conscious of mortal sin, suggested the possibility of a disobedient attitude toward the church and thus toward God, an attitude that was ritualized in the act of remaining in the pew while others received holy communion.

4.2. Good Enough Catholics

Despite the climate of collective guilt that characterized this period, strong suspicions around sexual desire or aggressive behavior did not scare ordinary Catholics into a state of chastity and meekness but rather produced a state of heightened anxiety as the cost of belonging to the church. Catholics sinned, and sinned frequently. The confessional data we have from the time period reveals that the sins commonly confessed were banal, often sexual in nature, and habitual.[27] For most Catholics, frequent confession did not provide a setting conducive to true repentance, if by that we mean the cessation of specific sins. Rather, it provided the means to maintain a good-enough conscience before a God whose standards were impossibly high but whose benevolence allowed obedience to substitute for purity. The local clergy were positioned to recognize, with an authority subsidized by the laity, the obedience that constituted penitents as good-enough-Catholics—good enough, that is, to receive communion. A dialectic of frequent confession and frequent communion thus facilitated the ongoing maintenance of a felt sense of belonging in exchange for a taxation on pleasure and the willingness to confess one's guilt according to a reductive and legalistic moral framework.

Participation in this world meant accepting, to some extent, the church's fear of instinctual pleasures, at least in terms of the ability to frame moral language around it. The emergence of frequent confession required a sense of ritual literacy that allowed Catholics to quickly name easily identifiable sins, without ever learning how to decipher their latent content within a theological context. In terms of their overall religious health, the world of frequent confession presented a challenge to the ability of Catholics to express themselves authentically. It viewed with great suspicion the enjoyment of normal pleasures and cast doubt on the ability of the laity to flourish spiritually. The Catholic laity accepted these impediments to healthy religious practice in exchange for a sense of belonging, of identity, and for sacramental access to God.

---

[27] For a thorough presentation of this data, see (O'Toole 2004, pp. 131–86). Among many such examples, O'Toole cites one priest as complaining, "We could teach a parakeet or myna bird to say the words" of the many confessions he was accustomed to hearing (O'Toole 2004, p. 168).

Frequent confession became, for a time, a constitutive part of the world of Catholic guilt, and through confession Catholics upheld this world—but they also appear to have subverted it. By enacting the features of the moral landscape in which they found themselves frequently and in great numbers, the Catholic laity ritually performed both to themselves and the clergy the limitations of the practice of confession and its cultural context. The laity were willing to submit themselves to the discipline of the confessional, and they were willing to use the moral material at hand. Absent egregious transgression or a consistent program of self-inventory and reform, what was left to the laity to confess but hosts of minor behavioral issues that were somehow associated with not being quite good enough? Ritualizing this guilt, a sense of not being quite good enough, permitted Catholics to feel worthy enough to approach the communion rail.

4.3. Frequent Confession for Unhealthy Guilt

Was such an attitude a manifestation of a healthy sense of guilt? In the first part of this article, I argued that one of the psychological signs of unhealthy religious practice is the inability to communicate one's experience to others through the play of language available. As Vergote explains, "if a religious language fails to hold a possible meaning for others, or if it radically shatters the structure of language, or if it is no longer consonant with the reality envisioned, we may justifiably identify it as a pathological product of a religious consciousness" (Vergote 1988, p. 18). The foregoing analysis reveals that the juridical and legalistic moral culture surrounding frequent confession impeded the ability of Catholics to conceive of and translate their experiences into accurate and meaningful moral theological language. The moral language made available to the Catholic laity from the pulpit and parochial system was juridical and oversimplified, intended to identify express violations of the church's rules in order to adjudicate a layperson's status before God and church. Thus, as historian James O'Toole reports, "many parishioners complained increasingly that their confessions never touched on genuinely serious moral or spiritual matters. If, as the proverb maintained, the law was not concerned with trifles, confession often seemed to be concerned only with trifles, and the perfunctory nature of much of it was unsatisfying" (O'Toole 2004, p. 168). To return to John Paul II's own language, the culture of frequent confession promoted a sense of sin fixated with "the mere transgression of legal norms and precepts," a clear sign of unhealthy guilt by his own criteria (John Paul II 1984, no. 16). This state of affairs encouraged in ordinary Catholics a division between the world of the church, in which moral matters were a matter of what the church said was sinful and what was not, and the world of everyday life, in which decisions were messy, obligations complicated, and moral theology irrelevant.

The net effect of this division was to encourage the Catholic laity to articulate their sins as a violation of rules, rules whose justification lay in church's spiritual power over subjects identified by their obedience. Verbal confession within the culture of frequent confession served to express the penitent's disobedience before God and the Church. The content of the confession—the specific sins—was less important than the act of confessing itself. *That* the penitent confesses before the priest reestablished her or him as acceptable to God, and the priest's words of absolution provide the formal and effective acceptance of the penitent's confessing act. For ordinary penitents, the achievement of the sacrament of penance was in mustering the will to confess, to overcome the reluctance that spelled disobedience. Worse than any actual sin was the refusal to confess sin itself. This, then, is the infamous "Catholic guilt" at work: Catholics confessed because they were guilty, and they were guilty not because they sinned in this or that way but because their very constitution as desiring subjects demonstrated a resistance to law that the surrounding religious culture associated with sin. Absolution was not the removal of guilt, for this did not disappear. Absolution was the removal of the condition of having not confessed, that is, of disobedience.

Confession, then, answered the self-doubt created in the midst of unhealthy guilt with an ecclesially sanctioned assurance that depended only on the penitent's willingness to manifest obedience by confessing any sins of which he or she was aware and promising to avoid them in the future. A mostly unconscious internalization of God together with church and clerical authority, this sense of guilt tied Catholics to the church in ways analogous to how fear of failing one's parents can tie children to the family's unspoken or spoken rules. God, for such Catholics, was mediated by and contacted solely through the clergy. The effect of the church's expectations, as perceived by the laity in a moral climate of suspicion and guilt, was to facilitate and maintain a constant anxiety in the face of confession and to promote an attitude of ambivalent obedience. This suggests that normal Catholics confessed their sins not because of the gravity of the sins themselves but because not to confess—to withhold confession—was implicitly to consent to a disobedience that marked them as disobedient, no longer good-enough Catholics.

For early American Catholics, the distinction between church and God was barely visible for the laity. God lay on the other side of the church, beyond the horizon of the church's liturgies, disciplines, feasts, and, for the laity, beyond the horizon of death and the time of purgatory that awaited the just-good-enough Catholic. Being recognized by the church was as close to being recognized by God as was fitting for Catholics pilgrimaging through this life's vale of tears. The crises of the postwar years and the rise of weekly communion together effected a gradual loosening of the close bonds between church and God, as well as a decline in the moral authority of the Catholic priesthood. The ability of the teaching authority of the church to speak persuasively and decisively for God was challenged by the American laity's access to other authoritative discourses. Backed by an affluence that permitted the free play of imagination with respect to the market within the context of a much more welcoming non-Catholic America, American Catholics were able to question the church's conditions for sacramental access to God. Not only was the necessity of the clergy to recognize, on God's behalf, the obedience of the penitent called into question, but the conditions for divine recognition themselves shifted from outward signs of obedience to God's will as revealed by the Church's positive laws to an inward and imagined condition of spontaneity and freedom unrestrained by external regulation.[28]

The locus of the church's authority among the laity remains its liturgical power, for it is the church's liturgical rites that continue to confer meaningful identity on the Catholic faithful. But participation in these rites is seldom contingent on the orthodoxy of practical reasoning. Catholics do not go to confession, but nearly everyone present at the Sunday Mass receives communion. Where confession used to confer identity through the authority of the priest to recognize the penitent's recognition of their sins, now communion confers identity through an act of individual self-expression, a quintessentially private rite whose meanings are almost solely up to the communicant (Morrill 2011).

To be clear, none of the foregoing justifies the claim that the contemporary practice of private confession facilitates unhealthy guilt or that Catholics ought not practice it frequently. Rather, my more modest argument is that contemporary narratives about the decline of confession that depend upon a corresponding cultural decline in a healthy sense of sin are based upon an idealized and imaginary picture of early United States Catholicism. If contemporary Catholic clergy and theologians wish to promote the practice of private confession, they need to examine how the laity respond to church authority and how they tend to experience their faults. While the simplicity and availability of private confession once served a Catholic culture in which obedience was linked to a positive sense of self, most Catholics no longer experience their faults within the matrix of Church authority. For those few who do, private confession might make sense. But even for those who are attracted to private confession to a priest, its viability as a healthy religious practice depends on the wider cultural, ecclesial, and political context in which it is situated.

---

[28] On this point, see Catherine Bell's 1989 riposte to Victor Turner's criticism of the Vatican II liturgical reforms (Bell 1989). Taylor likewise charts the emergence of self-expression and authenticity as significant characteristics of contemporary religious life (Taylor 2007, pp. 473–504). Finally, see Hellwig's illustrative depiction of the conflict between the "catechism god" and the "other god" in the experience of Catholics after the Second Vatican Council (Hellwig 1982, p. 6).

5. Conclusions

Most rituals do not create emotions; rather, by ritualizing the obligations and desires that constitute their cultural landscape, ritual participants negotiate their way into a newly configured and empowering space. Ritual theorist Catherine Bell terms this aspect of ritual its "redemptive hegemony," a "construal of reality as ordered in such a way as to allow the actor some advantageous way of acting" (Bell 1992, p. 82). Ritualization is more than demonstration or repetition. When people ritualize, they make use of the cultural and religious sources available to them, performing and reperforming roles within the networks of social relatedness in which they find themselves. By incorporating the moral theological language and the clerical dynamics that underpinned their culture, penitents used ritual confession as an opportunity to take action in their religious worlds, to move themselves around within it in order to attain a new sense of belonging and self-worth.

Throughout history, Christians have adapted a variety of penitential forms to their own culturally constituted needs. And yet under the influence of what is arguably the most authoritative teaching on penance in our time, John Paul II's *Reconciliation and Penance*, the penitential vision of the Catholic hierarchy remains fixated on private confession. Faced with a dramatic decline in confessions that began in the late 1960s and showed no signs of stopping, John Paul II directed the Catholic Church to work toward the recovery of a sense of sin, something like the healthy guilt to which Pius XII had referred thirty years earlier.

Evidence that an attempt toward such a recovery was already underway can be seen in the Rite of Penance promulgated in 1973 in response to the Second Vatican Council's mandate for reform. In contrast with the traditional language of venial and mortal sin that had previously dominated the moral theological language of American Catholicism, the reformed Rite of Penance bears witness to a more complex and multivalent notion of sin (Rite of Penance, Decree of the Sacred Congregation for Divine Worship 1990). Sin disrupts the friendship with God given to Christians in baptism, but addressing sin also requires reconciliation with those others whom sin inevitably harms (Rite of Penance, Decree of the Sacred Congregation for Divine Worship 1990, no. 5). Furthermore, people sin not only individually but in cooperation with one another (Rite of Penance, Decree of the Sacred Congregation for Divine Worship 1990, no. 5). Thus, according to the text, the reform of confession requires a correspondingly multifaceted set of rites that can facilitate healing and reconciliation on individual, relational, and communal levels.[29]

But as we have seen, the moral and theological climate in the United States during the rise of frequent confession did little to encourage Catholics to cultivate such a multivalent sense of sin and a correspondingly healthy guilt. The evidence shows instead that the moral theological imaginations of Catholics well before the 1950s were taxed by the morbid and legalistic guilt that John Paul II had charged the postwar generations with producing. The Catholic Church may well need to recover a sense of sin, but given the overly reductive notion of sin that dominated popular American Catholic discourse described in the course of this article, Catholics must look elsewhere than the confessional culture of the past two centuries for a positive model of religious health.

The emergence of private confession as a popular practice was an anomaly that arose alongside the practice of frequent communion just long enough to acclimate the laity to its newfound sacramental access to God. The authority of the church as communicated through the ritual life of the parish, the discourse of parochial education, and the religious language of the family was reinforced by the importance of maintaining a sense of Catholic identity together with an emphasis on obedience as constitutive of this identity. Appeals to the dangers of hell and separation from God and all good things exaggerated the dangers of ambiguous identity, necessitating a ritual which could dependably

---

[29] As the Rite of Penance declares, "Just as the wound of sin is varied and multiple in the life of individuals and of the community, so too the healing which penance provides is varied" (Rite of Penance, Decree of the Sacred Congregation for Divine Worship 1990, no. 7).

mitigate anxiety through the performance of obedience. Confessional practice provided the Catholic laity with a space in which to negotiate the demands made on them by the authority of the church with their desire for belonging and recognition: by dutifully recognizing themselves as having been disobedient, Catholics were recognized by the Church as good-enough for communion.

At face value, we might say simply that penitents gained freedom from sin, or relief from guilt, or the assurance of forgiveness. But these theological phrases acquire their lived significance and power from their proximity to actual relationships and felt obligations. By ritualizing Catholic guilt in the confessional, Catholics perpetuated the moral obligations that connected them to the community and its eucharist, and in confessing these obligations, found a sense of liberation, however limited and temporary. Indeed, perhaps the emerging practice of frequent communion itself, by providing Catholics with a means of ritualizing their worthiness, helped to dissipate the culture of Catholic guilt.

A tiny minority of adult Roman Catholics still make frequent use of private confession.[30] Like its earlier counterpart, contemporary private confession allows Catholics to situate and maintain their Catholic identities with respect to God through a filial religious obedience to the Roman Catholic Church. In the past, the church made use of strong connections between law, responsibility, and punishment in order to encourage sorrow for sins and the willingness to confess. Among self-identifying traditionalist Catholics, frequent private confession signals the possibility of revisiting a religious world that has otherwise all but disappeared, a "traditional Catholicism" reconstructed to deal with specifically modern problems. As such, this return is marked by ambivalence, cultural and ecclesial tension, and the perpetual threat of disillusionment. It is worth noting, however, that, like his predecessors, Pope Francis has repeatedly emphasized the importance of sacramental confession, going so far as to proclaim an extraordinary jubilee of mercy throughout 2016, a year dedicated to mercy, conversion, and consolation centered on the celebration of the sacrament of reconciliation. Given the pontiff's well-known impatience with traditionalism and false piety, it seems unclear how Pope Francis envisions that the ecclesial moral authority that undergirds frequent confession might be reestablished among the laity.[31]

For the most part, American Catholics are not overly concerned with their moral obligations to the Catholic Church.[32] Priestly authority, once the locus of moral authority in Catholic parishes, has declined among the laity in favor of a widespread emphasis on individual conscience as the source of moral authenticity (D'Antonio et al. 2011, pp. 284–85). The Catholic guilt that once spurred Catholic to go to confession and, to a more limited extent, motivated ethical behavior, has given way to a much more ambiguous web of cultural and social obligations. Guilt exists where these obligations are strained, but it exists alongside a myriad of other senses of personal and communal fault like shame and alienation. This points to the continuing necessity in Catholic language and ritual of what Vergote calls the demythologization of morality: the recognition that the capacity for moral life develops gradually, in the midst of faultiness and guilt, into a precarious and ambiguous balance that must be consistently renewed and renegotiated in the midst of cultural influences and concrete personal interactions (Vergote et al. 1998, p. 71).

Indeed, as this article strives to demonstrate, psychoanalytic insights into the structure and function of guilt offer a promising resource for theological thinking about how the church ritualizes complex theological-psychological experiences like guilt, sin, and forgiveness. If consciousness of these phenomena involves a theological judgment about the human freedom involved in culturally

---

[30] According to research conducted in 2008 at Georgetown University by the Center for Applied Research in the Apostolate (CARA), only a quarter of American Catholics report that they go to confession at least once a year (Gray and Perl 2008, p. 5). While there appear to be no reliable studies that examine the rate of Catholic confessions in other cultural contexts, nothing suggests that this trend is anything but consistent throughout the rest of the world.

[31] The apostolic letter *Misericordia et misera*, disseminated at the end of the extraordinary jubilee year of mercy, provides a clear sample of Pope Francis's support for the centrality of the sacrament of reconciliation (Francis 2016).

[32] To cite a single straightforward example, according to the 2008 CARA study cited above, only twenty three percent of Catholics report attending Mass every Sunday, something required of every Catholic by Catholic church law (Gray and Perl 2008, p. 20).

and psychologically constituted experiences, psychoanalytic thinkers like Freud, Vergote, and Lacan might help to articulate how this freedom takes place and develops within, not somehow transcendent to, these experiences. Simplistic notions of guilt and sin denote simplistic understandings of the human condition. By contrast, a critical understanding of guilt as a complicated and multifaceted reality, attentive to issues of psychological development and cultural influence, challenge clerics and theologians to respect the moral and spiritual complexity of the children and adults who use, or reject, the church's rituals of penance.

If they are to be a source of healing, these rituals must provide a cathartic and self-reconciling context in which mercy and tolerance cooperate with law and restitution. Fault and the transgression of law are necessary aspects of a moral conscience, but they are insufficient. Rather, as Vergote argues, the ability to tolerate the ambiguity of pleasure and aggression and their relationship to our obligations to others is necessary to cultivating an ethical conscience. Conversely, a religious obsession with personal guilt, besides being a source of profound suffering, constitutes an impasse in the ethical becoming of the religious subject (Vergote et al. 1998, p. 74). Someone who cannot tolerate the ambivalences of aggression and desire will have difficulty encountering others as similarly ambivalent, ambiguous others deserving of respect. I can do no better here than to point us toward Freud's critique of the commandment to love one's neighbor in his *Civilization and Its Discontents* (Freud 1962, pp. 55–63). Whether and how the Catholic Church might incorporate these insights into its penitential rituals and practices is another question, but this much is clear. The ritualization of guilt promotes religious and psychological health only where it provides a sound basis for a renewed attempt to pursue the hard work of ethics: to balance the quest for personal authenticity with the obligation to others in the midst of work and love.

Funding: This research received no external funding.

Conflicts of Interest: The author declares no conflict of interest.

References

Bell, Catherine M. 1989. Ritual, Change, and Changing Rituals. *Worship* 61: 31–41.

Bell, Catherine M. 1992. *Ritual Theory, Ritual Practice*. New York: Oxford University Press.

Belzen, Jacob A. 2001. The Future Is the Return: Back to Cultural Psychology of Religion. In *Religion and Psychology Mapping the Terrain: Contemporary Dialogues, Future Prospects*. Edited by Diane E. Jonte-Pace and William Barclay Parsons. New York: Routledge.

Benedict XVI. 2011. Address to Participants in a Course Sponsored by the Apostolic Penitentiary. Rome, March 9. Available online: https://w2.vatican.va/content/benedict-xvi/en/speeches/2012/march/documents/hf_ben-xvi_spe_20120309_penitenzieria-apostolica.html (accessed on 4 April 2019).

Carey, Patrick W. 2018. *Confession: Catholics, Repentance, and Forgiveness in America*. Oxford: Oxford University Press.

Catholic Guilt. 2019. Wikipedia. Available online: https://en.wikipedia.org/w/index.php?title=Catholic_guilt&oldid=892184055 (accessed on 4 April 2019).

Coffey, David. 2001. *The Sacrament of Reconciliation*. Collegeville: Liturgical Press.

Collins, Mary, David Noel Power, and Marcus Lefébure. 1987. *The Fate of Confession*. Edinburgh: T. & T. Clark.

Council of Trent. 1848. *The Canons and Decrees of the Sacred and Œcumenical Council of Trent, Celebrated under the Sovereign Pontiffs, Paul III, Julius III and Pius IV*. Edited by James Waterworth. Chicago: The Christian Symbolic Publication Soc.

Curran, Charles E. 2008. *Catholic Moral Theology in the United States: A History*. Washington: Georgetown University Press.

D'Antonio, William V., James D. Davidson, Dean R. Hoge, and Mary L. Gautier. 2011. American Catholics and Church Authority. In *The Crisis of Authority in Catholic Modernity*. Edited by Michel J. Lacey and Francis Oakley. Oxford: Oxford University Press.

Dallen, James. 1986. *The Reconciling Community: The Rite of Penance*. New York: Pueblo Pub. Co.

Delumeau, Jean. 1990. Sin and Fear: The Emergence of a Western Guilt Culture, 13th–18th Centuries. New York: St. Martin's Press.

Dolan, Jay P. 2002. *In Search of an American Catholicism: A History of Religion and Culture in Tension*. Oxford and New York: Oxford University Press.

Dougherty, Joseph. 2010. *From Altar-Throne to Table: The Campaign for Frequent Holy Communion in the Catholic Church*. Lanham: Scarecrow Press.

Francis. 2016. Misericordia et misera. November 20. Available online: https://w2.vatican.va/content/francesco/en/apost_letters/documents/papa-francesco-lettera-ap_20161120_misericordia-et-misera.html (accessed on 5 May 2019).

Francis. 2019. Address to Participants in the Course on the Internal Forum Organized by the Tribunal of the Apostolic Penitentiary. Rome. Available online: http://w2.vatican.va/content/francesco/en/speeches/2019/march/documents/papa-francesco_20190329_penitenzieria-apostolica.html (accessed on 4 April 2019).

Freud, Sigmund. 1962. *Civilization and Its Discontents*. New York: W.W. Norton.

Gray, Mark M., and Paul M. Perl. 2008. *Sacraments Today: Belief and Practice among US Catholics*. Washington: Center for Applied Research in the Apostolate at Georgetown University, Available online: http://cara.georgetown.edu/sacramentsreport.pdf (accessed on 4 April 2019).

Hellwig, Monika. 1982. *Sign of Reconciliation and Conversion: The Sacrament of Penance for Our Times*. Wilmington: M. Glazier.

John Paul II. 1984. *Reconciliation and Penance*. Priests and Bros. of the Sacred Heart. Available online: http://w2.vatican.va/content/john-paul-ii/en/apost_exhortations/documents/hf_jp-ii_exh_02121984_reconciliatio-et-paenitentia.html (accessed on 4 April 2019).

Jordan, Mark D. 2006. *Rewritten Theology: Aquinas after His Readers*. Malden and Oxford: Blackwell Pub.

Lewis, Helen Block. 1971. *Shame and Guilt in Neurosis*. New York: International Universities Press.

Lewis, Marc D. 2000. The Promise of Dynamic Systems Approaches for an Integrated Account of Human Development. *Child Development* 71: 36–43. [CrossRef] [PubMed]

Lonergan, Bernard J. 2007. *Method in Theology*. Toronto: University of Toronto Press for Lonergan Research Institute of Regis College.

MacIntyre, Alasdair C. 1984. *After Virtue: A Study in Moral Theory*. Notre Dame: University of Notre Dame Press.

Mahoney, John. 1987. *The Making of Moral Theology: A Study of the Roman Catholic Tradition*. Oxford: Oxford University Press.

Mitchell, Nathan, ed. 1978. *The Rite of Penance: Commentaries: Background and Directions*. Washington: Liturgical Press.

Morrill, Bruce T. 2011. Holy Communion as Public Act: Ethics and Liturgical Participation. *Studia Liturgica* 41: 31–46. [CrossRef]

Morrill, Bruce T. 2014. Sign of Reconciliation and Conversion? Differing Views of Power—Ecclesial, Sacramental, Anthropological—among Hierarchy and Laity. *Theological Studies* 75: 585–612. [CrossRef]

O'Toole, James M. 2004. *Habits of Devotion: Catholic Religious Practice in Twentieth-Century America*. Ithaca: Cornell University Press.

Pius XII. 1953. On Psychotherapy and Religion: An Address of His Holiness Pope Pius XII to the Fifth International Congress on Psychotherapy and Clinical Psychology. National Catholic Welfare Conference. April 13. Available online: https://www.ewtn.com/library/PAPALDOC/P12PSYRE.HTM (accessed on 4 April 2019).

Rite of Penance, Decree of the Sacred Congregation for Divine Worship. 1990. *Rites of the Catholic Church: Volume One*. Collegeville: Liturgical.

Rizzuto, Ana-Maria. 1979. *The Birth of the Living God: A Psychoanalytic Study*. Chicago: University of Chicago Press.

Sacred Congregation of the Council. 1905. Sacra Tridentina Synodus. Available online: https://www.ewtn.com/library/CURIA/CDWFREQ.HTM (accessed on 29 May 2019).

Speziale-Bagliacca, Roberto. 2004. *Guilt: Revenge, Remorse and Responsibility after Freud*. New York: Brunner-Routledge.

Tangney, June Price, and Ronda L. Dearing. 2004. *Shame and Guilt*. New York: Guilford Press.

Tartaglia, Philip. 2015. The New Evangelisation and the Sacrament of Penance. Paper presented at Meeting of the European Doctrinal Commissions, Esztergom, Hungary, January 15; Available online: http://www.vatican.va/roman_curia/congregations/cfaith/incontri/rc_con_cfaith_20150115_esztergom-tartaglia_en.html (accessed on 4 April 2019).

Taves, Ann. 1986. *The Household of Faith: Roman Catholic Devotions in Mid-Nineteenth-Century America.* Notre Dame: University of Notre Dame Press.

Taylor, Charles. 2007. *A Secular Age.* Cambridge: Belknap Press of Harvard University Press.

Tentler, Leslie Woodcock. 2004. *Catholics and Contraception: An American History.* Ithaca: Cornell University Press.

Tracy, Jessica L., and Richard W. Robins. 2006. Appraisal Antecedents of Shame and Guilt: Support for a Theoretical Model. *Personality and Social Psychology Bulletin* 32: 1339–51. [CrossRef] [PubMed]

United States Conference of Catholic Bishops. 2013. God's Gift of Forgiveness: A Pastoral Exhortation on the Sacrament of Penance and Reconciliation. Available online: http://www.usccb.org/prayer-and-worship/sacraments-and-sacramentals/penance/upload/Penance-Statement-ENG.pdf (accessed on 4 April 2019).

Vergote, Antoine. 1988. *Guilt and Desire: Religious Attitudes and Their Pathological Derivatives.* New Haven: Yale University Press.

Vergote, Antoine. 1993. What the Psychology of Religion Is and What It Is Not. *International Journal for the Psychology of Religion* 3: 73–86. [CrossRef]

Vergote, Antoine, Josef Corveleyn, and Dirk Hutsebaut. 1998. *Psychoanalysis, Phenomenological Anthropology, and Religion.* Leuven: Leuven University Press.

Westerink, Herman. 2009a. *A Dark Trace: Sigmund Freud on the Sense of Guilt.* Leuven: Leuven University Press.

Westerink, Herman. 2009b. *Controversy and Challenge: The Reception of Sigmund Freud's Psychoanalysis in German and Dutch-Speaking Theology and Religious Studies.* London: Global.

Article

Converting Consumerism: A Liturgical-Ethical Application of Critical Realism

Benjamin Durheim

Theology Department, College of Saint Benedict/Saint John's University, St. Joseph, MN 56374, USA;
bdurheim@csbsju.edu

Received: 1 May 2019; Accepted: 19 May 2019; Published: 24 May 2019

Abstract: Critical realism as a lens of thought is not new to theological inquiry, but recently a growing number of theologians have been using its conceptual frameworks to guide their thought on how social structures function theologically, and how ethics might function in light of its insights. This article pulls these developments into the nexus of liturgy and ethics, applying critical realist categories to contemporary understandings of how liturgical celebration (and the structures thereof) form, inform, and/or malform Christian ethical imaginations and practices. The article begins with a brief survey of the main tenets of critical realism and their histories in theological inquiry, and argues that a main gift critical realism can offer liturgical and sacramental theology is a structural understanding of liturgical narrative- and value-building. Having described this gift, the article moves to a concrete application of this method in liturgical theology and its implications for ethics: addressing consumerism as a culture that can be both validated and challenged by liturgical and sacramental structures. The article ends with some brief suggestions for using and shifting liturgical structures to better facilitate the Christian conversion of consumerism.

Keywords: critical realism; social theory; liturgical theology; sacramental theology; theological ethics; Margaret Archer; social structures; agency

1. Introduction

Consumerism is so deeply a part of the cultural landscape of the United States that to critique it from a theological point of view might seem at once overly obvious (given the penchant of consumerism to reduce all entities to objects of commerce) and borderline futile (given consumerism's breadth and vitality). That said, at the confluence of liturgical theology and theological ethics, there is space for critiquing cultural currents in the context of ritual formation, lending to the project a method that moves beyond only argument. This article situates itself in that confluence, and uses a critical realist framework to situate critiques of consumerism, and suggests how liturgy might better embody something other than consumerist tendencies.

While critical realism as a method or hermeneutical approach to theology is not new, recently scholars have moved beyond its applications in biblical studies and systematics, to employing its precepts in theological ethics and theological accounts of social realities. Into this burgeoning milieu this article begins to introduce another area of use for critical realism: in liturgical/sacramental theology and its relationship with ethics.

To do so, the article proceeds in three parts. First, it outlines a brief history and background of critical realism, and especially those of its tenets that have given rise to much of its contemporary application in social theory, and subsequently in theological ethics. The main gifts that critical realism brings to sacramental and liturgical theology, I argue, are its conceptions of the interplay between structures and agents, and the ways in which the two emerge from one another, and interact with culture. Second, in order to sketch one concrete application of critical realism to an issue in liturgical/sacramental theology, the article describes consumerism, or consumer culture, from a theological perspective, and argues that the ethical impact of consumer culture upon liturgy (and *vice versa*) can be best appreciated through the lens of critical realism. Finally, the article unpacks how critical realist categories can provide insights for how to approach and respond to consumer culture liturgically, and ends with two concrete examples of structural elaboration,[1] which can either liturgically buttress or weaken consumer culture.

2. Critical Realism

One might best conceive of critical realism not as a single theory or school of thought, but as a common set of shared convictions that have bled across philosophical, theological, and social-scientific disciplines in various attempts to give an adequate account of reality and humans' experiences thereof. According to Stanley E. Porter and Andrew W. Pitts, philosophical approaches that took the name critical realism began in the early twentieth century in North America, but while they share some of the aspects of what is currently meant by critical realism, most contemporary critical realists would find their intellectual roots in the seminal work of Roy Bhaskar.[2] Others have argued that critical realism's roots are best located as far back as Kant,[3] but regardless of the lineage, critical realists' convictions (and conclusions) tend to orbit at least three precepts. First, ontology and epistemology are distinct, in that what is real cannot be reduced simply to what is known. Second, while events occur due to real forces that do not depend upon humans' recognition of them for their efficacy, science properly understood is a socially constructed process, and therefore produces socially conditioned perceptions that describe those forces while remaining distinct from the real. Critical realists are keen to insist that there are no laws in nature, just forces, which human creations called "scientific laws" attempt to describe. Third, reality is stratified, which is to say that complex entities or structures emerge from less complex ones.[4] What follows is a brief summary of why these precepts matter philosophically, and how they have been used in social theory (which sets the stage for their use in theology, and therefore liturgy).[5]

The first precept, that ontology is not reducible to epistemology, is where Bhaskar diverges from (and responds to) Kant.[6] For Bhaskar and the critical realism that follows him, what *is* does not depend upon humans' perception of it. What Bhaskar sees himself combating by adopting this precept is a kind of "classical empiricism" that limits the real to human scientific inquiry, that is, to what humans can perceive or have perceived with the five senses.[7] Beyond the strictly scientific implications of this view of reality as "transcending"[8] human perception or context, Bhaskar's insight allows human knowing to circumvent the problems of "imprisoning" humans in the context of language or social

---

[1] This is not my term. I take it from critical realist Margaret Archer, as shown below.
[2] (Porter and Pitts 2015, pp. 278–83). I should note at this point that, in Roman Catholic circles, critical realism is often connected with the work of Bernard Lonergan. However, my choice to engage Bhaskar and those who follow him (Archer, etc.) results from my interest in specifically social theory and applications of critical realism. Lonergan, for his part, tended to continue the line of critical realism as a cognitional theory, and developments of biblical hermeneutics tended to follow that (see, for example, Denton 2015, p. 240). Denton develops this explanation further in (Denton 2004), and points readers to chapter 1 of (Lonergan 1972). The Lonerganian strain of critical realism is not irrelevant to the current project, but Archer's development (springing from Bhaskar) is more immediately applicable to this discussion.
[3] (Niiniluoto 1999, pp. 91–94).
[4] Porter and Pitts, citing Bhaskar, term these three precepts intransitivity, transfactuality, and stratification ("Critical Realism in Context," 283). Porter and Pitts cite Bhaskar's 1998, p. xiii as the source for these terms.
[5] Critical realism, like any other set of convictions, is not without its critics. See, for an example critiquing critical realism in the conversation between religion and science, (Robbins 1999). Critical realism has also been critiqued as needlessly complicated (Murphy 1988), and as overemphasizing events (Mearman 2006). Even in light of these critiques, I find its approach compelling, for reasons discussed below in the article.
[6] (Jerončić 2015, p. 357).
[7] (Bhaskar 2008, pp. 26–27).
[8] Bhaskar had originally termed this part of his formulation "transcendental realism" (Bhaskar, *A Realist Theory of Science*, 26).

context.[9] That reality exists regardless of perception by objects that inhabit it, pulls the object of human knowing beyond the linguistic.

This is also an initial point of contact for social theory and theology. According to Christian Smith, so-called "network structuralism" in the social sciences has attempted to definitively move the subject of social inquiry from the individual human to the "structured system of social relations that comprises the real social world."[10] For our purposes, very similar methodological moves in liturgical and sacramental theology have been championed by figures such as Louis-Marie Chauvet, for whom the primary subject of inquiry in liturgical/sacramental theology is the Christian assembly, conditioned by the linguistic, symbolic systems that construct it.[11] What this first precept of critical realism offers is a corrective that maintains that what is structurally, anthropologically, or even relationally real remains real, independent of humans' ability to perceive it. Put another way, anthropological reality is not reducible to context, community, and/or language. Instead, as Schilbrack notes, "critical realism seeks to defend a clearer recognition of the fact (a) that our perception and knowledge are conditioned by our social locations does not imply (b) that we cannot refer successfully to a world that exists independent of language."[12]

The second precept, that scientific (and all academic) inquiry is socially conditioned, provides something of a counterpoint to the first precept. For Bhaskar and critical realists, adherence to traditional philosophies of science (i.e., those that hold reality to be independent from human perception thereof) is only tenable in conjunction with the recognition that what science produces is not reality, but rather socially conditioned and socially articulated ideas about reality. In explaining this distinction, Daniel K. Finn uses the following example:

> "[When I drop a book], The book does not hit the floor "because of the law of gravity." It hits the floor because of the relation of the book and the earth, and the force (not a law) of gravity which that relation generates. The law of gravity is simply the scientist's summary of the ontologically real causal relationship between the earth and the book."[13]

While the first precept guarded against reductions of reality to that which humans perceive or can perceive (subject therefore to human language), the second precept guards against elevating human perception to ontology rather than epistemology. In a word, the second precept resists what Finn calls empiricism,[14] the perspective that claims what humans can know and demonstrate scientifically is what is ultimately true, real on the level of ontology.

The first and second precepts provide something like epistemological poles around which critical realism orbits, but the third precept about the stratification of reality provides the driving force for critical realism's application to social theory and ultimately theology. The fact that reality is stratified connects deeply with the concept of emergence, conceived of as the idea that higher-order or more complex realities are not reducible to or ultimately explainable only on the basis of those lower-order realities that make them up.[15] For example, a complex reality like the Christian liturgical assembly is made up of a number of other relational realities (e.g., a presider and congregation, a local and universal church, a religious group and its surrounding community, the assisting ministers and the presiding minister, the music ministers and those to whom they minister, etc.), but the liturgical assembly is

---

9 (Schilbrack 2014, p. 168).
10 (Smith 2010, p. 210).
11 See, for example, (Chauvet 2001, especially pp. 31–34). Chauvet also explains this in more depth in (Chauvet 1995, pp. 180–89). A more developed comparison of the parallels between recent social theory and recent liturgical/sacramental theology runs beyond the scope of this discussion. Suffice it to say here that critical realism's challenges to network structuralism have yet to precipitate a similar challenge to assembly-centered liturgical/sacramental theology.
12 (Schilbrack 2014, p. 168).
13 (Finn 2016, p. 148).
14 (Ibid., p. 148).
15 (Bhaskar 1998, p. xiii).

not reducible to any one or even the composite of all these realities that nevertheless constitute it. Or, to take an example from economics, Finn has argued that the "market" is a reality that exists on a higher level than the individual persons who inhabit or participate in it, and while persons' participation in the market is real, the market reality is not reducible only to the actions of the persons within it.[16]

Emergence is hardly the exclusive domain of critical realism, but the ways by which it is translated into social theory in relation to the first two precepts provide fertile ground to be tilled for liturgical/sacramental theology. Much of this translation has been done by Margaret S. Archer, for whom emergence and the stratified nature of reality provide a way of transcending (that is *not* to say resolving) the temptation to reduce human realities to either results of individual action (individualism) or to social context (collectivism).[17] For Archer, it is too simplistic to fall into an either/or between individualism and collectivism, and it is too sloppy to brazenly tout a both/and. Rather, as David Cloutier explains, "Critical realism seeks a framework in which the two [individual agency and social structure] are 'related rather than conflated,' with proper attention given to the distinct 'properties and powers' of each."[18] In Archer's view, individual agency and social structures *emerge* from one another, becoming newly irreducible to each other in the processes of emergence that play out over time. Emergence in this sense is conditioned by historicity,[19] because as an individual's agency emerges from the social structures that surround her or him, so also are those social structures continually emerging from the exercises of individual agency that make them up. These emergences must function on the basis of time, precluding any critical realist approach from ignoring concrete, embodied history when performing an analysis.

A brief word about exactly *how* agency and structure influence one another in critical realism will set the stage for this discussion to transition into its central application: consumerism as it encounters liturgy. For Archer, structure and agency emerge from one another in essentially a three-stage cyclical process she calls the "morphogenic cycle,"[20] a technically defined synonym for what nonsociologists might call social change. Archer calls the first step[21] in this process "structural conditioning," in which "systemic properties are viewed as the emergent or aggregate consequences of past actions."[22] This step is where structures exert causal force on agents, by defining the parameters within which agency is exercised. Structures, which have already emerged from past cycles of this process, provide the framework of possibilities within which an agent makes decisions. For example, the structure of presider-congregation within liturgy, already an emergent structure, makes up part of the framework within which a parent with a fussy child decides whether or not to take the child out of the sanctuary during the sermon/homily. If one's child begins crying during the preaching, what is a parent to do? The parent is free to leave with the child and also free not to do so, but liturgical structures, having emerged from previous actions and structures, will define in large part the costs and benefits associated with each possibility the parent/agent considers. Additionally, the congregation and the preacher will be evaluating costs and benefits of possible actions. Does the preacher simply speak louder? Do other congregants shoot dirty looks at the parent, or take a moment to appreciate the young life and growth of their community? As the parent, congregation, and preacher deliberate, they negotiate the

---

[16] (Finn 2019, p. 97, and all of chapter 7).

[17] (Archer 1995, pp. 33–64). Archer further explains these temptations with the terms "downward conflation," which is the temptation to conceive of human reality as the result of social context determining individual actions, "upward conflation," which is the temptation to see social context as *only* determined by individual actions, and "central conflation," which is an attempt at a both/and for agency and structure, but which ignores the importance of time for their interplay (Ibid., pp. 81–89).

[18] (Cloutier 2017, p. 70).

[19] (Archer 1995, pp. 66, 154).

[20] Archer notes that she borrows the term "morphogenesis" from (Buckly 1967), in large part because of its definition as elaborating (or beginning to change) the current forms that systems take (Archer 1995, p. 75, n. 11.).

[21] "First" here operates as conceptual only; in experience this "first" step is already emergent from previous cycles of this process.

[22] (Archer 1995, p. 90).

interplay between the structures they experience and what Christian Smith calls agents' "motivations," the beliefs, desires, and emotions that drive an agent to act.[23]

The second step is, as one might expect, "social interaction," by which Archer means the action(s) the agent chooses to take.[24] This step is also emergent in that it is not reducible *only* to a certain structure or set of structures that informed it. The parent's decision whether or not to remove the fussy child from liturgy is informed, but *not* determined, by the structures within which it occurs. The parent, if one asked, might explain the decision as a result of any number of reasons or structures, but the exercise of agency is essentially indeterminate; it *emerges* as a choice, rather than a deterministic result.

The third step that closes the morphogenic cycle (and opens it to endless further rotations) is what Archer calls "structural elaboration," which refers to "the modification of previous structural properties and the introduction of new ones ... [which is] the combined product of the different outcomes pursued simultaneously."[25] Structural elaboration is the unpredictable process of the reproduction or transformation of social structures from exercises of agency. If the parent leaves with the fussy child, what impact will that action (coupled with the actions of others in the assembly, the actions of the presider, among others) have on liturgical structures? If the parent remains with the fussy child, what impact will that have on the structures of liturgy? One might be able to predict likely outcomes, but these predictions are of their nature fallible. The structures will morph based on the actions of agents, but like the actions of agents in the second step, this is an emergent change, not reducible simply to the actions that occasioned it.

Overall, the morphogenic cycle Archer develops provides a conceptual framework within with to account for the mutual influence of agency and structures, but is a wild and sometimes volatile framework, rather than a determinative one. This unpredictability is exactly why Archer's critical realist approach to agency and structure is so fertile for liturgical/sacramental theology: in liturgy, Archer's morphogenic cycle repeats any number of times, again and again as a heartbeat within Christianity (and I have yet to meet a liturgist or sacramental theologian who would describe any liturgy as conclusively predictable).

3. Consumerism and Christianity

Why is consumerism a likely aspect of culture for critical realism to address within liturgical/sacramental theology? To answer, it would be good to explain why I have refrained from using the term "culture" thus far in the discussion. In critical realist social theory, culture refers to artifacts or systems of meaning or value, while structure (which has been our focus in this discussion thus far) deals with objective relationships between social entities. In the words of critical realist Douglas Porpora, "structure refers to social organizational relations ... [while] culture refers to ... anything with meaningful content produced by social intentionality."[26] In this light, consumerism is a culture, and a fairly strong one in the context of the United States.[27] However, cultures and structures inform one another, such that while structures may be interpreted through cultural lenses, so also are those cultural lenses conditioned by structures, which are themselves continually modified in and through the morphogenic cycle of structural conditioning, social interaction, and structural elaboration. My goal in this section is to describe a culture of consumerism as it encounters Christianity, especially in the United States, which will set the stage for thinking through how liturgy—with critical realist conceptions of structure and agency—may begin to convert it.

---

[23] (Smith 2015, pp. 69–82).
[24] (Archer 1995, pp. 90–91).
[25] (Ibid., p. 91).
[26] Douglas Porpora, qtd. in (Finn 2016, p. 138, n.11).
[27] Consumerism is hardly an issue *only* for the United States, but the attention of this discussion will remain on the context of the United States. That said, consumer actions of course carry global implications, both economic and religious. For a study of these implications and how they form Christianity, see (Miller 2010).

That consumerism exerts cultural influence is hardly debatable in the context of the United States, but whether or not it is a culture itself (and if it is, what that means) may be less readily apparent. Vincent J. Miller, in his work *Consuming Religion*, argues convincingly that consumerism is best treated not as a culture itself, but that neither is it reducible simply to beliefs or values.[28] Miller describes his experience teaching students at Catholic universities who readily "absorb the most radical reconstructions of Jesus' politics, the preferential option for the poor, and Catholic social teaching," and yet inhabit quite comfortably the disconnect between these beliefs and many of their eventual entries into consumer culture and the "professional managerial class."[29] Consumer culture seemingly trumps even sincerely held ideas or beliefs. Part of the reason for this, in Miller's view, is the totalizing commodification that saturates the lives of persons. For Miller, what he calls "commodity abstraction" separates persons—even those who value social justice and equity—from consideration of the background and implications of their consumer actions, even as the commodities stand before consumers in apparent utter clarity.[30] In his words, "like all seductions, [commodities] veil as much as they reveal."[31] The result for Miller is that a deeper account of what constitutes "consumer culture" is necessary in order for Christianity to adequately respond to it. Employing the work of Kathryn Tanner and Wendy Griswold, Miller maintains that to speak of consumer culture is best done in reference to "cultural habits of use and interpretation that are derived from the consumption of commodified cultural objects."[32] Miller's choice in this regard allows him to recognize the potency of consumer culture without relegating it exclusively to any specific social location. Instead, persons from diverse social locations can and do participate in consumer culture in varying degrees, informed not simply by value or belief, but also by their "habits of use and interpretation."

For the purposes of this discussion, two central aspects of consumer culture that Miller discusses are of significant interest (Miller discusses many more, but these two warrant our attention here): the "Fordist" move from domestic production to consumption, and the religious "style" of spirituality. Miller cites Michel Aglietta to first use the term Fordism, which connotes the shifts in production and labor that took place in the first two-thirds of the twentieth century. The vast increase in industrialization and production precipitated (among other things) a kind of "deskilling" of labor that, according to Miller, "had consequences that went far beyond the shop floor. Combined with the ever more complete exhaustion of the worker's energy in the course of the workday, it helped transform the home from a site of domestic production into a place increasingly dependent on mass consumption."[33] This shift moved consumer culture into home life in a new, totalizing way, wherein nearly every aspect of domestic existence became an occasion for asking, "what can we consume (rather than produce) in order to satisfy this need?"

This shift was further solidified according to Miller by the rise of single-family homes and the consequent cultural isolation of the nuclear family.[34] While previous models of family life likely included the support and maintenance of relationships with extended family, the cultural shifts that enshrined the nuclear family as the fundamental social unit carried with it the likely unintended consequence of replacing that extended family support with devices to consume. In the same way that domestic production was supplanted by domestic consumption, extended-family support was largely supplanted by reliance on consumption of devices (for example, appliances). Additionally, reliance on these devices did not bring with it an increase in leisure time or freedom from necessary labor, but rather (and overwhelmingly), it precipitated an increase in standards of domestic work

---

28 (Miller 2003, pp. 15–31).
29 Ibid., p. 19.
30 Ibid., pp. 37–38. Miller discusses here also the problems of recognizing value only in things, and further only in the *exchange* of things. Such valuing, he argues, is not so much a conscious choice as it is "our cultural default" (37).
31 Ibid.
32 Ibid., p. 30.
33 Ibid., p. 41.
34 Ibid., pp. 46–51.

that such devices provided (laundry, cooking, cleaning, shopping, etc.).[35] Miller does acknowledge that Fordism eventually gives way to a post-Fordist context of consumption,[36] but that development seems to only exacerbate the totalizing tendency of consumer culture. Whereas Fordism ushered in a focus on the nuclear family and domestic consumption in that context, post-Fordism seems to isolate even the individuals within families, bringing with it similar substitutions on an individual level of consumption for production, and devices for support. Such consequences are not without parallels in the lives of liturgical communities, as we will see in the next section.

The second aspect of consumer culture, and the one that bears directly upon theology, is the religious style of spirituality. Much can be said about approaching religion through the lens of spirituality (taken as a popular term rather than the academic discipline of spirituality), but for our purposes, of central concern is Miller's point that "spirituality as the emergent form of religious life is consonant with the workings of commodification."[37] In popular forms of spirituality in the United States, what tends to be of paramount importance is how well certain aspects of religion can satisfy whatever religious needs or desires an individual experiences, how efficiently they can do so, and in what combination they are most appealing. Timothy Brunk, writing on consumerism and liturgy, locates this tendency not primarily in Fordism or even secularization as Miller tends to, but rather specifically in the "consumerist mindset" that transforms the dignity of persons into the absolute priority of individual desires and concerns.[38] Individualism, for Brunk, precipitates what he calls the consumerist mindset because it translates religiously into a perpetual question of "What do I need now?"[39] Like the dissolution of domestic productivity and extended family support in the wake of Fordism, the religious style of individualized spirituality tends to dissolve, as Brunk points out, both the understanding of the importance of liturgical assembly, and also many notions of both religious permanence or loyalty.[40]

Brunk also moves further in this direction, explaining that consumerism tends toward a culture that values immediate gratification, which encourages individuals to constantly ask themselves whether what they have or are is sufficient, and which products (religious or otherwise) could best reinvent them into some better version.[41] When one's culturally formed mindset in any activity—especially liturgy—is to constantly evaluate whether the activity is satisfying one's perceived needs with adequate efficiency and strength, the very category of participation can be compromised. Or, at least, participation becomes a carrier primarily of evaluation, and thereby transforms from production (adding one's participation to some activity, like a liturgical assembly and community) to consumption (consuming a liturgical assembly or community as a product or device). This attention to self-evaluation is akin to what Tom Beaudoin calls "branded culture," by which he means that, in the context of religion like any other context, what persons consume (by wearing certain clothes, eating certain things, etc.) continually builds or rebuilds who they are, even as spiritual persons.[42] The liturgical-theological problems with this are well-documented,[43] but such problems diffuse also into the realm of theological ethics. To the degree that liturgical celebration accommodates or especially appropriates the consumerist mindset, it also participates in the ethics that operate in consumer culture.

---

[35] (Schor 1991, pp. 88–94). Schor also documents the significant increases in time required for labor over the last few decades of the twentieth century (17–82) and argues that Americans have essentially become captives of a work-and-spend cycle in which consumerism is totalizing (107–38).
[36] (Miller 2003, pp. 66–71).
[37] Ibid., p. 106.
[38] (Brunk 2011, p. 55).
[39] Ibid., p. 56.
[40] Ibid., pp. 56–57.
[41] Ibid., pp. 57–67.
[42] (Beaudoin 2003, volume 7, p. 59).
[43] See also (Cavanaugh 2002, or Veiga 2012, or even the earlier essay by Kiesling 1978).

Theological-ethical appraisals and critiques of consumerism have already been done extraordinarily well,[44] but to them I would like to add one ethics-based interpretation of consumer culture as it applies to liturgy: consumer culture as ethical egoism. By ethical egoism, I mean an ethics that takes self-interest as the basis for discerning what is good. At first blush, this may seem so obviously contradictory to coherent Christian approaches to ethics as to not warrant discussion, but when I teach ethics to undergraduate students, my experience has been that many if not most students find it fairly easy to both espouse Christian ideals of justice, love, forgiveness, selflessness, and mercy, and also to hold self-interest as the primary, necessary criterion for what constitutes good living. Or at the very least, relatively few students seem willing to depart from what they view as the practicality of ethical egoism when it conflicts with the ideals of more explicitly Christian ethical systems, or they attempt desperately to deny that there might be any such conflict between naked self-interest and Christian ethics.

Few writers have helped me elicit this more clearly in the classroom than Ayn Rand, for whom the virtues of rationality, productiveness, and pride lead to the desired state of happiness, a state for which at least the self-interest of maintaining life (and ideally a rational, productive, and proud life) is necessary.[45] Almost without fail, there is no learning curve here for students, who have been formed by consumer culture, among other things, to operate according to the propagation (production) of their own views of life, rationality, and pride, and to consume whatever goods or services will most efficiently accomplish that production. So deep does this formation run that when I dare to suggest that some principle other than self-interest may be suited to ethical living, the reactions tend to hover around questions like, "that would be less efficient or practical," "why would I want to pursue something other than my own interests," or "how would that lead me to get what I want out of life?"

My point here is not about ethics writ large. Translated into reactions about liturgy, the questions I get from my students about moving away from self-interested consumption could remain essentially unchanged when discerning one's possible participation in liturgical communities. Consumer culture, as we noted with Vincent Miller above, is far more than a set of values; it is woven into the fabric of American Christians' self-understanding. In this context, the question is not only about Christians treating liturgical communities as commodities to be consumed; it is also about the ways in which liturgical communities can—intentionally or unintentionally—affirm the consumerist approach to religion, and thereby give a religious mandate to consumerist ethics (read: ethical egoism). If liturgy is, among other things, a place of ethical formation, then reactions to and accommodations of consumer culture within liturgy give flesh both to consumer culture's impact on liturgy (*ad-intra*) and liturgy's validation and/or repudiation of consumer culture (*ad-extra*). To develop this line of thought further, we must return to critical realism's treatment of structures and agents, as well as the ways by which they interact with culture.

4. Converting Consumerism

Critical realism is not new to theological inquiry,[46] but relatively little has been done in applying its insights to liturgical or sacramental theology. However, critical realism's approach to the interplay between structures and agents, and therefore between these two and culture, provides a potent way forward in areas where liturgical and sacramental theology has sometimes dissolved into vagueness (i.e., the oft-unspoken presumption that if we get our theology just a little more correct, then right liturgy or right liturgical/ethical formation ought to organically follow) or defeatism ("all we really need is better catechesis!"). Into these rather unsatisfying theological endgames, critical realism can inject a

---

[44] See, for example, (Beabout and Escheverria 2002, or Himes 2007).
[45] (Rand 1964, pp. 9–24).
[46] Many of its uses thus far have been relegated to biblical studies and systematic theology. See, for example, (Meyer 1994, or Achtemeier 1994). See also note 2 above, for my reasoning in bypassing the critical realism of Bernard Lonergan in this discussion.

helpful framework for contriving concrete possibilities for cultural conversion, if a community is brave enough—or, admittedly, possibly also foolhardy enough—to take hold of and shift the unpredictable structural levers of the morphogenic cycle. What follows are some suggestions for doing so in order to address consumer culture and its challenge to liturgy.

The first section of this discussion outlined a critical realist conception of the interplay between structure and agency, namely one of mutual emergence, which Archer terms the morphogenic cycle. However, in order to apply this framework to the issue of consumer culture, we need to recognize that a parallel interplay takes place between culture and agency. For Archer, while the morphogenic cycle between structure and agency rotates through the processes of structural conditioning, social interaction, and structural elaboration, the morphogenic cycle between culture and agency similarly proceeds through processes of cultural conditioning, sociocultural interaction, and cultural elaboration.[47] Additionally, the central causal forces of the structure–agency cycle hold in parallel with the culture–agency cycle, in that cultural conditioning comprises the social backdrop for an agent's decision-making, and exerts indeterminate causal force on the agent. The agent then acts (sociocultural interaction), having been formed by the cultural factors of which she or he is a part, and that action, coupled with the actions of other agents in the sociocultural interaction, gives way to cultural elaboration, the formation, re-formation, and malformation of which closes the cycle and begins it again.

One ought to note at least two things in this conception of the relationships between structure and agents, and agents and culture. First, as Archer points out, the two morphogenic cycles "intersect in the middle element of the basic cycle."[48] Agency, it turns out, is the unit common to both structure and culture, and the unit that provides the bulk of translation between the two. It is important to note that for Archer, agency does not necessarily imply *only* the agency of individual persons. Rather, she speaks also of the agency of "interest groups,"[49] recognizing that the exercise of individual agency is almost never that of an isolated, solitary actor. Still, agency remains weighted toward the individual, and to that extent it implies that the translation of social reality between structures and culture essentially takes place through the actions of persons—enstructured and encultured agents certainly, but nevertheless persons.

Second, the intersection of the two cycles, while mediated through social interaction and sociocultural interaction—that is, the actions of agents—does not imply a direct nexus point between the two cycles. Rather, in Archer's view, it is actually the third steps of the cycles that cross over to inform the first step of the cycles parallel to them.[50] Structural elaboration emerges into cultural conditioning, and cultural elaboration emerges into structural conditioning. The import of this point is, for our purposes, to caution against thinking that a change in structural conditioning can lead to a change in culture (through social interaction of agents) without continued elaboration of that structure beyond the initial change, or that vice versa, a shift in structural conditioning can, through sociocultural interaction of agents, lead to a shift in structure without continued elaboration of culture as well. In a word, this process is messy. It is also unpredictable. It is also, for Archer, quite real. Changes in structure, culture, and agency can be both intentional and unintentional, but they are not mechanistic. The morphogenic cycles of structure–agency and culture–agency are not determinative cycles; they are cycles of emergence, where each revolution of the cycle will bend the trajectory of the cycle in a slightly new, unpredictable way. There are ways in which shifts to agency, culture, and structure may steer that bending, but these are far from deterministic processes.

With this humility of purpose in mind, I would posit the thesis that liturgical and sacramental theology, especially in the context of liturgy and ethics, has paid admirable attention to culture and

---

47 (Archer 1995, pp. 168–69, 309).
48 Ibid., p. 305. Emphasis removed.
49 Ibid.
50 Ibid., p. 309.

agency, but it has tended to either ignore or shy away from structure. What I mean by this is that when problems appear in liturgy, the bulk of theological energy tends to be spent in the meaning-building or clarification of cultural realities, or in suggesting and refining practices intended to shape agency culturally. To be clear, these are good and necessary things to do (for example, Timothy Brunk's article, cited above, after working through an account of consumerist culture, ends with some very helpful suggestions about forming agency and culture).[51] However, critical realism suggests that there is a potent third area of social reality that is open to analysis and even change: that of structures. Structures, as objective entities distinct from agency and culture, nevertheless both build and are built by agency and culture. Liturgical/sacramental theology, especially as it encounters ethics, would needlessly hinder itself by ignoring structures and their ability to change.

To show what I mean, I'd like to suggest two examples of structural conditions that have shifted (and continue to shift) as a result of cultural elaboration that, according to the morphogenic cycle, emerged from sociocultural interaction and the cultural conditioning that preceded it. I do so with the conviction that changes (elaborations) in these structures have and can continue to shift cultural conditioning in the context of liturgy, for good or ill. One should take care not to expect a quick-fix or silver bullet solution here. Recall that for Archer, the historicity of the relationship between agents and structures is integral to their reality, and so shifting of structures is not something that takes place instantaneously. In fact, not only do changes not take place instantaneously, but shifts to structure would best be approached stepwise, in order to avoid falling into the illusion that one might reduce structures to mere tools of agency. If an agent or group of agents shifts a structure, at best they may have in mind a general trajectory toward or away from which such structures will elaborate as they continue to develop. Structures shift through the morphogenic cycle, and not necessarily quickly. With this humility of purpose in mind, what follows are two examples of how liturgical/sacramental structures might change in order to begin bending the morphogenic cycle away from consumerism. There may be other beginnings, and better ones depending on the specific context of a liturgical community; these are examples, not solutions.

Example 1. *Who makes the communion elements?*

Simply asking this question may reveal my agenda in asking it (and, it is important to note, I am far from the first one to raise this particular issue).[52] There is a relational structure between the baker of the bread and the liturgical community, as well as between the winemaker and the liturgical community. My assertion here is that elaboration of consumer culture has so driven the structural conditioning of these relationships that for a great many liturgical communities, parallel to the supplanting of domestic production by mass consumption we saw in Vincent Miller's work above, these relational structures do not even register as embodiments of consumerism. This of course would come with notable exceptions (certainly some liturgical communities maintain direct and ethical relationships with local producers of bread and wine), but the pervasiveness of sleeves of wafers and gallon jugs of Mogen David in many liturgical celebrations suggest to me that the exceptions remain exceptions.[53]

---

[51] (Brunk 2011, pp. 68–72).

[52] This question has been asked from a variety of theological vantage points, but many thus far tend to connect the question to environmental concerns, and/or questions of returning eucharistic practice to that of a full meal for community sustenance. These are certainly important aspects of the question, but for our purposes in this discussion, I would like to ask it specifically in relation to consumer culture and the possibility for structures of eucharistic practice to shift that cultural paradigm. For other engagements of this question, see (Jung 2006, pp. 130–40; Hostetter 2017, p. 54; Northcott 2007, pp. 261–66). Laura M. Hartman does ask this question in passing relationship to consumerism, but I would like to push further in this direction than her project initially goes (Hartman 2011, p. 163).

[53] It may also be good to recognize that some mass production enterprises are nevertheless cast as much as possible as sustainable, family-owned businesses, indicating a recognition of the tensions of consumerism even in its execution (see, for example, Zezima 2008).

I am not suggesting that switching from mass-produced wine to a local (even parishioner) winemaker and from mass-produced wafers to a church bread-baking group will magically equip a liturgical community to resist the totalizing commodification of persons and communities that consumer culture heralds. Rather, I am suggesting that basing structures—for example the structures of relationships between a liturgical community and those who produce its communion elements—on elaborations of consumer culture already weights the social interactions of that community toward cycling ever deeper into consumer culture. This is more than a matter of hypocrisy (though it is that as well, because how can I critique consumerism while consecrating its fruits?) because hypocrisy is nearly exclusively the realm of the agent (contradictory words and actions). This is instead a matter of the structural frameworks that pave the way for hypocrisy in the first place. To shift the structures of sourcing a liturgical community's communion elements could—slowly, ever slowly—elaborate into a cultural conditioning that is something other than consumerism. It also might not. But the question at this point is, even in the context of slow historicity and unpredictability, why not bet on structures that depart from consumerism, rather than ignoring the structural realities by exclusive focus on culture and agency?

Example 2. *Who sets the communion table?*

About two years ago, the liturgical community in which I worship adopted a structure of communion preparation in which the children of the congregation—as many or as few as are present—do the work of preparing the communion table. During the offering, the children leave their seats in the pews and make their way to where the dishes and elements are stored (they neither need explicit invitation anymore, nor do they process; it's a beautifully malleable and rather uncoordinated process). Then, they take turns bringing the wine, the bread, the plates, the chalices, the towels, and whatever else happens to be present up to the altar, where they are received by the presider, and having been thanked for their help, the children return to their seats. To be clear: this is a process, not essentially a structure. However, it was made possible by a structural elaboration in which the community (most especially the presider) recognized the structure of presider–table-setter and shifted at least one aspect of it, namely, that the table-setter was no longer the usually adult assisting minister of the day, and instead became the assembly's young ones.[54]

This structural elaboration has made possible an area of meaning-making, that is, cultural conditioning, that was not available before the structure shifted. Certainly the meanings derived are unpredictable—just as many likely see this as an opportunity for an "isn't-that-cute" precious moment as for anything deeper—but even in that context of unpredictability, the emergent cultural conditioning has paved the way for other emergent sociocultural interactions and cultural elaborations. Child agents, on the whole, have taken quite seriously their new role, with older children guiding younger children in how to participate, and often helping them when underdeveloped motor skills threaten to send some piece of pottery crashing to the floor. The assembly, for its part, has begun to recognize the value not simply in "letting kids participate," but in treating children's contributions as both real and necessary to the celebration.[55]

---

54 I should mention here that structures are not primarily concerned, in critical realism, with *who* exactly is filling them, so one might argue that I have misused the term structure in this example. I would reply that what changed in the structural relationship *was* actually a set of aspects that were seen either as obvious or even essential: age (from adult to the young), number (from one to an indeterminate number), and efficiency (the current structure produces longer, less reliable table-setting).

55 It might be helpful to note here that, in this particular liturgical community, the children are also welcome to participate in the Holy Communion they have helped set up if they desire to (with the understanding that they are ideally being formed in ever-greater understanding of the mystery they participate in). I readily acknowledge that this may not be possible for all liturgical communities, but again, what I am trying to elucidate here is not imitation of these specific structural shifts, but community-appropriate structural shifts that would tend to elaborate away from consumer culture.

The point at which this example touches consumer culture is that ultimately this process is not efficient (it does not easily lend itself to instant gratification), nor does it prioritize the consumption of religion for the nuclear family (families are physically separated when their children go to set the table and their parents/guardians remain in the pews) or the interests of any single individual (some like the practice, and some do not). The children's witness is that this labor makes a difference, and the meanings consequent upon consumer culture do not fit easily into this structural conditioning. The kids haven't bought or merited a place at the table, other than by being invited. However, this structure, perhaps by its novelty and perhaps by other factors, is pronounced; it is highly visible and accentuates by its makeup the other structures at work in the liturgy. In this way, what one might derive as ethical implications from the celebration of the liturgical assembly is formed, at least in part, by a structure that is not soaked in consumerism. Again, such a structure does not "fix" consumerism on its own, not by a long shot. Rather, this structure opens the door for further structural and cultural elaborations, which may continue to twist away from consumer culture, or they may not. In either case, the liturgical community has elaborated this structure in order to embody something true about the liturgical celebration and its ethical implications beyond, and I believe that is a gamble from which liturgical and sacramental theology can learn.

5. Conclusions

This article has argued that critical realism provides fertile conceptual ground in which to sow liturgical/sacramental theology, especially as it encounters ethics. Beginning with a summary of the development of critical realism and the ways in which it was translated into social theory, I then argued that Archer's model of the morphogenic cycle provides a compelling way to conceive of the mutual emergence of structure and agency. Following this, the article presented a theological view of consumer culture, and named both liturgical and ethical problems with consumerism. Finally, I argued that the parallel morphogenic cycles of structure–agency and culture–agency provide an illuminating framework for understanding the underappreciated importance of structure in liturgy and ethics, alongside agency and culture. Given the examples of both the structure of who provides the communion elements to liturgical communities and who sets the communion table, I argued that structures can, albeit slowly and unpredictably, provide another avenue for conditioning liturgical-ethical engagement with cultural forces like consumerism. This is not a silver-bullet fix, but critical realism's treatment of structures can provide another worthy tool to studies in liturgy and ethics.

Funding: This research received no external funding.

Conflicts of Interest: The authors declare no conflict of interest.

References

Achtemeier, P. Mark. 1994. The Truth of Tradition: Critical Realism in the Thought of Alasdair Macintyre and T.F. Torrance. *Scottish Journal of Theology* 47: 355–74. [CrossRef]

Archer, Margaret S. 1995. *Realist Social Theory: The Morphogenic Approach.* Cambridge: Cambridge University.

Beabout, Gregory R., and Eduardo J. Escheverria. 2002. The Culture of Consumerism: A Catholic and Personalist Critique. *Journal of Markets and Morality* 5: 339–83.

Beaudoin, Tom. 2003. *Consuming Faith: Integrating Who We Are with What We Buy.* Lanham: Sheed & Ward.

Bhaskar, Roy. 2008. *A Realist Theory of Science.* New York: Routledge. First published in 1975.

Bhaskar, Roy. 1998. General Introduction. In *Critical Realism: Essential Readings.* Edited by Roy Bhaskar, Margaret Archer, Andrew Collier, Tony Lawson and Alan Norrie. New York: Routledge, pp. ix–xxiv.

Brunk, Timothy. 2011. Consumerism and the Liturgical Act of Worship. *Horizons* 38: 54–74. [CrossRef]

Buckly, Walter. 1967. *Sociology and Modern Systems Theory.* Upper Saddle River: Prentice Hall.

Cavanaugh, William T. 2002. *Theopolitical Imagination: Rediscovering the Liturgy as a Political Act in an Age of Global Consumerism.* London: T & T Clark.

Chauvet, Louis-Marie. 1995. *Symbol and Sacrament.* Collegeville: Liturgical Press.

Chauvet, Louis-Marie. 2001. *Sacraments: The Word of God at the Mercy of the Body.* Collegeville: Liturgical Press.

Cloutier, David. 2017. Grimes and Cavanaugh on Structural Evils of Violence and Race: Overcoming Conflicts in Contemporary Social Ethics. *Journal of the Society of Christian Ethics* 37: 59–78. [CrossRef]

Denton, Donald L., Jr. 2004. *Historiography and Hermeneutics in Jesus Studies: An Examination of the Work of John Dominic Crossan and Ben F. Meyer.* London: T&T Clark.

Denton, Donald L., Jr. 2015. Being Interpreted by the Parables: Critical Realism as Hermeneutical Epistemology. *Journal for the Study of the Historical Jesus* 13: 232–54. [CrossRef]

Finn, Daniel K. 2016. What is a Sinful Social Structure? *Theological Studies* 77: 136–64. [CrossRef]

Finn, Daniel K. 2019. *Consumer Ethics in a Global Economy.* Washington: Georgetown University.

Hartman, Laura M. 2011. *The Christian Consumer: Living Faithfully in a Fragile World.* New York: Oxford University.

Himes, Kenneth R. 2007. Consumerism and Christian Ethics. *Theological Studies* 68: 132–53. [CrossRef]

Hostetter, Derek. 2017. An Integral Eucharist: Pope Francis, Louis-Marie Chauvet, and Ecology's Relationship to Eucharist. *Journal of Moral Theology* 2: 34–55.

Jerončić, Ante. 2015. The Quest for "La Sapienza:" Roy Bhaskar's Critical Realism and the Science and Religion Dialogue. *Andrews University Seminary Studies* 53: 355–68.

Jung, L. Shannon. 2006. *Sharing Food: Christian Practices for Enjoyment.* Minneapolis: Fortress.

Kiesling, Christopher. 1978. Liturgy and Consumerism. *Worship* 52: 359–68.

Lonergan, Bernard. 1972. *Method in Theology.* New York: Herder and Herder.

Mearman, Andrew. 2006. Critical Realism in Economics and Open-Systems Ontology: A Critique. *Review of Social Economy* 64: 47–75. [CrossRef]

Meyer, Ben F. 1994. *Reality and Illusion in New Testament Scholarship.* Collegeville: Liturgical Press.

Miller, Vincent J. 2003. *Consuming Religion: Christian Faith and Practice in a Consumer Culture.* New York: Continuum.

Miller, Vincent J. 2010. The Body Globalized: Problems for a Sacramental Imagination in an Age of Global Commodity Chains. In *Religion, Economics, and Culture in Conflict and Conversation.* Edited by Laurie Cassidy and Mareen H. O'Connell. New York: Maryknoll, pp. 108–20.

Murphy, Nancey C. 1988. From Critical Realism to a Methodological Approach: Response to Robbins, Van Huyssteen, and Hefner. *Zygon* 23: 287–90. [CrossRef]

Niiniluoto, Ilkka. 1999. *Critical Scientific Realism.* Oxford: Oxford University.

Northcott, Michael S. 2007. *A Moral Climate: The Ethics of Global Warming.* Maryknoll: Orbis.

Porter, Stanley E., and Andrew W. Pitts. 2015. Critical Realism in Context: N.T. Wright's Historical Method and Analytic Epistemology. *Journal for the Study of the Historical Jesus* 13: 276–306. [CrossRef]

Rand, Ayn. 1964. *The Virtue of Selfishness: A New Concept of Egoism.* New York: Signet.

Robbins, Wesley. 1999. Pragmatism, Critical Realism, and the Cognitive Value of Religion and Science. *Zygon* 34: 655–66. [CrossRef]

Schilbrack, Kevin. 2014. Embodied Critical Realism. *Journal of Religious Ethics* 42: 107–12. [CrossRef]

Schor, Juliet B. 1991. *The Overworked American.* New York: Basic Books.

Smith, Christian. 2010. *What is a Person?* Chicago: University of Chicago.

Smith, Christian. 2015. *To Flourish or Destruct.* Chicago: University of Chicago.

Veiga, Carlos. 2012. Artistic Creativity in Liturgy as Christian Identity and Freedom: Against Consumerism and a Liturgical Monopoly. *Journal of Latin American Theology* 7: 83–91.

Zezima, Katie. 2008. Bread of Life, Baked in Rhode Island. *The New York Times*, December 28. Available online: https://www.nytimes.com/2008/12/25/business/smallbusiness/25sbiz.html (accessed on 16 May 2019).

Article

Drones and Eucharist

Jason M. Smith

Liberal Studies, Tougaloo College, Tougaloo, MS 39174, USA; jason.m.smith521@gmail.com

Received: 31 May 2019; Accepted: 26 June 2019; Published: 28 June 2019

Abstract: In the post-9/11 world, the use of drone strikes has become a critical aspect of U.S. Military strategy in the War on Terror. While the ethics of drones have been argued from a theological perspective, this essay argues that a deeper, more theoretical understanding of drones is necessary in order to mount an adequate theological response. The author argues that the particular epistemological foundations by which drone strikes are justified must be given a theological corrective and that the Eucharist is the site for such a correction. This essay ultimately argues that the Eucharist shows the epistemology that undergirds the use of drones to be severely lacking and that under the judgment of the Eucharist the use of such technology is incompatible with the identity of the Church.

Keywords: drones; Eucharist; theology; ontology; apophaticism

1. Introduction

On 7 September 2013 an unaccompanied red pickup truck rumbled along a gravel path in the district of Watapur, taxiing a group of passengers to a nearby village. Watapur is a treacherous area to traverse so the drivers in this region have developed something of a buddy system. The truck in question was expected to arrive at its destination around nightfall. It contained a dozen or so members of a family from the area, as well as a lone female passenger hitching a ride through the boggy road ahead. Among the members of the family on board were women and children, one as young as eighteen months old. They would never reach their destination.

At around 5:30 PM they were attacked by what the locals call the *ghanghai*. They never got a good look at it. It killed several of the right side passengers first, then returned for those trying to flee on foot, then came back one final time and killed any that might have remained hiding in the truck. Most of the trucks passengers were found dismembered or disemboweled when help arrived. A four-year old girl was the sole survivor of the attack, and she was left horrifically mutilated. She was missing her nose, her bottom lip, and her faced was bloodied to the point that her uncle, who was the first to arrive at the scene of the attack, did not recognize her until she spoke to him. "Where is my Father? Where is my Mother?" she asked him.

The ghanghai is a creature with which the denizens of Watapur and surrounding provinces are quite familiar. They have adapted to its intrusion into their country. Locals are known to scatter when they hear the telltale buzzing sound that foretells its approach in order to limit the number of people it can kill. They hear the sound of its approach several times a day. The ghanghai is not, however, a creature, strictly speaking. It is a creation.

"Ghanghai" is the local word for "drone" (Jeong 2018).

2. Theorizing and Theologizing the Drone

Why must theologians speak of drones? This will be the central question to which this essay hopes to give an answer. There are, however, several ways to ask this question, each with its own specific emphases. We could ask, "why *must* theologians speak of drones?" This is to make the question out to be an entirely ethical one that theologians, perhaps because of their metaphysical commitments or social locations, have neglected to ask. Those who see the wisdom in asking the question in this way would want to say that the ethical catastrophe of drone warfare must awaken the theologian from their political and, therefore, dogmatic slumber. With the Obama administration's striking admission in 2015 that drone strikes in Pakistan, Yemen, Somalia, and Afghanistan had killed somewhere between 64 and 116 civilians (though many human rights organizations contend the real number is much higher) and the Trump administration's recent refusal to report the number of civilian casualties caused by drone strikes, the ethical questions that press themselves upon the global Church need little assistance in making themselves known (Savage and Shane 2016; Savage 2019).

Another way to ask the central question is, "why must theologians *speak* of drones?" Those who would ask the question this way imply that speaking is precisely what we do *not* need. The answer to be given is not a theoretical but a practical one. In this case, to answer the question at all would be to say why theologians in particular ought to join the movements of protest and political resistance against the use of drones. Talk is cheap, after all. Yet, how shall we believe if we have not heard? These two divergent modes of asking obviously caricature a great many aspects of a complex conversation, but they demonstrate what might be described as two tempting directions to take a conversation about drones amongst theologians. Either direction seems to take the question off of terrain we call "properly" theological. That is to say, if we ask the question of drones in either way we seem to be admitting that theologians have very little to say at all about the matter *as theologians*. They engage the issue only in their role as ethicists or activists.

My intent in this essay is instead to ask the question in this way: why must *theologians* speak of drones? In other words, what is it about theology, and Christian theology in particular, that ought to compel the theologian, as in keeping with their vocation, to speak about drones? The real heart of the matter will be to answer what it is that such a theologian can or ought to say about the particular problems that drones present to Christian orthodoxy. That means that very little of what I am about to say will have to do directly with *ethics*. Much of what I will have to say has to do with questions limited to the realm of ontology or metaphysics with an eye towards an ethical correlate of that theory. I imagine this essay as attempting to stand in the tradition of thinkers like Donald MacKinnon who afforded to metaphysical discourse an inevitable ethical correlate since both were concerned with saying what was actually the case (Mackinnon 1982). Thus, to write a 'theology of the drone' is decidedly not to say only what the Christian ought to *do* or to say only what the Christian ought to *believe*. As obscure as it may sound, drones require a theological response rooted in matters of ontology and theory precisely because they resist ontological and theoretical categorization. The drone, after all, is a soldier without a body.

The methodological quibble over the true nature of the question at hand is not a new technique by any means in theology. The unique aspect of my argument will be that I take it to be impossible to speak about drones as a theologian, to give a theological response to the problem of drones, without speaking of the Eucharist. Indeed, the central claim of this essay will be that a theological response to the drone must see the drone as nothing less than an "anti-sacrament" so the only source from which to draw a theological corrective must be the sacrament that makes the truth of the Church in the first place, namely, the Eucharist.

In order to reach this claim I want to examine first contemporary responses to the problem of drones, focusing in particular on the recent genealogical account of drones from French theorist Grégoire Chamayou. His work shows, I think, that an idolatrous vision of the human being lies at the heart of what I will call "drone reasoning" or the "drone *episteme*," i.e., the epistemic frame that allows for the justification of the use of drones in war. Second, I shall turn to a theological genealogy to try and ascertain what a theological response to the problems of drones might look like. For that, I turn to the recent and characteristically ambitious political theology of John Milbank. Thus, I will argue that, seen through a Milbankian framework, a theological response to drones is all the more essential since drones are shown to be the secular weapon *par excellence*. A theological response to drones is thus an ontological and an ethical response or, more accurately, an ethical response *because* it is an ontological response. Drones, to put it again in Milbank's terms, must be read on theology's terms and not vice versa.

Thus, in my final section I shall turn to the work of this theological account of drones from a Eucharistic perspective. In this theological account, drone reasoning no longer reads the human subject but rather drone reasoning is read by the Eucharist, a rite that displaces that which is knowable about the human person through their encounter and incorporation into mystery. Drones are thereby shown to be an anti-sacrament, the embodiment of communal life that is fundamentally alienation rather than incorporation, ignorance rather than knowledge, absence rather than presence. Thus, that community which is thrown into being by the Eucharist, the Church, is shown always already to be an anti-drone community.

So I begin with the elemental question: what is a drone? There are technical answers to this question, obviously. According to the U.S. Army, a drone is "a land, sea, or air vehicle that is remotely or automatically controlled" (U.S. Department of Defense 2011, p. 109). Yet, any attempt to answer this question more fully—to "theorize" the drone, rather than merely define its use—will inevitably run aground upon negativity and absence. The drone is a weapon without a body. The drone is a gaze without a physical eye. The drone is a soldier that cannot be sacrificed. Grégoire Chamayou charts this series of absences in his *Theory of the Drone* by giving an account of the changes that the use of drones have loosed upon the world, particularly as it pertains to the way in which traditional norms of warfare have been changed by the emergence of this new technology. For our purposes, however, I want to focus on the theoretical or epistemological changes that the justification for such technology relies upon, as chronicled within Chamayou's genealogy.

According to Chamayou, in striving to emulate the traditional theological dictum that "omniscience implies omnipotence," drones attempt to fulfill a series of strategic principles (Chamayou 2014, p. 37). They are as follows:

1. The principle of persistent surveillance or permanent watch.
2. The principle of a totalization of perspectives or a synoptic viewing.
3. The principle of creating an archive or film of everyone's life.
4. The principle of data fusion.
5. The principle of the schematization of forms of life.
6. The principle of the detection of anomalies and preemptive anticipation (Chamayou 2014, pp. 38–42).

Within these principles, I want to argue that there is present to us a particular sort of epistemology—a series of presumed notions about how knowledge is gained, what we can and cannot know about human persons, and what such knowledge allows us to conclude as certain or established. The use of drones, so I think Chamayou is trying to argue, is only justifiable so long as this presumed epistemic frame holds, so long as archiving forms of life and studying their patterns can lead to successful preemption of certain actions. Allow me to analyze each principle in further detail.

The first two principles show that drones aim to establish a permanent watch on a given target or network and to couple that watch with synoptic viewing. To do so, drones must overcome what is called the "tyranny of distance" (Scahill and the Staff of the Intercept 2017). The tyranny of distance in this case is the forced series of "blinks" in the drone's gaze on its targets caused by the distance drones and other aircraft must traverse in order to reach their mark's location and keep the surveillance feed uninterrupted. In this sense, then, drone reasoning is both literally and theoretically a refusal of distance and an embrace of closure. The subsequent principles of drone reasoning are a consequent to the first two: in overcoming the tyranny of distance one can create an archive of everyone's life, fuse the various sorts of data involved in that archival construction together (video surveillance, cell phone intercepts, etc.), and then construct a schematization of forms of life within a given social network of persons. The permanent gaze of the drone ought to allow one to map out an individual's movement in and out of various social groups so as to fulfill the final principle—to identify emergent threats via the identification of deviations from normal forms of life and take preemptive action. In the case of "signature strikes," i.e., drone strikes based on nothing more than a "signature" of deviant behavior, this sort of preemptive action can be undertaken without even having to identify the persons targeted.

It is not difficult to predict Chamayou's critique of this epistemology. The typical rules of drone warfare operate based upon an epistemic overreach that leads directly to dire political consequences. As Chamayou puts it, "[T]he whole problem—at once epistemological and political—lies in [the] claimed ability to convert a series of probable indices into a legitimate target" (Chamayou 2014, p. 49). The overreach, in other words, lies in the epistemic leap from an ambiguous pattern deviation to a matter of actionable certainty. I would argue that such a leap is only possible because drones offer us an imagined world in which people can be known as threats simply by overcoming the tyranny of distance—a world in which terrorists are 'texts,' if you will, which if read completely, or perhaps just *sufficiently*, will fully reveal their true nature. The distance that prevents this reading is the only barrier to the mission objectives of "Find, Fix, and Finish" (Scahill and the Staff of the Intercept 2017). Drones find their targets through a regime of permanent watch, *fix* them as targets through pattern of life analysis, and finish them with supposed precision. But, as Chamayou so delicately puts it, "There is a crucial difference between hitting the target and hitting only the target" (Chamayou 2014, p. 141).

Chamayou's ultimate conclusion is that the introduction of the technology of drones portends a concomitant shift in the underlying martial philosophy of war itself. Military action has now become governed by the logic of "manhunting," a logic immune from the typical *ethos* that once governed what we might call "traditional" warfare (Chamayou 2012, p. 5). This changes fundamental aspects of warfare—the way that States behave towards one another, the distinction between civilians and combatants, and the political calculus involved in waging war. Chamayou is here worth quoting at length:

> What is emerging is the idea of an invasive power based not so much on the rights of conquest as on the rights of pursuit: a right of universal intrusion or encroachment that would authorize charging after the prey wherever it found refuge, thereby trampling underfoot the principal of territorial integrity classically attached to state sovereignty. According to such a concept, the sovereignty of other states becomes a contingent matter. Full enjoyment of that sovereignty is recognized only if those states take imperial tracking to heart—"failed" states cannot, "rogue" states will not—their territories can legitimately be violated by a hunter-state (Chamayou 2014, p. 53).

Yet, for my purposes, what is more striking is that drones have introduced a new matrix of military jargon—coupled inexorably to the logic of manhunting that Chamayou describes—that seems to steer certain situations that ought to be innocuous towards disastrous results. Andrew Cockburn's *Kill Chain* opens with such an incident, wherein twenty-three civilians were killed by an air strike coordinated by drone operators and spurred on by anxiety over the two to five second delay in the relay of images from the drone itself. More than just the delay, however, is the linguistic covering over of human beings that turns men, women, and children into something different. Cockburn writes, 'The crews spoke a language almost incomprehensible to outsiders, so laden with acronyms that plain English was often supplanted. But that night's conversations show that the military jargon, like the two-second video delay, imposed another layer between them and the reality on the ground. Any MAM (military-aged male) became by definition an enemy fighter, irrespective of age, and therefore a legitimate target" (Cockburn 2015, p. 8). Ultimately, what becomes clear is that using drones insulates one from the typical manner of experiencing human beings, both physically and linguistically. The arresting nature of a genuine human encounter, that which causes one to recognize the limits of one's knowledge in encountering an Other, is displaced in and through the visual and linguistic experience of drone operation.

It is that linguistic displacement that Solmaz Sharif attends to masterfully in her recent collection of poems, *Look*. Sharif interpolates terminology from the Department of Defense's *Dictionary of Military and*

Associated Terms into her poetry so as to throw light upon the ways in which the language of the D.O.D. is at odds with the poetic way in which we seek to understand our own being as humans. The contrast between the spartan mode of military speech and the intimate nature of Sharif's re-presentation of embodied particularity reveals the displacement of human mystery that is at the heart of the drone's gaze. "It matters what you call a thing," Sharif begins, and in this beginning is perhaps the whole of what one needs to criticize in the U.S. Drone Program (Sharif 2016, p. 3). Yet, there are several moments of *poesis* that seem to make present for the reader the precise linguistic displacement of which I am speaking. Some are quite direct, (note: the words in ALL CAPS are drawn from the DOD Dictionary): "Daily I sit with the language they've made of our language to NEUTRALIZE the CAPABILITY of LOW DOLLAR VALUE ITEMS like you" (Sharif 2016, p. 64). Some instances utilize religious allusions: "Whereas *ye know not what shall be on the morrow. For what is your life?* It is even a THERMAL SHADOW, it appears so little, and then vanishes from the screen" (Sharif 2016, p. 4). Sharif shows, in sum, that the ultimate effect of this sort of linguistic innovation is, in fact, a calculus removed from humaneness: "In EXECUTION PLANNING, they weighed/the losses, the SUSTAINABILITY/and budgeted/for X number,/they budgeted for the phone call/to your mother and weighed that/against the amount saved in rations/and your taste for cigarettes" (Sharif 2016, pp. 64–5).

Ultimately, what Chamayou, Cockburn, and Sharif reveal is that the thinkability or imaginability of the use of drones is not merely a byproduct of technological innovation. It is not merely, in other words, that we have built the bombs and therefore are going to drop them. The problem of drones runs deeper. Drones are the end result of a particular epistemology or, perhaps better, a *desire* for a certain epistemological state of affairs that makes thinkable a certain relationship between war and the state, combatant and civilian. It is a way of knowing that sees human life as subject to surveillance, classification, and pattern of life analysis. It is a way of knowing that relies upon a particular linguistic distortion of human life and finite reality—a displacement, through language, of the natural yet excessive mystery at the heart of being itself. Hence, theology cannot respond to the ethical quandary of drones with an ethical recommendation for new modes of action—though this will certainly be a part of any theological critique—but instead must respond in kind. The way of knowing at the root of the use of drones must be read theologically and a theological corrective as a form of counter-ontology must be offered. It is to the beginning of that counter that I now turn.

3. The Drone as Secular Weapon

When faced with this linguistic displacement of human mystery, I want to claim that theologians can do more than simply suggest a new vocabulary to the D.O.D. Instead, I want to claim that the particular gift theology can give in this moment is not just an ethical prescription but rather a theological account which shows the *episteme* at the root of drone reasoning to be incompatible with Christian orthodoxy. This will mean, ultimately, that drone reasoning is not merely mistaken but *idolatrous* and thus requires a theological corrective in order to begin the work of making thinkable an ethical alternative.

I would like to do this through a recent work of political ontology from John Milbank. In *Beyond Secular Order*, Milbank has attempted to trace the roots of how problematic ontological thinking, particular the ontological moves of modernity, becomes a problematic frame for political action (Milbank 2013). His argument rests on the notion that "ideas about being coincide with ideas about human action" (Milbank 2013, p. 3). Now, that is clearly a contestable proposition, but I want to assume it for the moment to show not only the usefulness of some aspects of Milbank's genealogy but also how that genealogy helps us to analyze the particular phenomenon of drone warfare. For if we assume that ideas about being really do coincide with ideas about human action then a genealogy of modern ontology ought to flow directly into a genealogy of modern political realities. This is the root of Milbank's fascinating decision to call a portion of his work a "political ontology" (Milbank 2013, p. 114). In short, political constructions are contingent realities whose origins can be traced genealogically, but for Milbank, if I have read him correctly, the theologian must trace these genealogies not merely through the vicissitudes of cultural or material realities, but ontological ones as well. So to peer into the history of the philosophy of being is also to peer into the bedrock of those systems of political legitimacy that have come to characterize modernity as a whole.

Thus, Milbank's genealogy begins with what he calls four pillars characteristic of modern ontology. They are: (1) univocity over analogy of being, (2) knowledge by representation instead of identity, (3) the priority of possibility over the mysterious depths of actuality, and (4) divine causality as concurrence within the same causal plane rather than influence through a series of hierarchical causal chains (Milbank 2013, p. 3). Here Milbank is singing a tune quite familiar to those who have followed the work of he and his cohorts associated with the Radical Orthodoxy movement. Milbank's broad claim here is still much the same as that which he advanced in *Theology and Social Theory* some decades ago, namely, that being itself—our idea of it and, therefore, the way in which we choose to act within it—was emptied of a mystery that was proper to it in the transition from the Middle Ages to the Secular Age (Milbank 1997). In other words, being was once held to be *naturally* mysterious, not as the secret bearer of some hidden divine presence. This natural mystery proper to being and, consequently, to beings, is drained away in the transition from pre-modern ontology into an ontology governed by the four pillars that Milbank is describing. For my purposes, I want to claim that when we take the four pillars together a compelling thesis comes into view: the drone can be classified as a *fundamentally secular weapon* because without the modern ontological turns I am about to describe the drone's primary foundation for the justification of its use would be rendered untenable.

As to the first pillar, one of the characteristic arguments of radical orthodoxy comes into view. First, the characteristic argument of much of what is known as radical orthodoxy berates John Duns Scotus' thesis of the "univocity of being." What this phrase entails is a dispute between Aquinas and Scotus on what the proper mode of predication was for God and for creatures. Now, before I recount Milbank's argument here I should note that his reading of both Scotus and Aquinas have come under heavy criticism, to the point that his readings of either figure is nearly untenable (Horan 2014; DeHart 2012). What use then can I have for his arguments? While I take Milbank's historical assertions to stand on highly questionable grounds I do believe his use of these two figures as paradigms of sorts for certain streams of thought within the broader current of modernity does stand. Thus, in the coming paragraphs perhaps it is best to think always of these two figures as "Milbank's Scotus" and "Milbank's Aquinas" respectively.

Milbank sees in Scotus' theory of univocity in religious language a disastrous misstep. Put in a less abstract way, Scotus thought that what we attribute to God could be attributed to creatures in the same voice, i.e., univocally (Scotus *Ordinatio*, 18/19). In other words, when we say that God is good and that this essay is good, we are using a notion of goodness that is common to both of them, though the latter possesses goodness to a far lesser degree than the former. Yet, critically, there is no inherent difference between what we mean by good in each instance. We are still speaking in the *same voice* about God being good and the essay being good. This is, so Milbank argues, a marked shift from the mode of predication that had been prevalent amongst theologians prior to Scotus. Before this inflection point in theological language, *analogy* had been the mode of predication that was seen as primary (Milbank 2013, pp. 50–57). Thus, when we say that God exists and that Liverpool Football Club exists, we *are not* saying that these two share the same sort of existence. We are speaking analogously. Under Scotus' paradigm, however, God and Liverpool Football Club would share the same sort of existence, albeit at different levels of intensity. To dramatically simplify the dispute, Aquinas sought to protect the distance between God and creatures by ensuring that theological language, while able to speak truthfully, is always out of its depth so to speak. Scotus sought to protect the legitimacy of theological claims by asserting that whatever is good about our created life must be held by God in spades.

This might seem like an inquiry confined solely to theoretical concerns but the implication of this thesis, in Milbank's estimation, is vast and far-reaching. The consequence of this shift towards univocity is that existence now must be predicated in precisely the same, univocal manner to God and creatures. This means, ultimately, that being is a neutral thing that both God and creatures possess in the same way. So any knowledge within this horizon of being will be fundamentally determined by this sameness and accessibility.

Secondly, knowledge by representation instead of identity refers, for Milbank, to the epistemological shift that came to see true knowledge as an accurate "copy" within the mind. This was in contradistinction to the traditional sense of knowledge that held to know something was to be united to it via one's intellect. For the first time, so Milbank's argument goes, an "object" emerged rather than a synthesis of form and matter. Thirdly, our idea of reality came to be dominated by what Milbank calls the priority of the possible. The big idea here is that in modernity we view reality as determined most fundamentally by a prior possibility or by a matrix of acceptable possibilities rather than by what is actually in front of us. So rather than reality disclosing a partial image of the divine glory, we are forever haunted in our knowledge of the world by the idea that it might have been otherwise. Perhaps this point is best understood if one notes the difference between the following phrases "reality as *gift*" and "reality as a *given*." Finally, and perhaps most critically, this view of reality changes the way in which God can be said to act within reality. The theological notion of concurrence is not necessarily invented during this period but comes to take center stage in explanations about how it is that God can be said to act within the causal order without overriding the freedom and dignity of creatures. There are many variations on this theme, but what Milbank wishes to hammer home is that the prior three pillars are theological moves that preeminently culminate in this move, which would see God as one causal actor among others within the same neutral field of being. Again, the view of reality here is what is critical. Beings, in order to be free, must be free from divine causality. Freedom of God and freedom of creatures becomes an either/or rather than a both/and—either God is acting freely or a creature is acting freely, but to say that both occur at the same time is a difficult proposition to defend from the univocal perspective.

Now, what I've just recounted surely invites critical responses from the perspectives of historical theology and contemporary systematic theology. As I said above, critiques of Milbank's *oeuvre* are certainly not few and far between. Adjudicating the accuracy of his readings of John Duns Scotus as the great boogeyman or of Thomas Aquinas as ur-theologian of radical orthodoxy is beyond the scope of my argument. What I do want to claim is that his genealogical sequence bears surprising fruit when put in dialogue with the problem of drones. Milbank's work is useful in bringing the following to light: whatever we are to make of his charge that the entirety of the secular order is grounded in a draining of mystery from reality, it is surely the case that drone warfare can only operate off of an anthropology that is based in an ontology like the one Milbank is describing. Thus, I think it is telling that Milbank's first step after leveling his critical faculties against modern ontology is to launch into a constructive effort aimed at rebuilding an adequate account of the human being. In short, the critical connection that Milbank makes is between the way we imagine reality and the way in which we then imagine what it ought to be like for human beings to belong together within said reality. If that reality is drained of a mystery that was once considered proper to it, then the human being is also now deprived of a particular type of dignity. My reading of Milbank thus brings forth the claim that it is only this loss of mystery that justifies a regime of permanent watch as a viable solution to violence. Whatever systems of thought drones might be grounded within—capitalism, neoliberalism, etc.—it is theology that reveals that the roots of the drone *episteme* I have been describing are not merely ontological but *theological*. The linguistic displacement of the natural, yet supernatural mystery inherent to an adequate ontology and a dignified anthropology requires not only a theoretical corrective, but a theological response.

4. Drones and the Judgment of the Eucharist

If theology is essential to the task of naming the problem of drones then theology ought also to be indispensable for the problem's solution. What we seemed faced with is the need for an orienting point that could both refute the ontological problems of drone reasoning without dealing in a similar refusal of mediation and mystery. It is my contention that the appropriate site of a theological response to the problems of drones, therefore, is the Eucharist, wherein we encounter the authentic presence of God *and of ourselves* in an embodied, mysterious act. If drones rely on a linguistic displacement of this sort of authentic presence, then it will be our focus to discover how it is that the Eucharist refuses such a displacement and does so precisely in and within language. The Eucharist will thus be shown to be a form of language that incorporates us into an authentic sort of human belonging. The Eucharist, in other words, fundamentally shapes the identity-forming waters that we swim in, so to speak, by calling forth particular forms of human belonging. Yet, crucially, what I want to claim is that the form of belonging that the Eucharist calls forth is made possible by a fundamentally *mysterious* form of belonging into which the Eucharist incorporates us—that is, the mystery of the Trinitarian life of the Godhead. Thus, the Eucharist does displace our identities in language, but it places us into the mystery of the Trinity's *perichoresis*, wherein our identity is only to be found in the identities of those to whom we belong as members of one Body. While Chamayou sought to claim, rightly of course, that the drone is a sort of "anti-kamikaze," I want to put a theological spin on this by arguing that the drone is a sort of "anti-sacrament." Where the Eucharist is an instituting sign of the "presence of absence," the drone is a vacuous sign of the "absence of presence."

To make this case, I want to turn to the work of Louis-Marie Chauvet, whose seminal work on the Eucharist has most closely investigated the relationship between the Eucharist and absence. Chauvet is primarily concerned with understanding the Eucharist according to two fundamental categories: *gift* and *symbol*. More importantly, the understanding gained by investigating these two categories ultimately reveals not just a clearer picture of the Eucharist, but a refined picture of what it means to be human. It is by traveling the path through gift and symbol—by *submitting to them*, as Chauvet will say—that we discover a proper understanding of the Eucharist and a proper sense of human identity as gifted therein.

For Chauvet, the Eucharist occupies an odd place within the economy of grace. The rite is located, so to speak, right at the heart of a dialectic between being "instituted" and "instituting." On the one hand, the Eucharist was given to the Church. Hence, the traditional claim that the Eucharist, along with the other seven sacraments, were in some way "instituted" by Christ. The Eucharist, in, "escapes" the Church—the Church does not have full control over the rite because it did not create it (Chauvet 1995, p. 377). Yet, on the other hand, the instituted nature of the rite is the foundation of the "instituting" nature of the Eucharist. Tellingly, Chauvet can only describe this instituting nature of the rite by referring to language. The Eucharist institutes us as human subjects into new identities as Christian subjects. The Eucharist brings us into what Chauvet calls the "language-game of faith." (Chauvet 1995, p. 378).

At the heart of this rite, however, is the more controversial question of transubstantiation. For Chauvet a great deal turns on the true nature of Eucharistic change: how we conceptualize this encounter with the grace of God in the rite will have tremendous effect on what kind of identity is instituted by the rite itself. Critically, for Chauvet the identity into which we are instituted by the Eucharist—the language-game within which we are submersed in and through our faith—is the mystery of the "presence of absence" (Chauvet 1995, p. 63). Avoiding the traditional axioms of Scholastic theology, which Chauvet thinks should be dismissed as ontotheological, Chauvet argues instead that the Eucharistic presence is not a graspable, objective presence. It is rather a presence the nature of which is constituted by absence. This is most seminally revealed in the fact that the bread only has its true essence *in being broken*. It is the fissure opened up in the bread—not simply the bread as a whole—that most truly signifies the presence of the One whose body was broken for us.

The Eucharist for Chauvet thus becomes a sort of sacred pedagogy—a rite by which we learn to come back to the real truth of the subject by *consenting to the presence of absence* (Chauvet 1995). For Chauvet, then, transubstantiation is not the indwelling of the presence of Christ in the bread that is whole. Rather, the Eucharistic presence is now something that escapes us, it is the presence of God *as absent* in the breach of the bread as broken. Chauvet walks a decidedly tight line, but it is an essential one: God communicates God's very self to us in the Eucharist, but this communication is the self-communication of a God who chooses to become present as the Absent One. Chauvet's great innovation here is insisting that presence and absence are not mutually exclusive realities in the Eucharist. The Eucharistic presence is the presence of the absence of God, but it is also true that in the absence of the broken bread God is indeed truly and fully present.

I said above that Chauvet's theology can go from the Eucharist to theological anthropology or vice versa. Thus, one could say that we learn to consent first to the presence of the absence of God so that we can learn to consent to the presence of absence in ourselves. Chauvet sees in the Eucharist almost a fitting anticipation of a great deal of postmodern theory. He appropriates the insights of those like Heidegger and Lacan who assert that true human subjectivity is not defined by an objective or static essence but by processes of becoming and mediation (Chauvet 1995). We, ourselves, are constituted by mediation because we come to be subjects in and through *symbol*—those communicative signs, either verbal or otherwise, by which we encounter and confront other people. Language itself forms a sort of gift-exchange wherein we gift to other people that recognition that forms their subjectivity and receive back in return a similar recognition for ourselves. Most importantly, and here Chauvet is absolutely adamant, this process is one that is continual and unending (Chauvet 1995). In other words, the Eucharist does not give to us the sort of epistemic assurance that the principles of drone reasoning outlined above purport to do. The Eucharist seems to be entirely at odds with such an *episteme*. For in the Eucharist we are confronted with our own immersion in symbol, and yet this immersion is not a barrier to the truth of our subjectivity but is itself the basis for our identity in the first place. We are symbolic beings and we show forth the same sort of mysterious presence as does the God whom we encounter in the broken bread. We are, in short, confronted, even within our own self-understanding, with the presence of absence. It is only in learning to consent to this absence, in learning to embrace rather than eschew the mediation of symbol, that we come to find our true selves.

Critically, however, the Eucharist is not *just* a pedagogy. Perhaps for our purposes it might be enough to say that the Eucharist teaches us a different vision of the nature of personhood as a counter to the epistemic frame that undergirds the use of drones. Yet, if as Milbank asserted "thoughts about being coincide with thoughts about human action" then it does, in fact, matter what sort of account we give of the presence of absence in the Eucharist. For Chauvet, it is not merely that the Eucharist challenges our ways of thinking about God and human beings, encountering sacramental grace in the Eucharist is an incorporation into the Trinitarian relations (Chauvet 1995, p. 531). This means, I would argue, that the "ontological scandal" of the Eucharist, so to speak, is an incorporation into *mystery*. In the wake of the Eucharist, there is then a necessary apophaticism to our "ideas about being"—we are bound by the Eucharistic presence to speak now of ourselves as having our identity in relations that fundamentally escape our epistemological capacity. I have my differences with Chauvet's account of the nature of such a mystery—he favors a more Reformed vision of the *deus absconditus* out of fear of ontotheology associated with more traditional apophaticism—but the overall point I am trying to make is still in line with much of his work. The Eucharistic presence is not just a pedagogy for consenting to the presence of absence, it is rather an incorporation into that very presence of absence—i.e., into the life of the Godhead that is fundamentally mysterious.

Ultimately, an adequate theological counter to drones must be rooted in a sort of counter-epistemology to the epistemic frame that helps to justify the use of drones. This counter-epistemology will be rooted in ideas about being and personhood that are inculcated in us, as all concepts that make up our deep background of the world are, through language. The Eucharist is, I am arguing, just this sort of epistemic frame—a counter-ontology to the ideas about being inherent in the drone *episteme* that see human beings as texts to be read and, if the patterns therein are found to be suspicious, erased. It is thus a particular "language-game" as Chauvet says that places the human person as first and foremost having their identity in symbolic mediation and having its final *telos* in the mystery of the divine *perichoresis* of the Trinitarian relations.

5. Conclusions

Ultimately, what I think this small work of *bricolage* leads to is something like the following claim: the Eucharist is the site in which a Christian vision of the ontological and political meaning of mystery is encountered. In receiving the sacrament, we find ourselves doing two things: first, submitting to the order of signs as the very site of divine revelation. Second, and more importantly, we find ourselves gifted with a new way of speaking of how we belong to one another, precisely in and through submitting to the order of signs. Our typical way of speaking about how we belong to one another is displaced in favor of a fundamentally new mode of belonging: sharing in a common mystery that is both radically transcendent and as mundane as our daily bread. But, there is ever the recognition that these new manners of speaking are not final, but rather, they point beyond themselves to a manner of belonging that shall one day *become* final. This means that if we try to build a Christian political theology from the Eucharist (or a foreign policy, for that matter!) it will have very little to say with finality. It will look more like what Derrida famously called the "democracy to come" (Derrida 2005, p. 8). What such a political theology can do with great emphasis, however, is to note the way that the Eucharist stands in judgment over all other forms of human belonging, precisely in its refusal to speak with the finality that so many other forms of political discourse ground themselves upon. It would look like a political theology of apophasis or a politics grounded in *askesis*.

Drones, therefore, when placed under the judgment of the Eucharist, are seen to be something like an anti-sacrament: a sign that signifies a poverty of true negativity, *a symbol of the refusal of symbol*. It is no wonder, then, that such a "sign" can form no community and can bring no justice. For drones rely on a covering over of that fundamental mystery at the heart of human belonging in favor of an epistemology that sees in "patterns of life" nothing further than nodes of a mappable social network. Thus, the drone gives rise to the peculiar state of military affairs in which our world finds itself—constantly at war with no one in particular.

An epistemology that refuses to consent to the presence of absence—whether in ontology, in subjectivity, or in the Eucharistic community of the Risen One who is "not here"—cannot adequately ground a community striving for the common good. And it is, I think, chiefly the ontological and subsequent political scandal of the Eucharist that brings this to light. The Church, therefore, is always already an anti-drone community. For the Church dares to give primacy to a particular, located flesh and to eschew a gaze other than that gaze which looks out in love and forgiveness. Indeed, it must do this, since the root of the Church's entire idea about its being comes from a rite in which our ready to hand ideas about subjectivity are displaced by locating the truth of all subjectivity in Trinitarian mystery. Such a community can only see reality as a *gift* to be received and, consequently, can only see those whom it comes into contact with as unsurveillable—in other words, as their neighbor.

Obviously, the Church does not always behave in this way. The form of belonging that the Eucharist calls forth—that incorporation into the Trinitarian mystery that constitutes our identities, both individually and communally, as mysterious—is often neglected or even contradicted by the lives of the faithful. I am also not arguing that simply partaking of the Eucharist will be enough to make Christian communities around the world into the sorts of communities where that type of being-with is the identity we seek to live out of each day. In this sense, as I have written elsewhere, one could say that every Eucharist fails. Each meeting at the Lord's Table promises the presence of a new community and with each meeting it becomes quite obvious that such a community will not have any lasting presence on this side of the veil of tears. What I am arguing, however, is that the vision of the Body of Christ—the momentary transfiguration of the crooked timbre of human community into the congregation of the glassy sea—is the proverbial north star of the Christian imaginary. Drones, I have argued, are simply not compatible with this theological vision of dignified human life.

Funding: This research received no external funding.

Acknowledgments: The author wishes to thank the Critical Theories seminar group of the North American Academy of Liturgy for their comments on an earlier draft of this article.

Religions **2019**, *10*, 407

Conflicts of Interest: The author declares no conflict of interest.

References

Chamayou, Grégoire. 2012. *Manhunts: A Philosophical History*. Translated by Steve Randall. Princeton: Princeton University Press.

Chamayou, Grégoire. 2014. *A Theory of the Drone*. Translated by Janet Lloyd. New York: The New Press.

Chauvet, Louis-Marie. 1995. *Symbol and Sacrament: A Sacramental Reinterpretation of Christian Existence*. Translated by Patrick Madigan S. J., and Madeleine Beaumont. Collegeville: Liturgical Press.

Cockburn, Andrew. 2015. *Kill Chain: The Rise of High-Tech Assassins*. New York: Henry Holt and Company.

DeHart, Paul. 2012. *Aquinas and Radical Orthodoxy: A Critical Inquiry*. New York: Routledge.

Derrida, Jacques. 2005. *Rogues: Two Essays on Reason*. Translated by Pascale-Anne Brault, and Michael Naas. Stanford: Stanford University Press.

Horan, Daniel P. 2014. *Postmodernity and Univocity: A Critical Account of Radical Orthodoxy and Jon Duns Scotus*. Minneapolis: Fortress Press.

Jeong, May. 2018. Losing Sight. *The Intercept*, January 27.

Mackinnon, Donald. 1982. Prolegomena to Christology. *The Journal of Theological Studies* 33: 146–60. [CrossRef]

Milbank, John. 1997. *Theology and Social Theory: Beyond Secular Reason*. London: Blackwell.

Milbank, John. 2013. *Beyond Secular Order: The Representation of Being and the Representation of People*. London: Wiley Blackwell.

Savage, Charlie. 2019. Trump Revokes Obama-Era Rule on Disclosing Civilian Casualties Outside of War Zones. *The New York Times*, March 6.

Savage, Charlie, and Scott Shane. 2016. U.S. Reveals Death Toll from Strikes Outside War Zones. *The New York Times*, July 1.

Scahill, Jeremy, and the Staff of the Intercept. 2017. *The Assassination Complex: Inside the Government's Secret Drone Program*. New York: Simon & Schuster.

Sharif, Solmaz. 2016. *Look*. Minneapolis: Graywolf Press.

U.S. Department of Defense. 2011. *Dictionary of Military and Associated Terms. Joint Publication 1-02*; Washington: The Joint Staff.

Article

The Sacrament of Revelation: Toward a Hermeneutics of Nuptial Encounter

Lauren Smelser White

College of Bible & Ministry, Lipscomb University, Nashville, TN 37204, USA; lauren.white@lipscomb.edu

Received: 11 July 2019; Accepted: 18 August 2019; Published: 22 August 2019

Abstract: This article addresses the notion of sacramentality in relation to revelation, framing revelation as a divine-human discursive encounter facilitated through semantic media. In doing so, it suggests disciplines for theological reflection that would preserve the import of human submission to the Holy Spirit's guidance in interpreting God's Word while also envisioning a positive place for subjective construction along that Spirit-led way. The article locates the basic tenets of such a methodological paradigm in the works of Sarah Coakley, Louis-Marie Chauvet, and Rowan Williams. Coakley's work provides the groundwork for a vision of ecstatic encounter with God as integral to the Spirit-led process of revelation. Next, engagement with Chauvet establishes how mediated revelation may be conceived as a sacramental and dialogical reality, which fundamentally evokes and includes human self-expression. The article closes by drawing upon Williams' theological reflection on sexuality as a resource for embracing subjective construction, as integral to our Spirit-guided, "nuptial" incorporation into the life of Christ. The results afforded by this analysis warrant spiritual-hermeneutic commitments from communities who desire to cooperate with the Holy Spirit in acts of theological interpretation.

Keywords: revelation; sacrament; hermeneutics; Holy Spirit; Pneumatology; spirituality; symbol; ekstasis

---

1. Introduction

Christianity is experiencing a revival of the Holy Spirit. This is true not only in the church, which is seeing the striking growth of Pentecostal-charismatic movements in the global South, but also in academic circles, where there is burgeoning interest in fresh engagements with Pneumatology.[1] Regarding the latter trend, in his plenary address to the 2007 Nordic Systematic Theology Conference (whose theme was "Spirit and Spirituality"), LeRon Shults offered this incisive observation:

> The one trend in contemporary Pneumatology that encompasses virtually all of the others is the trend represented in the very title of this conference: *Spirit and Spirituality*. Broadly speaking, the theme of spirituality deals with the ways in which we interpret and attend to the transformation of our relation to God and our neighbors. Most of the general developments—and many of the concrete proposals—in recent Pneumatology are oriented toward or flow out of this concern. (Shults 2007, p. 1)

On the face of things, the close relation of Pneumatology and spirituality may seem obvious: it would appear that theologians' giving formal attention to Christian spiritual experience would lead them quite

---

1 Specifically, for instance, as LeRon Shults remarked in his 2007 address to the Nordic Systematic Theology Conference, there is "growing interest in and generative use of the theological concept of the divine Spirit among those exploring issues in feminist and liberation theology, ecology, politics, ecumenism and the astonishing expansion of Pentecostalism" (Shults 2007, p. 1).

naturally into considering and constructing treatises on the topic of the Holy Spirit. But, in fact, this has not long been the case for contemporary academics, as Shults reminds his audience: the corpus of post-Enlightenment academic theology instantiates a marked gap between attention to spiritual practice and systematic treatments of the Holy Spirit. This fact is little wonder, given that, over the course of modernity, Christian spirituality had become predominantly circumscribed within the bounds of inner, individual states of psychological or transcendental experience.[2] It is only in the past eighty years or so that a robust body of academic literature began to expand that acknowledges, and demonstrates interest in mining, the overlap of Christian spirituality and theology in general. That movement—made possible largely by the work of the New Theology (*nouvelle théologie*) theologians,[3] and propelled by innovative figures like Simone Weil and Hans Urs von Balthasar—apparently succeeded because it shifted away from individualist, psychological framings of spiritual experience and instead situated spirituality in the contexts of liturgical practice, trinitarian faith, and the cooperation of nature and grace.[4]

The present essay's analysis represents an effort to honor the wisdom borne out in attending to spirituality in those three contexts. It seeks to do so specifically in the interest of unearthing practical implications for Spirit-guided hermeneutics, having conceived "spirituality" as does Shults—i.e., as the interpretation of and attention to transformed relations to God and neighbor. The essay works towards this goal by synthesizing certain intriguing contributions of three thinkers who have recently theologized at the intersections of systematics and spirituality: Sarah Coakley (looking closely at her recently acclaimed *God, Sexuality, and the Self*, 2013), Louis-Marie Chauvet (by way of his seminal work *Symbol and Sacrament*, 1987), and Rowan Williams (attending to his celebrated essay "The Body's Grace," 2002). In three broad moves, this engagement distills a pneumatological paradigm as a departure-point for framing mediated revelation as a sacramental event, which event presses toward what I call a "hermeneutics of nuptial encounter." First, it assesses Coakley's integration of Pneumatology and spiritual disciplines, drawing out key implications and questions vis-à-vis a doctrine of revelation. Second, the essay considers how those questions are illumined by the concept of sacramentality as articulated by Chauvet, thereby proposing how inspired revelation may be conceived as the occasion and outcome of a divine-human discursive encounter. Having thematized this rendering of revelation, the essay's third move takes up Williams' theological reflection on sexuality, thus suggesting how revelation as sacrament concurs with our "nuptial" incorporation into Sonship. The essay concludes by calling for a hermeneutics that accounts for the spiritual insights afforded by this constructive synthesis, which ultimately results in a proposal for theological method. Let us now turn to its first broad move.

2. Sarah Coakley and the "Spirit-Led" Experience of Mediated Revelation

In a memorable segment of *God, Sexuality, and the Self* (2013), Coakley takes issue with trinitarian formulae that she evaluates as relying upon something like a "linear' revelatory model," wherein "primary focus is given to the Father-Son relationship, and the Holy Spirit becomes the secondary purveyor of that relationship to the church" (p. 11). Coakley finds such a rendering of the trinitarian relations paradigmatically represented in the Gospel of John, wherein the Father-Son/Logos bond is prominent in Christ's earthly life, and the Spirit comes to "replace [Christ] and to remind the

---

[2] Spirituality came to be defined largely according to inner psyschological states under the significant impact of William James' *Varieties of Religious Experience* (1902), wherein James influentially asserted both the possibility and benefit of setting aside philosophical and theological concerns when analyzing religious experience. In theological sectors, this bifurcation of spiritual experience and theological interpretation was largely accepted by neoscholastic Thomists, whose "natural theology" envisioned an inherent division between divine activity and natural human experience; meanwhile, it was also accepted by transcendental Thomists who (in the vein of Schleiermacher) framed spirituality in the terms of pre-thematic, transcendental experience. For detailed analysis of this twofold development in Thomistic thought, see McCool (2002).

[3] Including, for instance, the work of such thinkers as Henri de Lubac, Marie-Dominique Chenu, and Yves Congar.

[4] See Anselm Stolz's (Stolz [1938] 2001) ground-breaking argument along these lines in *The Doctrine of Spiritual Perfection*, trans. Aidan Williams (1938; New York: Crossroad/Herder, 2001), chp. 9, "Mystical experience."

disciples of his teaching, after he has 'gone away' ... The Spirit's role here is to 'glorify' the Son by (secondarily) passing on his teaching and 'declaring' it to the disciples (John 16. 14)" (ibid., p. 101, fn. 1). In contrast with this linear model, Coakley argues for the importance of a "Spirit-led" model of God's self-disclosure as trinitarian, drawn paradigmatically from the contemplative prayer experience described in Romans 8: 15–27. In this passage, Coakley observes, "the priority ... logically and experientially speaking, is given to the Spirit" (p. 112), namely in that the pray-er who finds the Spirit "interced[ing] with sighs too deep for words" (vs. 26, NRSV) detects the Spirit's promptings "'reflexively' at work" within her, drawing her own expressed longings into the "circle of response to the Father's call" (Coakley 2013, p. 111), enabling us to echo Christ's own call: "Abba! Father!" (vs. 15). Otherwise said: by way of sensing the Spirit's activity within her, galvanizing her own response to the draw of divine desire, the contemplative is able to detect a distinctive reflexivity in God's life—a perpetual outgoing and return of divine desire—which she begins to detect as the perichoretic dynamism of the trinitarian life itself.[5] What's more, Coakley notes, this person who prays in the Spirit also finds that the Spirit's cooperative dynamism is "the primary means of incorporation into the trinitarian life of God" (p. 111): when she invites and accepts the Spirit's divine reflexivity via spiritual acts, she finds her own Christoform life made possible. Hence, the Holy Spirit does not simply point the believer to what has already been disclosed in the Father-Son bond. Rather, the Spirit's indwelling and incorporating activity constitutes the very experience whereby believers become aware simultaneously of God's existence as triune and their own experience of incorporation into God's life as "Sons."[6]

Coakley takes care to note that the linear and the Spirit-led models of trinitarian revelation are neither at odds with nor even necessarily distinct from one another. They can be seen as "presum[ing] each other, given their close contiguity and entanglement within the texts of the New Testament" (p. 111).[7] The crucial point she works to demonstrate, however (by closely examining the Trinity doctrine's historical development), is that when believers privilege the "linear" type of revelation, they tend to overlook—and neglect attending to, in practice—the Spirit's function as "that without which there would be no incarnated Son at all, and—by extension—no life of Sonship into which we, too, might enter by participation" (p. 56). Accordingly, Coakley finds reason in Paul's theology for emphasizing the Spirit's function as the primary *initiator of* the Son's being in the world.[8] In this "Spirit-led" trinitarian paradigm, Coakley proposes that we may think of the "Father" as "both 'source' and ultimate object of divine desire," the "Spirit" as "that (irreducibly distinct) enabler and incorporator of that desire in creation—that which makes the creation divine," and the "Son" as "that divine and perfected creation" (p. 114).

The Spirit-led paradigm augurs intriguing implications not only for a doctrine of trinitarian revelation, but for mediated revelation in general. We can locate its touchstones in Coakley's treatment of the Romans 8 theme of the believer's Spirit-afforded incorporation into Sonship. Here, as the Spirit labors to impart the Christoform shape of life to those who pray, Jesus Christ remains Sonship's

---

[5] Coakley explains it thus: "It is not that the pray-er is having a conversation with some distant and undifferentiated deity, and then is being asked (rather arbitrarily) to 'hypostacize' that conversation (or 'relationship') into a 'person' (the Spirit); but rather, that there is something, admittedly obscure, about the sustained activity of prayer that makes one want to claim that it is personally and divinely activated from within, and yet that that activation (the 'Spirit') is not quite reducible to that from which it flows (the 'Father')" (p. 112).

[6] My regular use of the language of the believer's participation in "Sonship"—and, here, her status as "Son"—takes a cue from Coakley's use of the same language, drawn from Romans 8. I understand the language as she does: not as indicating a masculinized identity or status, but as referring to the believer's redemption via being "conformed to the likeness of [the] Son" (Romans 8:29, qtd. in Coakley 2013, p. 112).

[7] Coakley notes that a tendency to prioritize one model over the other "arose partly and originally ... from an intrinsic ambiguity in the biblical resources for the later, developed, trinitarian thinking. For the 'ordering' of the language of Father, Son, and Spirit is varied in the biblical witness" (p. 101).

[8] It is worth noting that one may also find basis in the Gospels for the Son's worldly existence being Spirit-initiated. Consider, for instance, at the Annunciation scene in the first chapter of Luke, when the angel Gabriel declares to Mary that the Holy Spirit will bring about her pregnancy (see also Matthew 1:18).

supreme and orienting expression (*the* "divine and perfected creation," as Coakley says). Nevertheless, Coakley notes that—as this contemplative "groans" in the Spirit, moving agonistically toward her Christoloform goal—she discovers that "the whole creation has been groaning in labor pains" under the Spirit's influence as well (vs. 22). Hence,

> the life of 'Sonship' ... is not only not restricted to Jesus's human (male) life, but nor to the mystical 'body of Christ' which is the church; it is ... expanded even further to include the full cosmological implications of the incarnation, the whole creation 'groaning' to its final Christological telos in God (Romans 8: 18–21). What this underscores is the extraordinary ripple effect of prayer in the Spirit—its inexorably social and even cosmic significance as an act of cooperation with, and incorporation into, the still extending life of the incarnation. (Coakley 2013, p. 114)

In sum, as the contemplative prays in the Spirit, she detects the cosmic reach of the Spirit's ministry of incorporation, which highlights the nature of the Incarnation as "still extending" and the believer's participation in that unfolding life as she is incorporated into it. The Spirit-afforded bestowal of Christocentric revelation does not involve believers' reception of something like a "closed text," in other words. It took its definitive shape in the life, death, and resurrection of Jesus Christ, but it is still unfolding in the cosmic expanse of history, its meaningful contours arising out of concrete contexts wherein the Spirit is drawing all things to their Christological telos. Those who pray in the Spirit should expect to find, then, that "the authority of the revelatory Word is continually and freshly encountered and expounded—by a 'reason' *which is itself in process of disclosure*" (ibid., p. 88, emphasis added).

In her earlier work *Powers and Submissions* (2002), Coakley had already hinted at the character of this "reason-in-process" vis-à-vis a "deepening of vision" afforded by contemplative exercises: when taking up the process of wordless prayer, the contemplative commonly experiences "a profound sense of the mind's darkening, and of a disconcerting reorientation of the senses" (p. 19). This unsettling experience is both the cost and benefit of a "'love affair with a blank', such as contemplation is," Coakley says: costly, because it entails "a strange subversion of all certainties, a stripping, often painful, of what one previously took for granted" (p. 342)[9], but also beneficial, because—as one suspends one's rational agendas and waits for what may be disclosed—"what fills the waiting over time is a kind of seepage in the self, a recognition of rich unconscious elements, a transcendence of narrow rationality" (ibid.).

Coakley also identifies a hallmark of the Spirit-afforded supercession of narrow rationality in the discovery that "twoness, one might say, is divinely ambushed by Threeness" (Coakley 2009, p. 11). Sinful dichotomies—for instance, those accompanying certain formulations of gender or race—are thereby granted "an eschatological hope," an expectation that "what is fallen can be redeemed and sanctified—indeed rendered sacramental by participation in Christ" (Coakley 2002, p. 54). This transformation of "twoness" is, indeed, sacramental; for it is typified in the hypostatic union, as Coakley sees it:

> In Christ, I meet the human One who, precisely in the Spirit, has effected ... interruptive transfiguration of twoness. He has done so by crossing the boundary between [a] 'twoness' more fundamental even than the twoness of gender: the ontological twoness of the transcendent God and the created world. In crossing that boundary in the incarnation, Christ does not re-establish the boundary as before, nor—significantly—does he destroy it; rather, we might say that he 'transgresses' it in the Spirit, infusing the created world anew with divinity. (Coakley 2013, p. 57)

---

9   Coakley attributes the phrase "A love affair with a blank" to Dom Sebastian Moore (1977) description of contemplative practice in his "Some Principles for an Adequate Theism," *Downside Review* 95 (1977), pp. 201–13.

Hence, interpreters of revelation should also expect that, as the Holy Spirit infuses creation with the conditions of the sacramental, it also works towards the "transgressing"—though not necessarily the undoing—of ontological boundaries, towards the end of relational intimacy.

Coakley cites (what we could take to be) an example of and entry-point into the sacramental transfiguration of twoness by way of Pseudo-Dionysius's *Divine Names*—particularly his use of the notion of *ekstasis*, the profound experience of self-opening that involves "an implicit acknowledgement of love across difference" (ibid., pp. 316–17).[10] Dionysius, Coakley notes, attributes "ecstatic yearning not only to human lovers of God, but also, prototypically, to divine love of creation" (p. 314). The divine *ekstasis* may be understood as the incorporative reflexivity of the trinitarian life, the out-going and return of divine love that draws creation relationally towards Godself. For Dionysius, a similar ecstatic potential holds true between human parties; and while he may not have been thinking particularly of male-female relations, Coakley wonders what may come of applying his thinking on *ekstasis* in this context: "If the divine ecstasy returning to itself allows redeemed creation to participate in it, and so signals an 'incorporative' trinitarianism," she muses, "what, correlatively, might be the trinitarian implications of ecstatic love between the sexes?" (p. 317).

In a creative exposition upon that correlation, Coakley draws upon French theorist Luce Irigaray's thematizing of "the transcendence of the other which becomes an immanent ecstasy" in the act of love-making.[11] Coakley reflects upon how, analogously, we may imagine that

> human ecstatic loves (at their best) might ultimately relate to divine ecstatic love: not by any direct emulation of the trinitarian nature, but by the 'interruption' by the Spirit of any merely 'egological' duality inherent in their relationship, such that the human lovers are themselves aware of a necessary 'third' between them—both uniting them and protecting their integrity in their new ecstasy of exchange. What then is happening may even be a degree of participation in the divine life; but it comes with both the cost and the joy of truly 'ecstatic' attention to the other. (p. 318)

Coakley thus proposes not a lived entry-point into cooperating with the Spirit's incorporative dynamism—that is, a way of inviting sacramental union with God: by cultivating self-other distinction in relationship (whatever the cost) and enjoying that distinction to the point of its overturning. In that experience of *ekstasis*, one's perception is drawn not toward illuminated and fixed essences, but toward intimate embrace and noetic transformation. Entering into such relationship can teach us a way of stepping "willfully into an act of reflexive divine love that is always going on, always begging Christomorphic shape" (p. 343).

Even as this Christomorphic shape is ever arising, our theological reason remains ever *in via*, laboring towards its final telos of perfected union with God and neighbor. Coakley thus maintains that it is not possible (pre-eschaton) to guard absolutely against the danger of doctrinal language being impacted by "abuse and distortion" (p. 343). Hence, the hermeneutics of suspicion must always remain in play, keeping the socially-located and political complexion of contemplation and theological expression in view; and both the message and the structure of the church must remain open to amendment—though, notably, extant ecclesial structures ought not be reduced to rubble. While "authoritarian ecclesiastical Christian 'orthodoxy'" must not remain "cut off from the real 'sea' of lived religion by hierarchical avoidance or denial" (p. 72), says Coakley, there remains a practical

---

10 Coakley is looking at chapter 4, section 13 of *Divine Names*.
11 She draws upon a passage from Luce Irigaray's work wherein Irigaray is describing "the transcendence of the other which becomes an immanent ecstasy" in the act of love-making, as a "shared outpouring" and a "loss of boundary of the skin into the mucous membranes of the body, leaving the circle which encloses my solitude to meet in a shared space, a shared breath ... In this relation," Irigaray goes on, "we are at least three, each of which is irreducible to any of the others: you, me and our creation [*oeuvre*], that ecstasy of ourself in us [*de nous en nous*] ... prior to any 'child'" (Irigaray 1991, "Questions to Emmanuel Lévinas: On the Divinity of Love," in Robert Bernasconi and Simon Critchley, eds., *Re-Reading Lévinas*. London: Athlone, 1991. 109–18, at 88); quoted in Coakley (2013).

and even ethical necessity in *some* sort of hierarchizing in the human realm if we are to order our values properly.[12] It is *oppressive* hierarchies that we must cooperate with the Holy Spirit in seeking to overturn. In the end, the revelation-paradigm emerging from Coakley's work is fundamentally practical, one of "knowing by doing"—but the "doing" encompasses more than simply taking up traditional disciplines, or simply challenging them. Those who wish to render their perceptions labile to the Spirit's direction must enter into a patient, lifelong enterprise of *ascetic practice* (which, as she frames it, uniquely enables one's commitment to justice[13]), *ekstatic attention* (to "the other" in every relational context), and *continued discernment* (of unfolding, Christomorphic reason), individually and corporately. Under the influence of such ongoing efforts, interpretive communities may embrace the painstaking processes of theological and liturgical retrieval and refinement in expectation that "what is fallen can be redeemed and sanctified—indeed rendered sacramental" by the Spirit's transfiguring ministry (Coakley 2002, p. 54).

In Coakley's estimation, there is no surer way to take up this work than by embracing the "slow but steady assault on idolatry which only the patient practices of [non-discursive] prayer can allow God to do in us" (Coakley 2013, p. 325). Granted, she does allow that "symbolic bombardment," such as that characterizing the trinitarian tradition's numerous metaphors for the Godhead, "should not be seen merely as a theological problem" (ibid., p. 309). In keeping with the tradition of the kataphatic/apophatic dialectic, "metaphorical profusion can aid, just as much as distract from, the epistemic stripping necessary to right contemplation of the divine," says Coakley (ibid.). "We can start with ... outrageous multiple cultural meanings and move, through contemplative purgation, to an ascetic alignment with God's purposes." As this progressive sacrifice of "cultural meanings" ministers toward the purgation not only of the contemplative's will, but also of her intellect, it ultimately "contribut[es] to an expanded objectivity of standpoint, rather than an intensified subjectivity" (p. 26). Coakley thus highlights the revelatory value of the kataphatic/apophatic process as a discipline that invites the Spirit's transfiguring influence. One may question, however, Coakley's foremost association of "symbolic bombardment" and "multiple cultural meanings" with the need for purgative silencing rather than *also* with potential for facilitating communion with God. It is difficult to see how language is "rendered sacramental" within this formulation.

Coakley does highlight the sacramental potential, so to speak, that exists in certain communicative forms when she attends to artistic representation of the Trinity that "(in its most creative and original moments) point[s] out beyond literalism and ideology to something both richly symbolic and at the same time apophatic in its imaginative dimensions" (ibid., p. 260). She thus emphasizes the latent possibility in certain forms of dialogic expression—namely, here, in the representative mode of the visual arts—to hold together kataphatic and apophatic import, sacramentally weaving physical and spiritual together. Nonetheless, Coakley's "love affair with a blank"—that is, her steady emphasis on wordless prayer and silent contemplation as primary means of opening ourselves to the Spirit's transforming influence—seemingly exhibits a rather low view of our *less* creative, everyday semantic tendencies. They apparently number among the fallen realities that, if they need not be eliminated altogether, must become thoroughly subject to non-discursive discipline so as to be rendered sacramental. Could there be a sense in which our dialogic[14] expression itself may become a sacramental site of communion

---

[12] On this point Coakley refers to anthropologist Louis Dumont's underscoring of the necessity of a "system of ordered values" for social life, as well as to Mary Douglas's work on cultural analysis. Therein, Douglas points out that the "'hierarchical society' is not necessarily, let alone intrinsically, a repressive top-down system," but can be one wherein "'every decision is referred to the well-being of the whole ... transcending its parts'" (p. 320).

[13] Coakley says: "there is much talk of the problem of attending to the otherness of the 'other' in contemporary post-Kantian ethics and post-colonial theory; but there is very little about the intentional and embodied practices that might enable such attention. ... The moral and epistemic stripping that is endemic to the act of contemplation is a vital key here: its practiced self-emptying inculcates an attentiveness that is ... more discomforting, more destabilizing to settled presuppositions, than a simple intentional design on empathy" (p. 48).

[14] I am here employing the notion that all language is dialogical, endlessly responsive to what has already been said and in anticipation of what will be said in turn.

with the divine? The remainder of this essay works to develop such an account of communicative acts, locating the basic tenets of such a paradigm in Louis-Marie Chauvet's work with the notions of sacrament and symbol. In its light, we may begin to see how subjective human construction can be integral to the Spirit-led unfolding of Christic revelation. Let us turn now to identify those tenets.

3. Louis-Marie Chauvet and the Sacrament as Dialogical Occasion

One avenue of entry into Chauvet's theological endeavor in *Symbol and Sacrament* is by way of his engagement with Karl Barth therein. Chauvet affirms Barth's positions that "the Word of God is sovereign, that this Word gathers in Christ the entire unfolding of history," and that the visible church's status as Christ's body is a fact undergirded by mystery (p. 540). Chauvet expresses reservations with Barth's project, however, on the grounds that Barth has (ironically) reached too far with his mode of theologizing, which implies that the human can contemplate reality from some ahistorical, extemporal perspective.[15] To avoid this perceived error Chauvet affirms that, while the Christ-event certainly constitutes an "eschatological rupture" in history, that rupture must not entail the utter discontinuity "between 'profane' history and 'salvation' history" (p. 546). Instead, Chauvet believes that the sacred-profane distinction ought to be treated as fluid, for the Word *became* flesh; it did not simply "live in" the body as an instrumental organ. In keeping with this premise, and the fact that the flesh of the Word is necessary for our encounter with it—we could not and cannot conceive it otherwise—one of Chauvet's key proposals is that God's Word appropriates the human symbolic nexus, not as a "veil concealing the unique divine action" but rather as a sacred space of relational encounter between God and humanity (p. 539). For Chauvet, divine revelation unfolds as we are grasped by it in the mediating spaces of our historically, ethically, and symbolically constitut*ed* and constitut*ing* embodiment. Accordingly, we should see the entire corporeal realm, including language, as an "arch-sacramental" medium of grace.[16]

Maintaining this view of the corporeal nexus as a site of divine-human encounter, Chauvet establishes his basic purpose in *Symbol and Sacrament*: rather than subsuming the Christian sacraments into an abstract notion of "sacramentality," he wants to consider them as *"symbolic figures allowing us entrance into, and empowerment to live out, the (arch-)sacramentality which is the very essence of Christian existence"* (p. 2, italics in original). He believes that proceeding along these lines requires shifting away from the Scholastic metaphysical approach to the sacraments, which, broadly construed, conceptualizes them in terms of causality. To explain: unlike Barth's approach to human signification (which, for Chauvet, over-determines that system's deficiency), Chauvet critiques Scholastic thinking for presuming a natural capacity in the signifier to touch or even produce the reality it signifies. That thinking accordingly conceives of the sacraments "instrumentally," that is, as signifiers inherently able to affect the realities they indicate, however mysteriously (see Boeve 2008, p. 7). Chauvet resists this instrumentalist approach to the sacraments on the grounds that it fails to recognize humanity's essential constitution "inside language": any presence we encounter via the system of signification always operates in tandem with its absence, its "going beyond" language.[17] He roots this argument in Martin Heidegger's existential philosophy, according to which "humans do not possess language," as Chauvet explains it; "rather, they are possessed by it. *They speak only because they are always-already spoken*" (p. 57,

---

15   Chauvet connects his critique to an observation by H. Bouillard: "What bothers us the most is precisely that Barth has somehow placed himself in God's unique vantage point … in order to contemplate God's work from that vantage point" (quoted in Chauvet 1995, p. 540).

16   I previously engaged these hermeneutic features of Chauvet's work in (White 2016). In that article I considered in greater detail the epistemological implications of his work as an expression of a critically realist ontology, whereas here I engage in greater detail the theological import of his depiction of the human situation within language.

17   Chauvet operates with a broadly construed notion of "language": as the verbal and non-verbal web of signifiers. Though I cannot take up the task here, I believe Chauvet's critique of Thomas Aquinas (though perhaps not later Scholasticism) on these accounts warrants nuance: the Thomistic deployment of analogy could be seen as preserving the eschatological quality of theological utterance within a symbolic register.

italics in original). Chauvet also affirms Heidegger's observation that metaphysics mistakenly "believes itself to have produced an explanation of being, when in fact it has only ontically reduced being to metaphysics' *representations*, utterly forgetting that nothing that exists 'is'" (pp. 26–27). We cannot, then, instrumentally reach or bring about realities untouched by the system of signification, for that system is indelibly constitutive of our perception. The fact that we lack foolproof understanding of what becomes present to us via that system might be overlooked by frameworks such as that of analogical negation (which could be taken as circumventing the distressing reality of God's absence/unknowability). Chauvet finds such projects to be hazardous, for presuming that we can plot even the "fixed" nature of reality's *withdrawal* from language can render theology an idol of speculation.

Arguing in the above fashion, Chauvet proposes that if we imagine our interpretive engagement with the sacraments as existing in plottable connection *or* contrast with an external reality, we will take up those discourses in self-deception, laboring to construct "short-cut onto-(theo)logical approaches" in fear of "the consequences of a fully hermeneutical theology" (p. 23). From a "fully hermeneutic" theological perspective, we would contemplate the nature of the sacraments by setting aside the longing for reality's transparence, accepting the unknowing signaled by the withdrawal of signified reality while, nevertheless, responding to that reality's presence with bold creativity. Such is the hermeneutic way "inseparable from us," which is not a pre-determined path with a treasure at its end; rather, "the treasure is nothing else but the *work of journeying which takes place in ourselves, the labor of giving birth to ourselves* since it is *we ourselves* who are being plowed ... and who are bearing fruit by becoming different" (p. 54). It operates in the register of *symbolic* representation, in which we take up the semantic nexus, not as an instrument for control over reality, but as something like the Israelites' desert manna: "a question ... a non-thing ... a non-value" (p. 45), an occasion for transformative encounter with God and neighbor.

Chauvet's sacramental paradigm has been met by skeptics who flag the potential of fideism or self-constructed fantasy in a hermeneutic way "inseparable from us." Lieven Boeve, for instance, voices reservations regarding Chauvet's emphasis on the "absence" of what is signified, expressing concern that such a construal of reality renders sacramental ritual too mysterious to bear real meaning for its adherents. The epistemic results, he fears, could entail faith-communities' resorting to radical particularity or false universalism (here reminding us of Chauvet's worries over Barth's theologizing). Boeve accordingly wonders if Chauvet should develop what he calls "a more appropriate language to express Christ's sacramental presence in the church" (p. 14). A similar concern is evidenced in Elbatrina Clauteaux's effort to accept the tenets of Chauvet's hermeneutic way "inseparable from us" while articulating a more detailed account of sacramental presence. She employs a notion of symbol as dancing between *logos* and *bios*, "feed[ing] on the capacity of the cosmos to show its order" (Clauteaux 2008, p. 169). That capacity is evidenced in the phenomenon of interlocutors joining in dialogical relationship regardless of difference. Clauteaux thus emphasizes what she takes to be the intrinsic relationship between "the real" and the symbol, envisioning "the real" as spilling over into the "life of the symbolic," even as it (the real) "goes beyond ... discourse" (ibid.). The "absence" Chauvet emphasizes could be understood simply as discourse's inability to contain the fullness of the symbol. In like manner, Clauteaux infers, God becomes present via the sacraments' symbolic life, with the hypostatic union standing as the symbol *par excellence*.

Chauvet does, in fact, understand the symbol as a kind of meeting place of *bios* and *logos*, and so Clauteaux's suggestive description of reality's capacity to disclose itself via the symbol could prove helpful to Chauvet's followers' efforts to image how God becomes present through sacramental media. Clauteaux's project could turn attention away, however, from certain important implications in Chauvet's hermeneutic paradigm: namely, regarding how *we* offer ourselves to God in the sacramental meeting of *logos* and *bios*.[18] For Chauvet, it is critical that the bios-logos meeting does not entail "the

---

[18]   Cf. (Morrill 2009, pp. 116–18)).

real" (or "the order of subsistent entities," p. 438) simply "knocking up" against us as we attempt to make ordered sense of it via words and rituals. Rather, one might say that the symbol is a kind of "hyperreality": a merging of *bios* and our creative response to it, which forms a new reality. This is not to claim that Chauvet's understanding of the symbol accords with Jean Baudrillard's definition of the "hyperreal," as a simulation involving the perversion and pretense of reality.[19] Chauvet understands the symbol's hyperreality as sacramental, rooted in the nature of the Word's incarnation. Much as the divine Word truly *took on* the flesh it became, incorporating human life into the life of God, the incarnation discloses that the real, ever exceeding hermeneutic construction, also *incorporates* that construction. Thus, theological interpretation ought to take a way "inseparable from us" because only thus will it cohere with the truth: that we are simultaneously formed *by* and form*ing* that which we encounter. Because our discursive activity is an "order of the on-going transformation of subjects into believers" of one sort or another (p. 438), we only avoid idolatry when our thinking begins and ends in a kind of intellectual *kenosis* that "continually requires theology to take a step backwards, a step which both disenthralls it from itself and reopens it" (p. 73). In this posture of self-opening, we can experience truly graced encounter with the infinite.

Chauvet's vision of reality as the arch-sacramental order of "on-going transformation of subjects into believers" resonates with the epistemology Coakley employs in her emphasis that truth-claims are ever informed by extra-rational features of perception, and that Christological reason remains "in via." Also, in Chauvet's paradigm, human semantic improvisation is a risk required by reality's sacramental dynamism; this coheres with Coakley's take on the Spirit-led cosmic unfolding of Sonship, and our participation in that process. Chauvet goes further than Coakley on this account, however, by presenting hermeneutic construction in a way she does not: that is, Coakley discovers autonomy from God as illusory primarily through silent contemplation, while Chauvet cites the same discovery in the nature of language itself, on the condition that its process is taken up as "manna," an occasion of responsive reopening to God and neighbor.[20] Returning to the sacraments does not, in itself, instrumentally insure that we embrace this fully hermeneutic theological posture. But, as symbolic figures, the sacraments *do* illumine the arch-sacramentality of Christian existence, and by that light they empower us to live out that arch-sacramentality.

One could say that, in Chauvet's work, the semantic nexus' sacramental potential is anchored in the fact that the symbol's "hyperreality" is born of a discursive encounter between *bios* and *logos*—or, more fittingly, *Logos* and *logos*—which is akin to love-making as thematized by Irigaray: it entails a "shared outpouring," a "loss of boundary ... of the body, leaving the circle which encloses my solitude to meet in a shared space" (qtd. in Coakley 2013, pp. 317–18). Depending on "the *attitude*, idolatrous or not, they elicit from us" (Chauvet 1995, p. 43), our semantic constructions either result in the expansion or constriction of our own lives, and the life of the Incarnation itself. Rowan Williams makes use of such an analogy in his renowned essay "The Body's Grace," wherein he contemplates the comparable impulses driving sexual and communicative advances humans make toward one another. In light of those subtle parallels, we may find a key to understanding the sacrament of revelation as a "nuptial" event of our Spirit-led incorporation into Sonship.

4. Rowan Williams and the Dialogical Occasion as Nuptial Event

Williams opens his reflections in "The Body's Grace" (2002) with an observation: "Most people know that sexual intimacy is in some ways frightening for them ... that the whole business is

---

[19] See Baudrillard (1994).
[20] For Chauvet, *manna*'s fleeting nature invites its recipient into trusting relationship with God and neighbor; it is thus akin to the "presence of the absence" of Christ in the sacramental medium. This absence invites believers to seek Christ in all persons, especially those occupying the forgotten corners of society. Chauvet (1979, 1987) engages this idea in two of his untranslated works: *Du symbolique au symbole. Essai sur les sacrements* (Paris: Le Cerf, 1979), p. 99; and "L'avenir du sacramental," *Recherches de science religieuse* 75 (1987): 241–66, at 257.

irredeemably comic, surrounded by so many odd chances and so many opportunities for making a fool of yourself" (p. 310). Williams goes on to draw upon philosopher Thomas Nagel's observation regarding parallel vulnerabilities entailed in seeking sexual connection with another person and in seeking to communicate with an audience.[21] (p. 65)Specifically, attempts at communication (i.e., "any attempt to share, in language, what something means," p. 312) and sexual advances share a similar process: both are "aroused" by the presence of another with whom one wants to connect, and to whom one must expose that desire in hopes that it is reciprocated. And, indeed, that desire must be reciprocated, if one's effort is to come to fruition. If I initiate this exchange-oriented movement, I find (if I am honest) that "I am no longer in charge of what I am. *Any* genuine experience of desire leaves me in this position," Williams observes: "I cannot of myself satisfy my wants without distorting or trivializing them" (p. 313). We here find a reflection that complements Chauvet's assessment that our situation within language leaves us anxious for control. That anxiety can be seen as due not only to the elusiveness of assured meaning, but also to the vulnerability enshrouded by communicative efforts: one's hope for others' careful attention, and one's susceptibility to pain in the face of their potential rejection or misunderstanding of what one hopes to say.

Given the vulnerabilities we experience vis-à-vis sexual desire and its expression, it is hardly surprising that, as Williams notes, culture and religion "have devoted enormous energy to the doomed task of getting it right" (ibid.). (One could certainly say the same for communication as well, with another nod to Chauvet and the "short-cut onto-(theo)logical approaches" he decries.) To Williams' mind, the fact that efforts to secure a risk-free approach to sexuality have proven futile is a reality with transcendent implications, for it is not in "getting it right" that one discovers the graced nature of sexual desire and encounter. It is, rather, in the giving and receiving of the realization that one is desired by another. Williams explains:

> Grace, for the Christian believer, is a transformation that depends in large part on knowing yourself to be seen in a certain way: as significant, as wanted. The whole story of creation, incarnation, and our incorporation into the fellowship of Christ's body tells us that God desires us, *as if we were God*, as if we were that unconditional response to God's giving that God's self makes in the life of the Trinity. We are created so that we may be caught up in this, so that we may grow into the wholehearted love of God by learning that God loves us as God loves God. (pp. 311–12)

The economy of grace which Williams here outlines corresponds with a somewhat controversial understanding of our fleshly pleasures, for it is a picture of the human creature before God wherein the creature's joy is a graced end in itself. Such a construal of grace would supplement Chauvet's work, particularly his cautioning against instrumentalized renderings of the sacraments, with the following observation: when we doggedly seek to make our entry-points into "the shared world of language and (in the widest sense!) 'intercourse'" (Williams 2002, p. 312) instrumental to another process, we likely do so because we are overwhelmed by the "possibility not only of pain and humiliation without any clear payoff, but, just as worryingly, of nonfunctional joy—of joy, to put it less starkly, whose material 'production' is an embodied person aware of grace" (p. 318). Otherwise said, when we only make sense of our desire's frustration or fulfillment *instrumentally*—i.e., as a means to a "productive" end such as the generation of children through married sex,[22] or the manufacturing of secured knowledge through metaphysical reasoning (or perhaps even Christoform transfiguration afforded via purgative silencing)—we are disposed to overlook the grace of, in itself, the encounter with the (human or divine) other. One does not have to reach far from this observation to Coakley's: that when believers privilege the "linear" type of trinitarian revelation, primarily focusing on the illumined Father-Son relationship,

---

[21] See also a similar discussion in Chauvet (1979), *Du symbolique au symbole*, p. 65.

[22] This is to reference the view that sexual intercourse is justified only by the partners' intention to conceive a child as a result of the union. Williams takes issue with this viewpoint in "The Body's Grace."

they could miss how "human ecstatic loves (at their best) might ultimately relate to divine ecstatic love: not by any direct emulation of the trinitarian nature, but by the 'interruption' by the Spirit of any merely 'egological' duality inherent in their relationship" (Coakley 2013, p. 318).

Williams holds fast to this surplus economy of grace, along with our need to embrace the vulnerability it induces in us, if we are to learn to see ourselves as belonging to one another and as objects of "the causeless, loving delight of God" (Williams 2002, p. 317). He gives contours to that relationship via the biblical trope of "nuptial" relations between God and humanity. With a doctrine of revelation in mind, one may observe that Williams' use of the nuptial paradigm has little in common with other uses which render the church's "bridal" incorporation into Christ's life as a process of its becoming instrumental to the reproduction of God's self-expressing Word. Williams instead draws upon the observation that "sexuality beyond biological reproduction is the [metaphor] foremost in the biblical use of sexual metaphors for God's relation to humanity" (p. 318). In Hosea, for instance, Williams points out that "God is not the potent male sower of seed but the tormented lover," engaged in "exposing himself to humiliation" before the beloved and straying people: "God is at the mercy of the perceptions of an uncontrolled partner" (ibid.). Similarly, Williams notes that the marital imagery of Ephesians 5, "for all of its blatant assumption of male authority, still insists on the relational and personally creative element" in the nuptial metaphor "without using procreation as a rational or functional justification" (p. 319). The biblical writers repeatedly draw upon sexual imagery that represents the "complex and costly faithfulness" (ibid.) of God's love affair with God's people, rather than punctuating God's straightforwardly reproductive objective with those images.

In this picture of the nature-grace "nuptial" relation which Williams sketches, God's worldly self-disclosure occurs in a manner that wants to be "enlarge[d by] the life of others" (p. 313). That is to say, God's self-expressing Word invokes creative creaturely "collaboration" in determining the meaning of its material life, and the eschatological end of this incorporative process is "nonfunctional joy," productive of persons aware of being desired by another, whereby they may grow into the love of God. Coakley similarly recommends such a picture of divine longing for human self-distinction by way of Pseudo-Dionysius' "daring metaphysical move" of attributing "ecstatic yearning not only to human lovers of God, but also, prototypically, to divine love of creation" (Coakley 2013, p. 314). But Chauvet and Williams illuminate potential to extend the implications of that *ekstasis* further than Coakley does: by imagining "the cost and the joy" of God's "truly 'ecstatic' attention" to creation as the conditions of sacramental encounter, which also functions as a discursive occasion of mutual self-opening. We now imagine how the unfolding of creation, incarnation, and our Spirit-led incorporation into Sonship entails God desiring us, as a lover longs for the beloved's affections, and as a speaker longs to heard by the addressee: not as by an empty echo-chamber, neatly receiving and reproducing that speech, but as by an authentic other who receives the Word *into* and responds to it *out of* her distinctive other-ness; and who longs to be heard in turn, finding in God's responsive presence an occasion of joy. The Spirit indwells the "hyperreal" body of the semantic nexus because God's self-expression wants to be received, enjoyed, and reconstructed by those who are being drawn into the life of Sonship, i.e., who are growing into the devoted love of God.

5. Conclusions: Toward a Hermeneutics of Nuptial Encounter

This essay has drawn upon the insights of Sarah Coakley, Louis-Marie Chauvet, and Rowan Williams to propose that the "inspired" relation between human words and God's Word may be understood as both the sacramental circumstance *and* outcome of a graced, ongoing "nuptial" encounter: a giving and receiving of desire for discursive, delighted relationship between Creator and creature, in which process the Spirit cooperates with humans' improvised expressions of Sonship as it draws them into the life of God. A "hermeneutics of nuptial encounter"—that is, a mode of theological interpretation which honors this sacramental nature of linguistically mediated revelation—clearly cannot replace interpretive efforts trained upon close exegesis of texts, based upon the learning afforded by empirical disciplines. We should think here of the semiotic relation between sign (i.e., that which concerns intended reference, or "linear logic") and symbol. The two do not compete—rather, as Chauvet explains it, these concepts represent points in the same continuum of meaning-making, and one is never without some element of the other (see Chauvet 1995, pp. 111–13). For this essay's purposes, the important thing is to recognize that the symbolic is always at play in the creative construction that inevitably informs our construal of "the real." Thus, a "hermeneutics of nuptial encounter" ought to function as a form of discipline trained upon the symbol, which supplements those empirical disciplines concerned with the content of the linguistic sign. If we accept Shults' broad definition of "spirituality" noted at the opening of this essay—that it "deals with the ways in which we interpret and attend to the transformation of our relation to God and our neighbors" (Shults 2007, p. 1)—then we might say that hermeneutics of nuptial encounter begins and ends with spirituality, for it is fully trained upon the transformed relations with God and neighbor that may occur in the midst of our communicative and interpretive efforts. And it is oriented toward a pneumatological-cum-sacramental goal: that is, it is offered as a means for inviting the transfiguring presence of the Holy Spirit, who renders our expressions sacramental by incorporating them into the expanding life of the Word incarnate.

In closing, I propose that engaging in a hermeneutics of nuptial encounter would warrant the reading community committing itself to pursue the following six disciplines: first, setting aside the longing for reality's transparence, accepting the unknowing signaled by the withdrawal of signified reality; second, responding to that reality's presence with hopeful creativity, taking up the semantic nexus, not as an instrument for control over reality, but as an occasion for transformative encounter with God and neighbor; third, bearing in mind that "the authority of the revelatory Word is continually and freshly encountered and expounded—by a 'reason' which is itself in process of disclosure" (Coakley 2013, p. 88). Fourth, the Triune God retains sovereignty in shaping the terms, content, and outcome of this dialogical intermingling—not as a fellow agent, manipulating our responses by restricting our range of activity, but as the very source, context, and destiny of our agential responses. Those responses are, in a sense, the "children" born of our nuptial encounter with the divine, the orienting form of which we find in Christ. Hermeneuts thus discover their semantic categories "inspired," grafted by the Spirit into God's own self-expression.

Fifth, in this paradigm of revelation as sacrament, we must expect that our Spirit-led experience of God's self-disclosure will remain agonistic. Pre-eschaton, we cannot escape the fact that experience of "hyperreal" fusing of the Word and words is heavy laden by the systemic sins that darken perceptions and constrict our living. Thus, sixth and finally, as we are invited to contribute to the Word's incarnate meanings in an improvised sequence of answerable acts, we have also been given the ongoing task of discerning the profound yet subtle difference between our interpretations' capacities to expand one another's meanings and lives, and their capacities merely to project our desires upon each other (as "texts") and upon texts themselves, flattening their dimensions by treating them as voiceless objects. The first sort of expression is offered for returning response, out of desire for the joy and expression of the "other." It will go to the cross for that offer. The latter sort desires an audience only so as to ensure the speaker's security over or within the corporate network; such is the character of subjugation or enmeshment, both of which abdicate genuine responsibility vis-à-vis one's dialogue partners. Chauvet thus does well to remind us that the manner in which we construct our discourses—evidenced in "the *attitude*, idolatrous or not, they elicit from us"—either forms or *de*forms our experience of the sacramental meeting places in creation. The spiritual mishandling of interpretation occurs when we fail to embrace it as an occasion for offering ourselves to be reconstructed by God's and one another's reception and response.[23] As befits all sacraments, points of the overlap *of* or distinction *between* human signifiers and the divine Word remain obscure. Nonetheless, in this occasion of encounter with

---

23 From this perspective of grace, Williams says, "sexual 'perversion' is sexual activity without risk ... [it is] the effort to bring my happiness back under my control and to refuse to let my body be recreated by another person's perception" (p. 314).

Religions **2019**, *10*, 495

God, we are offered the grace of receiving that obscuring, not first as an indication of human sin and ignominy, but rather of our being God's beloved children.

Funding: This research received no external funding.

Conflicts of Interest: The author declares no conflict of interest.

References

Baudrillard, Jean. 1994. *Simulacra & Simulation*. Translated by Sheila Faria Glaser. Ann Arbor: University of Michigan Press.

Boeve, Lieven. 2008. Theology in a Postmodern Context and the Hermeneutical Project of Louis-Marie Chauvet. In *Sacraments: Revelation of the Humanity of God*. Edited by Philippe Bordeyne and Bruce T. Morrill. Collegeville: Liturgical Press, pp. 5–24.

Chauvet, Louis-Marie. 1979. *Du symbolique au symbole. Essai sur les sacrements*. Paris: Éditions du Cerf, p. 99.

Chauvet, Louis-Marie. 1987. L'avenir du sacramental. *Recherches de science religieuse* 75: 241–66.

Chauvet, Louis-Marie. 1995. *Symbol and Sacrament: A Sacramental Reinterpretation of Christian Existence*. Colledgeville: Liturgical Press.

Clauteaux, Elbatrina. 2008. When Anthropologist Encounters Theologian: The Eagle and the Tortoise. In *Sacraments: Revelation of the Humanity of God*. Edited by Philippe Bordeyne and Bruce T. Morrill. Collegeville: Liturgical Press, pp. 155–70.

Coakley, Sarah. 2002. *Powers and Submissions: Spirituality, Philosophy and Gender*. Malden: Blackwell Publishing.

Coakley, Sarah. 2009. Is There a Future for Gender and Theology? On Gender, Contemplation, and the Systematic Task. *Criterion* 47: 52–61.

Coakley, Sarah. 2013. *God, Sexuality, and the Self*. Cambridge: Cambridge University Press.

Irigaray, Luce. 1991. Questions to Emmanuel Lévinas: On the Divinity of Love. In *Re-Reading Lévinas*. Edited by Robert Bernasconi and Simon Critchley. London: Athlone.

McCool, Gerald A. 2002. *From Unity to Pluralism: The Internal Evolution of Thomism*. Oxford: Blackwell.

Moore, Dom S. 1977. Some Principles for an Adequate Theism. *The Downside Review* 95: 201–13. [CrossRef]

Morrill, Bruce T. 2009. *Divine Worship and Human Healing: Integral Theology at the Margins of Life and Death*. Collegeville: Liturgical Press.

Shults, LeRon. 2007. Current Trends in Pneumatology. Paper presented at Nordic Systematic Theology Conference, Copenhagen, Denmark, January 4–7.

Stolz, Anselm. 2001. Mystical experience. In *The Doctrine of Spiritual Perfection*. Translated by Aidan Williams. New York: The Crossroad Publishing Company. First published 1938.

White, Lauren S. 2016. For Comparative Theology's Christian Skeptics: An Invitation to Kenotic Generosity in the Religiously Pluralistic Situation. *The Harvard Theological Review* 109: 159–77. [CrossRef]

Williams, Rowan D. 2002. The Body's Grace. In *Theology and Sexuality: Classic and Contemporary Readings*. Edited by Eugene F. Rogers Jr. Oxford: Blackwell Publishers, pp. 309–21.

MDPI

St. Alban-Anlage 66

4052 Basel

Switzerland

Tel. +41 61 683 77 34

Fax +41 61 302 89 18

www.mdpi.com

Religions Editorial Office

E-mail: religions@mdpi.com

www.mdpi.com/journal/religions

www.ingramcontent.com/pod-product-compliance
Lightning Source LLC
Chambersburg PA
CBHW041140120626
46547CB00020B/3064